Influence

A Collection of Writings by Steven Lewis

Influence

A Collection of Writings by Steven Lewis

Longwoods Publishing Corporation
Toronto

Toronto

Printed in Canada

www.longwoods.com

ISBN: 978-0-9810089-6-7

Library and Archives Canada Cataloguing in Publication

Lewis, Steven, 1951-
Influence : a collection of writings / by Steven Lewis.

Includes index.
Also issued in electronic format.
ISBN 978-0-9810089-6-7

1. Medical care--Canada. 2. Medical policy--Canada. 3. Health care reform--Canada. I. Title.

RA395.C3L49 2012 362.10971 C2012-903245-X

Credits
Editor: Kira Leeb
Managing Editor: Ania Bogacka
Design and production: Jonathan Whitehead

Contents

CHAPTER TWO The Call for Professional Accountability

CHAPTER THREE Research to Inform Policy

CHAPTER FOUR The Reactionarian

Note from the Editor

Kira Leeb

Left up to Steven Lewis, this short (and grossly incomplete) collection of his writings might be called "The Golden Fleece." His choice reflects his own perception of his contribution to reshaping the healthcare agenda in Canada. We disagree. As chronicled by the comments – interspersed in this collection – of Steven's longtime friends and colleagues, his contributions have influenced, inspired and, at times, irritated us. Steven is an advocate for medicare. He believes in equitable access to healthcare for all, and he believes it can be achieved within a public-payer model. But he also believes that Canadian healthcare in the 21st century is in need of reform, and that those responsible for change should be held accountable.

Steven's writings are pointed and direct, and highly crafted. His gift for writing makes his work at once entertaining, thought-provoking and sometimes acerbic. Some essays are analytical, while others react to a situation or event. All reflect his passion and his ultimate desire to incite change where change is required, and to hold accountable those who have perpetuated a less than high-performing healthcare system.

It is no secret that some critics take issue with Steven's perspective and passion. But over the years that he has been writing for Longwoods, as well as his multitude of other academic journals and books, many critics have also commended him for his honesty and bravery

With his numerous publications and invitations to speak at public forums, Steven has had the ear of politicians and bureaucrats. He has lectured to nursing students and medical students, and has helped shape healthcare leadership in Canada.

In this 60th year of his existence, we pay tribute to our friend, whom we hope continues to influence and inspire us.

Foreword

Roy Romanow

Steven and I go way back. In fact, I can't pinpoint the day we met. Perhaps it was during the course of some campaign in the 1970s or 1980s when Allan Blakeney was leader. Or was it after I became premier in the early 1990s? But, of course, it doesn't matter – and besides, he may not be prepared to admit that he is really that old. What really matters is that from day one, I have always considered Steven to be one of the most knowledgeable healthcare policy experts I have ever worked with.

If I were asked to pick four words to describe Steven they would be *brilliant*, *energetic*, *committed* and *witty*. His brilliance and intelligence are demonstrated in his voluminous body of work on healthcare. The collection of writings contained herein is evidence of this. But his brilliance goes beyond this and impresses me every time we meet. Regardless of venue, Steven's gifts are obvious.

Steven's energy is perhaps the first notable characteristic. Energetic people are sometimes daunting, and this might be how Steven appears to some. However, I have often observed that those who suffer from extreme intellectual curiosity are confronted with difficult and competing interests all the time. For some, this might seem like a threadbare approach; for Steven, it simply adds to or complements his capacity to produce.

Committed. In all aspects of his life, Steven is committed. And, unlike many, Steven follows up his commitments with actions. This is reflected in both his written word and beyond. Where social issues are concerned, he works to influence his neighbours through hosting events and canvassing – or whatever is necessary. He recognizes that a healthy local community is the cornerstone of a healthy society, and he is willing to do what it takes to move that agenda forward.

But, at the end of the day, you can't talk about Steven without mentioning his wit. Steven's humour is at times cutting but is never without charm. I encountered his sense of humour when he was assisting on the Royal Commission. When the deadline for an interim report approached and there wasn't much to report, I asked Steven for his advice. He said, "Oh hell, just write them a short letter and tell them you have nothing to say!" I didn't take his advice. In hindsight, I sometimes think it would have saved much grief along the way.

Steven is a great speech writer, a wonderful writer, period; and among the best of many advisors I've had the pleasure to be associated with both professionally and personally. I foresee and hope that there are many, many more speeches, academic lectures, articles and exhibits of his community influence in the years to come.

Canadian Institute
for Health Information

Institut canadien
d'information sur la santé

The Canadian Institute for Health Information (CIHI) is pleased to facilitate the publication of "Influence: A Collection of Writings by Steven Lewis." For the past three decades Steven Lewis has contributed substantially to health policy development in Canada through his work and his writings. As this collection makes clear, a common element of Steven's contributions has been his unwavering ability to speak truth to power, to tackle some of the most contentious issues facing healthcare in Canada and to do so in very pointed but literate and engaging ways.

Not all of us will agree with Steven's perspective all the time, but all of us can learn from it. Steven's desire for change and his knowledge of the need for data to support it, aids our work at CIHI to ensure that he and others like him have the data required to ensure sound policy and decision-making at all levels.

Steven's passion inspires us to think about the possibilities of what can and should be achieved to ensure excellent healthcare is available for all. We hope everyone who reads this collection will be at once stimulated and engaged.

The Canadian Health Services Research Foundation (CHSRF) is pleased to help make possible the publication of "Influence: A Collection of Writings by Steven Lewis". Steven Lewis is one of Canada's most vocal and influential health services researchers and leaders – an important and credible voice calling for health system change. His writings are inspirational, and at times controversial, but always rooted in evidence and should renew our confidence in the possibility of health system improvement and transformation.

For over a decade, Steven Lewis and his work have helped CHSRF collaborate with health system leaders to examine and address difficult questions about how to organize, finance, manage and deliver high-quality, affordable, patient-centred healthcare for Canadians. Throughout his career, Steven has been an important voice for this. We hope this collection helps readers and health system leaders in their own health system improvement efforts.

CHSRF is dedicated to accelerating healthcare improvement and transformation for Canadians. Working at the nexus of health policy and delivery CHSRF enables leaders to tackle thorny and systemic barriers necessary to create breakthroughs with evidence-driven policy and implementation solutions.

CHSRF believes that together, we can improve healthcare for Canadians. We also believe there is much we can learn from the collected works of Steven Lewis as we tackle this important work.

CHAPTER ONE Advocating for Reform

Why Health Reform?*

Steven Lewis and Stephen Leeder

The call for sweeping health reform has become an international mantra. Like all mantras, repetition can become reflexive, and one can lose sight of its origins. It is hard to recall a time when governments, research workers and policy analysts were content with things as they are. A Google search finds about 60 000 sources with the exact phrase "health system transformation"; "health reform" pops up nearly two million times. No clear line separates quotidian change from major reform, but transformation entails an irreversible break with the present. The typewriter was a great invention but its day is done.

There is a case against reform. The health status of people living in advanced countries has been steadily improving. Life expectancy has increased, erstwhile rapid killers such as AIDS and several cancers are now chronic conditions, heart disease death rates have halved, and avoidable mortality rates have plummeted.[1] Health technology is ever more dazzling, from high-resolution medical imaging to robotic surgery. There are more effective drugs than ever before. From diagnosis to surgery, health care is steadily less invasive. Health care practitioners are rigorously trained and credentials required to enter practice are on the rise. *Citius*, *altius*, *fortius*: faster (technology, recovery, publication); higher (credentials, spending, intervention rates); and stronger (institutions,

* Lewis Steven J & Leeder Stephen R. Why health reform? MJA 2009; 191 (5): 270-272.

drugs, methods). Everything's coming up roses, so it's better to finetune here, innovate there, and stick with a model of proven success.

But where the optimist sees paradise, the analyst sees purgatory. Our contention is that the case for reform is compelling, but reform remains very difficult to achieve. One explanation for the lack of progress is that the case is fragmented, and the parts have not been assembled persuasively into a compelling narrative that both unifies and strengthens resolve. In this article, we attempt to create that narrative by weaving together the main strands of the case for reform. We review the evolution of our understanding of health, and health care effectiveness and efficiency; this evidence comprises the intellectual impetus for reform.

The population health revolution

Since the 1970s, biology, epidemiology, geography, sociology and economics have joined to create a fundamentally new understanding of health and the relationship (or lack thereof) between health and health care.[2] For centuries, it has been clear that rich people are healthier than poor people. The famous Whitehall civil servant studies revealed a gradient that added a new dimension of complexity to the determinants of health and the prospects for health improvement.[3,4] Geographers launched a friendly invasion into health territory, illuminating the connection between health and place, and major variability in health status within generally healthy jurisdictions. Health services research workers showed that, even in countries with universal, state-funded health care, non-financial barriers to quality care persist.[5,6] And biologists and geneticists produced the disheartening news that one's life course prospects carry the heavy freight of imprints from the very early years.[7-9]

These findings refuted the presumption that medical wizardry and innovation is the reliable pathway to better individual and population health. They also cast doubt on the relationship between health care spending and health outcomes. Many remained committed to the science and technology road despite apparent failures, such as the "war on cancer"[10,11] and other therapeutic setbacks.[12] For example, renowned physician and essayist Lewis Thomas argued that we are in an era of "halfway technologies"[13] that will, with more investment in material and time, become fully-fledged, brilliant successes. Even if one finds this plausible, the evidence is overwhelming that medicine and science alone cannot compensate completely for the effects of the non-medical determinants of ill health. Some estimate that health care accounts for no more than about 20% of the variance in health status.[14] If better health is the goal, there is good reason to take a hard look at the massive enterprise that is health care.

The intractability of health disparities

There is broad international consensus that reducing disparities is both a moral imperative and the key to improving overall population health.[15] Moreover, while we do not know how to increase the longevity or quality of life among the most advantaged, we do know something about how to enhance the health status of the disadvantaged.

Several countries have done better than most.[16] The northern European social democracies typically have shallower social gradients in health status; not coincidentally, they have shallower income gradients and extensive social support systems. Yet, they too seem to have hit the wall in reducing further disparities — if anything, disparities are widening despite strong political commitment to narrowing them.[17]

Health care can help reduce disparities,[18] or unintentionally exacerbate them. Well-off people often have disproportionately better access to specialists, even under health care financing arrangements that provide universal coverage and that are tax-funded single-payer systems.[19] In two-tier systems like Australia's, even though the publicly insured population formally has equal access to care, in practice, those who are privately insured have better access — precisely what they are paying for.[20,21] Solo or small group primary care practices that are isolated from other sectors and disciplines may deliver effective episodic care for healthy middle class people, but may not be able to meet the needs of patients with complex health problems and of disadvantaged groups. This is yet another rationale for full-scale reform.

"Flat of the curve" medicine

Within health care, value for money has emerged as a critical issue. The evidence is compelling at several levels.

Internationally, there is virtually no relationship between health status and health spending beyond about US$1000 or so per annum per capita.[22] The upward trajectory in health status flattens out beyond this threshold; in the language of economists, the marginal health benefits from additional health care spending become vanishingly small. Countries such as Costa Rica and regions such as Kerala in India achieve health status not much inferior to that of countries that spend orders of magnitude more on health care. The rich countries are all on the "flat of the curve".

Additionally, there appears to be no relationship between the per-capita number of health care practitioners and health outcomes in high-spending countries.[23] Sooner or later, these provocative findings must lead to hard questions about what we get for what we spend.

Defenders argue that democratic societies, fully aware of these facts, nonetheless invest heavily in health care for three reasons:

1. health care is the only available route to improved health for most people in advanced countries because their non-medical determinants of health (income,

food, housing, education) are already at high levels, and low marginal returns are acceptable because they are the only returns available;
2. much contemporary health care is designed to reassure, and reduce small risks to very small risks — the "just to be sure" magnetic resonance imaging scan, the call-back visit;
3. and the focus has shifted from longevity and survival to quality of life, and at this — arthroscopic surgery, joint replacements, medication — modern medicine excels.

Even if one concedes the logic and legitimacy of these arguments, governments recognise that the opportunity cost is massive; there are far more benefits to be had by investing elsewhere. But cutting even marginally effective services risks a middle class backlash. Better to look for outright waste and complete inefficiency in health care — the zero or negative return domains — and here, governments have found a rich lode to exploit.

It's not flat of the curve for nothing

The return on health care investment does not flatten only because health care has a relatively modest impact on population health status, or because it is hard to conceive of how to make healthy people even healthier. It is because a lot of health care is not very good and not very efficient. The large corpus of health services research documenting these uncomfortable truths is compelling evidence for reform.

That health care is not very good at the margins is not newsworthy; that it is not very good in the middle of the curve is quite shocking.[24] All countries that have studied hospital deaths have found that there is a high avoidable death toll in their hospitals.[25-27] This is not a question of halfway technologies, or the inevitable misfortune arising from uncertainty; it is a basic failure to avoid harm. Similar performance in aviation or any other industry would be viewed as both a performance and financial scandal.

The other side of that tarnished coin is waste. Variations in practice are rampant in health care. There are enormous differences in the use and cost of health care among similar populations,[28,29] and some high-performing health systems, such as Jönköping County in Sweden, spend the least and get the best results.[30] It is finally dawning on governments that improved quality costs less. There is no more revolutionary idea in health care than that.

The systems that do best are attuned to, and centred on, the users of services rather than being organised for the convenience of providers. They rely heavily on e-health for both direct care and analysis that informs continuous improvement. They are more serious about prevention and invest in programs — some of which are outside health care — that will defer or pre-empt costs. They have been much more successful in paying for success and not paying for failure.[30]

The authors of government-commissioned reports from around the world have recognised these realities for years. To a large extent, the evidence speaks for itself: the more one looks, the clearer it is that health care delivers neither processes nor outcomes commensurate with the level of spending. No industry — not even a publicly financed health care system revered by citizens — gets an infinitely renewable lease on the flat of the curve.

The evolving political economy

Health care systems do not exist in isolation; they are largely public entities, never far from the centre of political debates. Recent changes in the political and economic terrain are bound to affect health care.

Perhaps the most significant political change is the movement towards greater accountability. Governments are expected to measure, report, and account for themselves more transparently and openly than before. Auditors-General and their equivalents have begun to impose a value-for-money perspective on a sector that has historically been immune to such cold-hearted calculation. The size of health care budgets — approaching half of provincial government spending in many Canadian provinces, and around 25% for the larger Australian states — makes them obvious targets for scrutiny. If the emperor has no clothes, the accountability movement will be the first to publish the photos.

On the economic front, the Reagan–Thatcher neoconservative revolution reduced taxes and devalued and shrank the public sector. Governments deliberately reduced overall revenue growth while investing heavily in health care, particularly in the past decade. In Canada, critics pointed to health care's growing percentage of government budgets as proof of the public system's unsustainability. Some governments agreed, even though the problem was less the health care spending numerator than the total government revenue denominator.[31] However incoherent this discourse, one result was, again, heightened interest in reform.

The size and intensity of the current worldwide economic meltdown is bound to add further fuel to the reform fire. Governments are now forced to be Keynesians again, offering stimulus packages that run up massive deficits. Already there are forecasts of spending restraint. Having spent three decades or so reducing their roles, governments are nationalising banks and taking equity positions in large and failing corporations. Hence, the competition for government dollars is now stiffer, just when the balance sheets look more precarious. In such an environment, business as usual is no longer viable, not even in health care.

Conclusion

The case for major health care reform is persuasive. It rests on three main elements:

- The evidence for the obsolescence of traditional health care delivery is abundant and powerful. Quality and safety defects, the failure to provide evidence-based care, and huge and unjustifiable variations in practice are highly incriminating exhibits. Professions are still largely autonomous and uneasily allied with each other. Fragmentation compromises the continuity and effectiveness of care.
- Evidence confirming the enormous impact of the non-medical determinants of health on health status has diminished confidence that the solution to health problems lies mainly in health care. Understanding the extent and origins of health disparities obliges governments to promise to address them, and heightens concerns about persistent and widening gaps. Health care cannot overcome health disparities; hence, the calls for both health care reform and greater investment in non–health-care sectors. Meanwhile, obesity rates climb and preventable health breakdown abounds.
- No level of spending or rates of increase in spending definitively solve problems of access, quality, or equity. The natural experiment of the past decade has been to test whether it is possible to spend the way to excellence. The experiment failed because we mistook a structural and cultural problem for a financial shortfall. Buying more of the same proved ineffective, and it is now fiscally impossible to extend the experiment. The only option is to reinvent the delivery of care and invest more effectively in the production of health. These realities create a perfect storm. The wonder is not that there is so much call for major reform, but that it has not been pursued more vigorously.

The question is whether the stars are now aligned in favour of true transformation. As Nobel Laureate, Lord Rutherford, said to his laboratory colleagues a century ago, "We haven't got the money, so we've got to think."[32] For the foreseeable future, no country can continue to paper over the cracks in health care with hundred dollar bills. Abundance neither eliminated the fundamental problems in health care delivery nor reduced health disparities. Perhaps relative deprivation will create the urgency and courage to achieve both.

References

[1] Korda RJ, Butler JR. Effect of healthcare on mortality: trends in avoidable mortality in Australia and comparisons with Western Europe. *Public Health* 2006; 120: 95-105.

[2] Evans RG, Barer ML, Marmor TR. *Why are some people healthy and others not?* New York: Aldine de Gruyter, 2004.

[3] Marmot MG, Smith DG, Stansfeld S, et al. Health inequalities among British civil servants: the Whitehall II study. *Lancet* 1991; 337: 1387-1393.

[4] Marmot MG, Rose G, Shipley M, Hamilton PJ. Employment grade and coronary heart disease in British civil servants. *J Epidemiol Community Health* 1978; 32: 244-249.

[5] Asada Y, Kephart G. Equity in health services use and intensity of use in Canada. *BMC Health Serv Res* 2007; 7: 41.

[6] Saposnik G, Jeerakathil T, Selchen D, et al. Socioeconomic status, hospital volume, and stroke fatality in Canada. *Stroke* 2008; 39: 3360-3366.

[7] D'Angiulli A, Grunau P, Maggi S, Herdman A. Electroencephalographic correlates of prenatal exposure to alcohol in infants and children: a review of findings and implications for neuro-cognitive development. *Alcohol* 2006; 40: 127-133.

[8] Anderson JW, Johnstone BM, Remley DT. Breast feeding and cognitive development: a meta-analysis. *Am J Clin Nutr* 1999; 70: 525-535.

[9] Monteiro PO, Victora CG. Rapid growth in infancy and childhood and obesity in later life — a systematic review. *Obes Rev* 2005; 6: 143-154.

[10] Laurance J. The war against cancer has been lost. *The Independent* 2003; 18 Sep. http://www.independent.co.uk/opinion/commentators/the-war-against-cancer-has-been-lost-580308.html (accessed Jul 2009).

[11] Faguet GB. *The war on cancer: an anatomy of failure, blueprint for the future.* New York: Springer, 2005.

[12] Chapman Z. After Vioxx scandal, NEJM Editor-in-Chief Drazen calls for full data disclosure. *Brown Daily Herald* 2007; 26 Apr. http://www.browndailyherald.com/2.12235/after-vioxx-scandal-nejm-editor-in-chief-drazen-calls-for-full-data-disclosure-1.1673806 (accessed Jul 2009).

[13] Thomas L. *The lives of a cell: notes of a biology watcher.* New York: Penguin, 1974.

[14] Nolte E, McKee M. Population health in Europe: how much is attributable to health care? *World Hosp Health Serv* 2004; 40: 12-14, 40, 42.

[15] World Health Organization. *Social determinants of health. Commission on Social Determinants of Health — final report. Closing the gap in a generation: health equity through action on the social determinants of health.* Geneva: WHO, 2008. http://www.who.int/social_determinants/thecommission/finalreport/en/index.html (accessed Jul 2009).

[16] Mackenbach JP, Stirbu I, Roskam AJ, et al; European Union Working Group on Socioeconomic Inequalities in Health. Socioeconomic inequalities in health in 22 European countries. *N Engl J Med* 2008; 358: 2468-2481.

[17] Walsh D, Whyte B, Gordon DS. Changing places? A comparative analysis of area-based health trends in Scotland through the 1980s and 1990s. *Public Health* 2007; 121: 889-897.

[18] Health Disparities Task Group of the Federal/Provincial/Territorial Advisory Committee on Population Health and Health Security. *Reducing health disparities — roles of the health sector: discussion paper.* Ottawa: Health Canada, 2005. http://www.phac-aspc.gc.ca/ph-sp/disparities/pdf06/disparities_discussion_paper_e.pdf (accessed Jul 2009).

[19] Roos NP, Mustard CA. Variation in health and health care use by socioeconomic status in Winnipeg, Canada: does the system work well? Yes and no. *Milbank Q* 1997; 75: 89-111.

[20] Segal L. Why it is time to review the role of private health insurance in Australia. *Aust Health Rev* 2004; 27: 3-15.

[21] Van Doorslaer E, Clarke P, Savage E, Hall J. Horizontal inequities in Australia's mixed public/private health care system. *Health Policy* 2008; 86: 97-108.

[22] Leon DA, Walt G, Gilson L. Recent advances: international perspectives on health inequalities and policy. *BMJ* 2001; 322: 591-594.

[23] University of California Atlas of Global Inequality. Health care professionals. Does having more doctors extend life expectancy? Life expectancy vs. physicians per capita (graph). http://ucatlas.ucsc.edu/professional.php (accessed Jul 2009).

[24] McGlynn EA, Asch SM, Adams J, et al. The quality of health care delivered to adults in the United States. *N Engl J Med* 2003; 348: 2635-2645.

[25] Kohn LT, Corrigan JM, Donaldson MS. *To err is human: building a safer health system*. Washington, DC: National Academy Press, 1999.

[26] Wilson RM, Runciman WB, Gibberd RW, et al. The quality in Australian health care study. *Med J Aust* 1995; 163: 458–471.

[27] Baker GR, Norton PG, Flintoft V, et al. The Canadian Adverse Events Study: the incidence of adverse events among hospital patients in Canada. *CMAJ* 2004; 170: 1678-1686.

[28] Fisher ES, Bynum JP, Skinner JS. Slowing the growth of health care costs: lessons from regional variation. *N Engl J Med* 2009; 360: 849-852.

[29] Welch WP, Miller ME, Welch HG, et al. Geographic variation in expenditures for physicians' services in the United States. *N Engl J Med* 1993; 328: 621-627.

[30] Baker GR, MacIntosh-Murray A, Porcellato C, et al. *High performing healthcare systems: delivering quality by design*. Toronto: Longwoods, 2008. http://www.longwoods.com/home.php?cat=571 (accessed Jul 2009).

[31] Evans RG. Economic myths and political realities: the inequality agenda and the sustainability of Medicare [working paper]. Vancouver: Centre for Health Services and Policy Research, Jul 2007. http://www.chspr.ubc.ca/node/791 (accessed Jun 2009).

[32] Think Exist [website]. http://thinkexist.com/quotation/we-haven-t-got-the-money-so-we-ve-got-to-think/408460.html (accessed Jul 2009). *(Received 28 Apr 2009, accepted 29 Jun 2009)*

Commentary on the Sustainability of Canada's Healthcare System*

Steven Lewis

Despite the huge spending, quality is uneven (Katz et al. 2004) and utilization rates vary widely and mysteriously (Fisher et al. 2000). Emergency rooms are backed up, wait times vary and public confidence has dropped precipitously in the past 15 years. Many things go right in healthcare, but the system is demonstrably unsafe (Baker et al. 2004). Compared with any other industry that has enjoyed such huge public support and massive spending increases, in terms of the quality of service and outcomes, healthcare must be termed a colossal failure.

It's not like we don't know how to fix it – there are countless examples in the Canadian experience (Rachlis 2005) and international literature of quality improvement and major reductions in wait times (Wales Audit Office 2006). Yes, expectations rise; yes, there is more technology all the time; and, yes, Canadians are willing to spend a lot of money on healthcare. Given its flaws, the system is indeed unsustainable, but not in the way unsustainability is normally portrayed, as a fiscal crisis.

What's truly unsustainable is doing business the same old way. We cannot continue to consume expensive new drugs when less expensive, older ones are just as effective most of the time. We cannot continue to have specialists do what family doctors ought to do, family doctors do what nurse practitioners ought to do and nurses do what licensed

* Originally published in *Longwoods Review* appearing in *Healthcare Quarterly* 2007, 10(2): 103-04

practical nurses ought to do. We cannot persist with a voluntarist, incremental model of quality improvement, where practitioners and institutions are free to embrace or refuse to adopt smarter and cheaper ways of delivering care. We cannot continue to accept the prices of goods and services that have no relationship to what they deliver.

That is why the article by Stuart and Adams[1] is so depressing: it accepts premises it should not accept, and assumes that the best we can do is tinker with eligibility, diminish expectations and allow the deeply flawed beast to roll merrily along. The single biggest problem in Canadian healthcare is the failure to apply ingenuity on a grand scale. The salient feature of most dramatic stories of quality improvement is that the cost actually goes down while outcomes improve.

When I first met you in your role at the Saskatchewan Health Research Board, you championed the need for health research to take place across the country, not just in a few centres, and made individuals and institutions pay attention.

Glenda Yeates

If, in 1986, someone had asked, "Is it sustainable to install massive computational capacity and storage on every office worker's desktop and in most people's homes?" the answer would have been a resounding no. Big consulting firms and think tanks would have rolled out straight-line projections that painted a terrifying financial picture. And they would have been right, if people and institutions had continued to pay $20 million for what can now be had for $179, or paid 10 times as much for a new microprocessor that had the same general specifications as the old one. Healthcare doesn't make errors of this magnitude, but it has long passed the point of zero return on investment at the margin.

Although there are encouraging calls for enhanced accountability and financial prudence, by and large Canadian healthcare remains a cottage industry of autonomous clinical and managerial decision-makers, where bad practice costs more than good practice. Unsustainable? Absolutely. But contrary to the conventional account, it is a failure of will, not the inexorable result of ingenuity and expectation.

Note

[1] Stuart, N. and J. Adams. 2007. "The Sustainability of Canada's Healthcare System: A Framework for Advancing the Debate." *Longwoods Review* in: *Healthcare Quarterly* 2007, 10(2): 96-103

References

Baker, G.R., P.G. Norton, V. Flintoft, R. Blais, A. Brown, J. Cox, E. Etchells, W.A. Ghali, P. Hebert, S.R. Majumdar, M. O'Beirne, L. Palacios-Derflingher, R.J. Reid, S. Sheps and R. Tamblyn. 2004. "The Canadian Adverse Events Study: The Incidence of Adverse Events among Hospital Patients in Canada." *Canadian Medical Association Journal* 25;170(11): 1678-86.

Fisher, E.S., J.E. Wennberg, T.A. Stukel, J.S. Skinner, S.M. Sharp, J.L. Freeman and A.M. Gittelsohn. 2000. "Associations among Hospital Capacity, Utilization, and Mortality of US Medicare Beneficiaries, Controlling for Sociodemographic Factors." *Health Services Research* 34(6): 1351-62.

Katz, A., C. De Coster, B. Bogdanovic, R.-A. Soodeen and D. Chateau. 2004. *Using Administrative Data to Develop Indicators of Quality in Family Practice.* Winnipeg: Manitoba Centre for Health Policy. <http://www.umanitoba.ca/centres/mchp/reports/pdfs/quality_wo.pdf>.

Leon, D.A., G. Walt and L. Gilson. 2001. "Recent Advances: International Perspectives on Health Inequalities and Policy." *British Medical Journal* 322(7286): 591-94.

Rachlis, M. 2005. *Prescription for Excellence.* Toronto: Harper Collins.

Wales Audit Office. 2006. NHS Waiting Times: Follow-Up Report. Author. <http://www.wales.nhs.uk/documents/NHS_waiting_times_update.pdf>.

A WestJet Healthcare System?*

Steven Lewis

I fly a lot – too much actually. I am chagrined by my carbon footprint. Most of my flights are on Air Canada (AC), indisputably an international-class, full-service airline. You can go pretty much anywhere in the world on AC or its Star Alliance partners. You can pick your fare, frills, seat and class. I've been an Elite AC member for about 15 years, so I get to wait for my flights in swanky lounges with free food, booze, newspapers, magazines and business centres. I get free flights from the Aeroplan miles I accumulate and an annual stack of upgrade certificates. I get a special number to call if I need to change a reservation or seek help. Cool, eh?

But I fly WestJet (WJ) whenever I can, and would happily abandon AC altogether if WJ decided to go after the Saskatoon-to-wherever (especially Toronto) business traveller markets. Why? What would lead me to turn my back on the airline that gives me all this stuff, and what accounts for the almost giddy affection for the one that doesn't? Here's my hypothesis: it's because Canada's airlines are akin to the health system we have (AC) and the health system we need (WJ). Here's how: What do I need? Business class to Kuala Lumpur? Single malt scotch in the lounge? Special meal? AC can do it. WJ? No can do. AC is pretty good at tertiary air care; WJ is the primary care airline. Most travel needs are primary: a reasonably priced ticket, an on-time departure, decent legroom, a modern

* Originally published in *Longwoods Essays*, March 10, 2011

aircraft. My own travel life is, well, pedestrian: Calgary, Vancouver, Toronto, Ottawa, Winnipeg (quit smirking, I like Winnipeg). WJ gives me a Boeing 737 with good overhead luggage capacity and a quiet ride – every time, all the time. AC gives me cramped Bombardiers that force passengers to compete for comically little carry-on baggage room. Advantage: WJ for the basic journeys; AC for the continental transplant operation.

What happens when there's a problem? Planes break down and weather mocks schedules. The test of an airline is not when things are tickety-boo; it's when misery descends. AC appears to believe that keeping the passengers in the dark about why a flight is delayed is reassuring, and that parcelling out the delays in two-hour increments is comforting. "The two o'clock flight that was to leave at four is now departing at six. We can't tell you which gate." WJ makes it a point to tell you what's happening. Call AC with a problem and you almost feel the blame-the-passenger vibes as the agent leafs through the policy manual to confirm your non-entitlements. WJ seems to want to help. AC has done some nice things for me, but WJ has performed truly heroic feats of creative problem solving, and in one case was generous beyond the call of duty. Advantage: WJ on both comportment and delivery.

Surprise, it's a service industry. Aviation is incredibly safe. Planes of equal size are pretty much interchangeable. The highway up there is the same for everyone, and an airport is an airport. WJ offers no business class, no hot meals, no fancy lounges, no air miles of its own. It pursues advantage by other means: the attitude of its people and their capacity to solve problems. Their entire ethos is built around the customer. I used to think the "AC attitude" was the inevitable result of an aging workforce fatigued by the wear and tear of a zillion flights and alienated by repeated labour strife and restructuring. Likewise, I was sure that the happy-faced, fun-loving, energetic WJ honeymoon would end.

Well, WJ is a decade old and still no sign of passive aggression; not all their employees are fresh-faced kids. AC actually tries, but there is too much ennui and complexity. Its own agents can't figure out their absurd Aeroplan mileage redemption rules, and its website produces some legendarily idiotic itineraries. Small wonder AC can't reliably produce quality service in the crunch. Pleasantness and can-do are hard-wired into WJ's DNA: I once bought a ticket from a WJ baggage service agent. WJ gives you more while giving you less. It has chosen the right quality indicators. Advantage: WJ.

Simple, reliable, effective, pleasant: whether from an airline or from healthcare, that's what we need most of the time. And where simple won't cut it, more than ever we need reliable, effective and pleasant. AC is besotted with complexity and covets the overseas, long-haul market segment. You can tell it doesn't really care about most domestic routes outside the big cities. Though they try their best, it's clear the employees have no great love for the corporation for which they work.

AC is to air travel what our acute care–obsessed, high-tech-envy healthcare system is to health. It's great that we can find the cystic fibrosis gene and separate Siamese twins, but not so good that chronic disease management is a national catastrophe. The vast majority of people don't need glitzy miracles; we need sound, evidence-based, timely, respectful and well-communicated primary healthcare from a team dedicated to getting it right.

In the end, it's about culture, that maddeningly elusive notion that signals what an organization or system is about. The truly successful put the customers first and pay attention to the workforce and the workplace. They get the fundamentals right and understand where their bread is buttered. WJ has mastered primary air care; it makes money where AC bleeds red ink. Healthcare, take a lesson.

Decoding Mazankowski: A Symphony in Three Movements*

Steven Lewis and Colleen Maxwell

The Mainstream Movement: Exhortation and Optimism

The first recommendation of the [Mazankowski][1] report exhorts Albertans to stay healthy as individuals, and to invest in programs that would alter the determinants of health that result in morbidity and mortality. Its wellness message may be the most forceful yet seen among the Royal Commission and similar reports produced in the last two decades. It even goes so far as to propose Alberta's "taking the lead in updating Canada's food guide" (p. 6).[2] It advocates stronger efforts to control tobacco use.

The report is equally strong on information technology, the centrepiece of which is the development of an electronic health record. Interestingly, there are two highlighted uses of the EHR: one is to "track and improve outcomes in health," the other is to "allow individuals to track their own use of health services and the costs involved, and provide the essential tools if further steps are taken to introduce new approaches to funding health services" (p. 6).[3] It further recommends a long-term investment strategy for both IT and healthcare technology acquisition and assessment.

* Originally published in *Healthcare Papers* 2002, 2(4): 20-26

Quality should be "the top priority for Alberta's health system. Set standards, measure results, and hold people accountable for achieving better outcomes in health" (p. 8).[4] To support this goal, there should be a permanent, independent Outcomes Commission, presumably an expanded version of the already-established Health Utilization Commission. The report continues the Alberta tradition of major investments in health research, advocating a greater focus on multidisciplinary centres of excellence, and further development of evidence-based decision-making capacity.

These elements of the report are rooted firmly in the tradition of mainstream health reform. They are often elegantly framed and forcefully argued. The report's emphasis on changing behaviour is short on specifics, doubtless because there is precious little evidence on how to move beyond exhortation to action. Awareness of risk factors and choices does not in itself create change; one need only observe the emerging obesity epidemic among children.

The language of the other two movements is more veiled and enigmatic. Here is where the music changes and the decoding begins.

The Financing Movement: Pessimism and Default

The report advances a number of propositions about healthcare financing. Among these are:

1. "[A]ll Albertans should have fair and equitable access to health services. No one should be denied access to essential health services because they are unable to pay" (p. 5).
2. "We need to extract maximum value for every dollar spent on health care" (p. 5).
3. "More money doesn't necessarily buy better health."
4. "The answer doesn't lie in rationing healthcare services … "We know what we want from the health system. Now we need to explore new ways of paying for it" (p. 5).
5. "We can only afford to spend more on health if Alberta's economy grows faster than spending" (p. 27).
6. "[O]pen up other sources of revenue … to improve access, expand health care services, and realize the potential of new techniques and treatments" (p. 7).
7. "Spending on health care cannot be allowed to crowd out other vital forms of public spending, including education, infrastructure, and other social services" (p. 31).
8. "Circumstances in Alberta and elsewhere in North America are such that the overall tax burden cannot be expected to rise to match increasing costs in health care. Instead of relying almost exclusively on the tax base, we need to diversify the revenue stream to support the health care services people want and expect" (p. 31).
9. "The natural and logical incentive for fee-for-service physicians is to treat more people, order more tests, or perform more procedures" (p. 33).

These assertions, crucial to the report's agenda and retailed as self-evident truths, are as a package highly controversial, and convey mixed and sometimes contradictory messages. Alberta is Canada's richest and lowest taxed province. Proposition 8 may indeed be a constraining competitive reality in many jurisdictions, but not in Alberta. Healthcare consumes a smaller percentage of its budget than is the case in any other province. The legitimate concerns about rising healthcare costs and crowding out of other programs are attributed in the report to the irresistible forces of aging, technology and unquenchable expectations. But there are more prosaic explanations, among them the Alberta government only a year ago awarding nurses a two-year, 22% wage increase and doctors an average of $40,000 in increased fees, setting off a "race to the top" that has fiscally destabilized much of the country. Propositions 2, 3 and 9 above imply – accurately – that the system is fraught with perverse incentives, unremedied inefficiencies and severely diminished marginal returns. Yet propositions 4 and 6 imply that utilization will and should rise, spending more is better because that's what Albertans want – only the government ought not to cover the additional costs. The peculiar message is that Albertans should use non-governmental revenues to purchase more services that the report notes are likely to have little impact on health status, simply to satisfy their always-rising expectations. Corollary: healthcare has been significantly redefined as a commodity, while medicare is premised on the notion that it is a public good, to be used prudently to meet needs rather than satisfy often manufactured wants.

Elsewhere the report accepts the doom-and-gloom scenario for cost increases put forward by the provincial/territorial health ministers in 2000 (Provincial and Territorial Ministers of Health 2000). That document was an advocacy piece designed to extract as much new money as possible out of Ottawa. It presents highly selective, unbalanced, worst-case analyses and scenarios, and bases 30-plus year cost projections on extrapolations of short-term trends. It relies heavily on the often-refuted assumption that an aging population creates unsustainable costs, despite abundant evidence that aging is not, in fact, a significant independent cost driver (Canadian Health Services Research Foundation 2001; Barer et al. 1987; Doblhammer and Kytir 2001; Khaw 1999; Manton et al. 1997; Manton et al. 1998; Statistics Canada 1999; Lubitz et al. 1995). The Mazankowski Report itself calls for more and better health technology assessment, much of which exposes the unrealized promise and inappropriate utilization of expensive innovations. Yet it concedes there is no turning back the technology tide, and in any event, regardless of value added, Albertans will not and should not settle for anything but the latest and best. Such logic is already extant in the system, an example being the government of Alberta's target of 24 MRI scans per 1,000 population being set in the absence of any evidence as to what doubling the year 2000 rate is expected to accomplish in concrete terms (Alberta Health and Wellness 2001).

Finally, the report is highly pessimistic about the prospects for successful and financially effective internal reforms. Research and real-world experiences have shown that where quality is the main objective – as the report commendably recommends – the savings are often massive, on the order of 30% or more (Kizer 1999; Findlay 2000). The report, however, assumes that prospects for increased efficiencies are dim, and any amount saved will be dwarfed by the new money required to fuel anticipated demands. This conclusion seems at best premature in that long-called-for reforms to reimbursement mechanisms, the distribution of personnel, the division of labour in healthcare, utilization management, primary care organization, etc., have yet to be widely implemented. Here the report is plaintive, almost mournful: an elegy for a system that might have been, but cannot be.

After carefully constructing the logic that the system is unsustainable, the report turns to "diversifying the revenue stream." In the end it stops short of recommending any particular mechanism, but urges further exploration of Medical Savings Accounts and variable premiums. Both notions, and in fact all financing proposals, require careful scrutiny.

Many forces have contributed to the sea-change in the valuation and application of evidence, with one being the role of the knowledge "broker". ... Steven will bristle at the notion that he is a knowledge broker (he holds a deep suspicion of the field of "knowledge transfer/ translation and exchange", within which the role "broker" firmly sits). But, this is precisely the role he has played over many years.

Lillian Bayne

The report assumes that telling people the costs of the services they use and creating some sort of account or mechanism whereby the more they use, the more they pay (or the less that remains in their account) will trigger wiser use of the system. This implies that ordinary citizens can and will master the knowledge to make prudent decisions about diagnostic tests and care options; will share decision-making authority with providers; and will be price-sensitive – all of this when they may be sick, scared and left alone to navigate the complexities of the system. It further implies that people knowingly misuse the system now, and that they, to a far greater extent than providers, generate activity and costs. There is clear Canadian (Tamblyn et al. 2001) and American (Foxman et al. 1987) evidence that when people reduce their use of services because of financial incentives or circumstances, they forego appropriate as well as inappropriate care. Despite noting the volume-driven logic of the supply side of the system, the report's financial reform discussions are reserved almost exclusively for the demand side.

The report clearly states that no one should be denied access to essential health services because they are unable to pay. The devil here lies in the details. Elsewhere the report recommends reducing the scope of covered services, implying that some now covered are nonessential. Does "unable to pay" mean absolutely unable to pay – literally, the person has no money – or that it would be unreasonable or unfair to expect the person to pay because of the hardships or opportunity costs incurred? At its core, medicare is a subsidy scheme: the healthy and wealthy finance the care of the sick and poor through the mechanism of a progressive tax system. The report nowhere clearly takes a position on cross-subsidization, but there are clues inherent in the mechanisms that excite its interest.

Consider the variable premium. If collected by the government from all citizens (with some exceptions), it is in fact a hypothecated (targeted) tax. If the premium rates are less progressive than the income tax system, and if premiums are expected to generate a higher proportion of revenues than is currently the case, there would be a shifting of burden from the well off to the less well off. If the variable premium rates are based on utilization, they will discriminate against the sick, who are also, on balance of probabilities, the poor; hence the result will be seriously regressive (which is why the report rejects the notion of making receipt of healthcare services a taxable benefit).

The Medical Savings Account notion is yet another matter. If the government creates and administers the (3 million!) accounts, the scheme preserves equity only if the size of one's initial account and annual additions are adjusted for age, sex, socio-economic status and other key variables affecting health status, needs and utilization. If, when the account is drawn down to zero, there is a "corridor" where all or most individuals pay out-of-pocket for subsequent services, the system would be highly regressive in that (a) the poor and the sick are more likely to use up their accounts than the healthy and wealthy; and (b) among those who do deplete their accounts, the disadvantaged will pay higher portions of their income for services. The approvingly cited Singapore experience with MSAs actually appears to discriminate against the elderly and the poor (Barr 2001). Empirical American evidence suggests that mechanisms relying on individual financial incentives to improve efficiency fail to achieve their goals (Schweitzer et al. 1996).

All healthcare financing proposals embed certain values. Proponents of these often-complex schemes have an obligation to declare and defend their value assumptions clearly and transparently. The only way non–income-tax-based finance mechanisms preserve or enhance equity is if they are fine-tuned, tweaked, means-tested and otherwise adjusted so that in the end they are equally or more progressive than the income tax system. Similarly, decreasing the scope of services financed by taxes invariably means that services that are essential to some must be paid for by other means. Delisting services by category has proved difficult, and the adverse consequences for at least some people become obvious. It is conceptually far more attractive, and financially significant, to find ways to reduce inappropriate utilization, but the report expresses no faith in prospects for doing so. Here again, pessimistic assumptions paint the report into a corner from which the only exit is either to raise taxes by another name, or leave people to their own devices and decisions about insurance and service use.

The Ideological Movement: The Code Revealed

"Alberta's health system, like other systems across the country, operates as an unregulated monopoly ... In short, it's a command and control system ... The system is organized by government, paid for by government, insured by government, and evaluated by government ... There are no choices ... There's no competition and no incentive to provide the most efficient and effective services available" (p. 21). The system needs to be "unbundled" and freedom and creativity need to be "unshackled."

This ostensibly factual description of the system could hardly have been more strident and provocative. It conjures visions of a Stalinist nightmare of impersonal functionaries robotically providing substandard service to a choice-deprived populace waiting endlessly in lines, yearning for glasnost and perestroika.

Government can't get anything right; all it should do is finance "most" care.

The reality, of course, is vastly different. Decision-making in healthcare is probably more decentralized than in any other sector in the world. Physicians practise with considerable autonomy; patients have a virtually unconditional right to see their family practitioners (if they can find one); clinical decisions, even demonstrably bad ones such as inappropriate prescribing (Hanlon et al. 2001) or unnecessary cataract surgery (Wright and Robens-Paradise 2001), go unchallenged. The great majority of physicians work as independent contractors, unbeholden to any organizational structure. The medical association, not government, largely determines how various services will be priced. Government does set out a general regulatory framework, but the real authority is legislatively delegated to self-governing professional bodies. Citizens can seek care wherever they want; they do not have to accept referral to the specialist suggested by the family practitioner and can (and do) bypass local services altogether. Physicians are free to opt out of the public system. The government provides almost no direct service; the great bulk of healthcare is delivered by private not-for-profit organizations and independent contractors.

"Canadians and Albertans understand and support competition, and we're reluctant to accept a situation where we have only one choice" (p. 21). Since the public clearly has (albeit theoretically in some cases) abundant choice of providers and services, and far more than is the case in the American managed-care environment, the assertion needs decoding. The meaning clarifies as one reads the references to greater roles for the private sector, and the implied growth of a parallel system as services are delisted. Regardless of one's philosophical predilections, it is clear that private-sector options promoted by effective marketing are not designed to encourage the public to make better choices, but more lucrative choices – for the providers. Utilization and costs rise. In any event, the public's main concerns are rarely expressed as choice per se, but in the more substantive terms of quality and access.

Far from evaluating its own services, government evaluates very little. Most evaluation is conducted by consultants or academics with peer-reviewed grant money. Regionalization was expressly designed to diminish whatever central government command-and-control elements remained in the system. And if there is such a powerful government monopoly, why does the report repeatedly deem the government powerless to control costs and expectations, or implement the internal reforms it and dozens of other government-commissioned reports have recommended?

Here is where the report is its most seductive, and why its internal inconsistencies and unsupported premises have not stood in the way of a generally respectful and attentive reception in the media and among politicians. The report nowhere explicitly advocates an American-style healthcare system, but it does adopt a thoroughly American neoconservative political stance that declares government the worst of all possible actors, and taxation the worst of all possible financing mechanisms. Acceptance of this perspective dooms the argument that internal reforms, tax-based financing and sound public policy-making – all in one way or another endorsed in the Mazankowski Report – are the keys to a higher quality, responsive and sustainable system. The field is then opened wide to any number of reforms, from those gingerly promoted in the report itself, to those unstated but lurking in the background. Ultimately the fate of the report will depend on which music decision-makers and the public find most appealing, and whether any consensus is likely to emerge among devotees of the classical, the dirge, and the cacophonously post-modern.

Notes

[1] Alberta, Premier's Advisory Council on Health. A Framework for Reform. 2002. Edmonton.

[2] Ibid, p. 6

[3] Ibid, p. 6

[4] Ibid, p. 8

References

Alberta Health and Wellness. 2001. Government of Alberta News Release – Alberta to Lead Country in MRI Scans. April 9. <http://www.gov.ab.ca/acn/200104/10508.html>.

Barer, M.L., R.G. Evans, C. Hertzman and J. Lomas. 1987. "Aging and Health Care Utilization: New Evidence on Old Fallacies." *Social Science and Medicine* 24(10): 851-62.

Barr,M.D. 2001. "Medical Savings Accounts in Singapore: A Critical Inquiry." *Journal of Health Politics, Policy and Law* 26(4): 709-26.

Canadian Health Services Research Foundation. 2001. "Myth: The Aging Population Will Overwhelm the Healthcare System." Ottawa: The Foundation. <www.chsrf.ca>.

Doblhammer, G. and J. Kytir. 2001. "Compression or Expansion of Morbidity? Trends in Health-Life Expectancy in the Elderly Austrian Population between 1978 and 1998." *Social Science and Medicine* 52: 385-91.

Findlay, S., ed. 2000. *Reducing Medical Errors and Improving Patient Safety: Success Stories from the Front Lines of Medicare.* Washington, DC: National Coalition on Health Care.

Foxman, B., R.B. Valdez, K.N. Lohr, G.A. Goldberg,J.P. Newhouse and R.H. Brook. 1987. "The Effect of Cost Sharing on the Use of Antibiotics in Ambulatory Care: Results from a Population-Based RandomizedControlled Trial." *Journal of Chronic Disease* 40(5): 429-37.

Hanlon, J.T., K.E. Schmader, C.M. Ruby and M. Weinberger. 2001. "Suboptimal Prescribing in Older Inpatients and Outpatients." *Journal of the American Geriatrics Society* 49: 200-09.

Khaw, K.T. 1999. "How Many, How Old, How Soon?" *British Medical Journal* 319: 1350-52. <www.bmj.com>.

Kizer, K.W. 1999. "The 'New VA': A National Laboratory for Health Care Quality Management." *American Journal of Medical Quality* 14: 3-20.

Lubitz, J., J. Beebe and C. Baker. 1995. "Longevity and Medicare Expenditures." *New England Journal of Medicine* 332: 999-1003.

Manton, K.G., L. Corder and E. Stallard. 1997. "Chronic Disability Trends in Elderly United States Populations: 1982-1994." *Proceedings of the National Academy of Science* 94: 2593-98.

Manton, K.G., E. Stallard and L.S. Corder. 1998. "The Dynamics of Dimensions of Age-Related Disability 1982 to 1994 in the US Elderly Population." *Journal of Gerontology: Biological Sciences* 53A: B59-B70.

Provincial and Territorial Ministers of Health. 2000. *Understanding Health Care's Costs: Interim Report.* <www.gov.on.ca/health/english/pub/ministry/ ptcd/ptcd_doc_e.pdf>.

Schweitzer, M., J.C. Hershey and D.A. Asch. 1996. "Individual Choice in Spending Accounts. Can We Rely on Employees to Choose Well?" *Medical Care* 34(6): 583-93.

Statistics Canada. 1999. "How Healthy Are Canadians?" *Health Reports* 11 (Winter).

Tamblyn, R., R. Laprise, J.A. Hanley, M. Abrahamowicz, S. Scott, N. Mayo, J. Hurley, R. Grad, E. Latimer, R. Perreault, P. McLeod, A. Huang, P. Larochelle and L. Mallet. 2001. "Adverse Events Associated with Prescription Drug Cost-Sharing among Poor and Elderly Persons." *Journal of the American Medical Association* 285(4): 421-29.

Wright, C. and Y. Robens-Paradise. 2001. "Evaluation of Indications and Outcomes in Elective Surgery." Centre for Clinical Epidemiology and Evaluation, Vancouver Hospital and Health Sciences Centre. May, www.resio.org. (Health Transition Fund project sponsored by Health Canada and Vancouver/Richmond Health Board.)

Regionalization: Making Sense of the Canadian Experience*

Steven Lewis and Denise Kouri

In Canada, regionalization of healthcare has entailed more than devolution and decentralization of services from provincial governments to regional authorities. It included consolidation of authority from local boards and agencies, and some centralization of services. Regionalization was the remedy proposed for the diagnosis of fragmentation and incoherence made by commissions across the country in the 1980s. Regionalization addressed the organizational dimensions of the perceived problems, but provincial governments added goals unrelated to structural change to its mandate.

The authors assess the potential impact of regionalization on health system goals and take stock of current Canadian circumstances. Even where regionalization's impact is theoretically high, there are many practical limits to its effect. Although it can facilitate or impede change, in the end the will and actions of provincial governments, providers and other actors in the health system are fundamental to attaining more substantive goals. Many health reform goals require nothing less than a transformation of how soci-

* Originally published in *Healthcare Papers* 2004, 5(1): 12-31

ety views health, and in the culture of healthcare delivery. Further, the authors argue that the implementation of regionalization in Canada has been limited. Devolution has typically been halting and provisional; there has been little stability; and there have been constraints on the ability to act. These limitations have reduced its potential effect.

The authors conclude with proposals for increasing regionalization's contribution to health reform goals. These include a more stable and transparent provincial–RHA relationship, information and measures to better align resources to needs, increased regional-level system integration and changes to organizational culture and practice in the health system.

Introduction

Nine Canadian provinces have regionalized healthcare (and in some cases, related services). With a decade or so of regionalization behind us, it is timely to revisit its purposes and achievements. What is healthcare regionalization supposed to accomplish, and how could we tell if it realized its potential? What proportion of changes in healthcare concepts, emphasis and delivery can reasonably be attributed to regionalization? The most sweeping structural reform since medicare became a coast-to-coast program in 1971, regionalization has taken different paths in different jurisdictions. There is no common definition of a health region, no uniform understanding of what services should be regionalized and no consensus on governance. The universal theme in Canadian regionalization may well be instability: governments have constantly revisited their regional schemes, making changes ranging from marginal to dramatic. Making sense of the Canadian experience in healthcare regionalization is at one level relatively straightforward, but understanding its virtues and flaws, achievements and failures becomes complex.

For these and other reasons, it is impossible to tally up the scorecard – balanced or otherwise – for regionalization. It is too diverse and too short of evaluative data. It is but one factor – albeit a crucial one – in the ongoing evolution of the health system. In healthcare, structures don't "do" anything; they enable or hinder certain developments, but they are not independent actors. Yet they can provide a directional nudge to the system and create the potential for major change. It is therefore important to try to understand regionalization as a phenomenon, revisit its origins and take stock of where we are a decade or so after its becoming the Canadian norm.

This paper addresses four main questions. First, what, conceptually, is regionalization in healthcare, and what distinguishes it as a structure? Second, how was regionalization intended to contribute to the achievement of the goals for the health system articulated in the 1980s and 1990s? Third, how has regionalization been implemented in Canada – its formal configuration, the degree of flux and stability, the "rules of the game" – and how have these factors affected its potential to achieve its intended impact? Fourth, with the experience gained over the last decade, how might we now (re)design regionalization to better contribute to health system goals?[1]

What Is Regionalization?

There is no consensus definition of regionalization in healthcare. Here we focus on the similarity of the Canadian experience rather than the differences. Put simply, Canadian regionalization has four main features. First, the regions are defined by geography – they occupy specific territory. Second, their existence and authority are at the pleasure of the provincial government – they are devolved authorities rather than self-defining entities. Third, they consolidate, at the regional level, authority previously distributed among many programs and communities. Fourth, they are responsible for a considerable range of health services – most frequently spanning at least community, long-term care residential and acute care services, and often extending to mental health and addictions, public health, and health promotion (Canadian Centre for Analysis of Regionalization and Health 2004).

These four features describe, more or less, the regional structures in nine provinces and how they differ from Ontario. While Ontario has cancer care regions, and has geographically defined planning bodies (the District Health Councils), it does not have regions defined by the four features described above.

There are two axes to regionalization, and it is important to recognize their distinctness. One axis is the continuum of authority, ranging from complete devolution to complete consolidation. The second axis is the centralization or decentralization of services, which refers to location. We use these terms consistently throughout this paper: consolidation and devolution invariably refer to authority, while centralization and decentralization invariably refer to physical location/configuration.

Regionalization of healthcare in Canada has played out along both axes. Provincial governments have devolved power to regional health authorities, which in turn have consolidated power previously held by local boards. Some provincial programs, such as mental health, were in some provinces devolved and decentralized to the regions, while others, such as acute care services, underwent consolidation but not always centralization at the regional level.

However, while in some instances RHAs have a mandate or at least the latitude to centralize services, they are often constrained by provincial action or policy from doing so. Some centralization reaches across RHA borders either through interregional agreements, or more likely as a result of provincial policy or the practical impossibility of doing otherwise due to the highly specialized or unusually expensive nature of the service in question.

Why Regionalize?

Regionalization was almost unanimously recommended by the provincial commissions and task forces of the 1980s charged with charting a new direction for healthcare

(Mhatre and Deber 1992). There was general agreement on overall health system goals: cost savings, efficiency, equity, enhanced citizen participation, increased accountability of decision-makers, emphasis on prevention and health promotion, all seen through the lens of an emerging needs-based, population health perspective (Church and Barker 2003; Williamson et al. 2003). But how was regionalization intended to contribute to the achievement of the goals for the health system?

One goal was to overcome the atomization of the system – Saskatchewan alone had 435 health boards for a population of 1 million – which invariably created difficulties in coordination, engendered narrow and sometimes parochial loyalties and forced the public to deal with a labyrinthine array of structures. Critics noted that the excess of governance meant that no one was actually in charge, able to implement a coherent and seamless program.

The diagnosis led to the proposed remedy of regionalization. Where fragmentation is the main problem, the first preoccupation is not devolution, but to consolidate power held by highly localized and service-specific boards. Provinces wanted to deal with fewer authorities and break down the barriers between programs and sectors. This left two main organizational options: eliminate sub-provincial boards altogether and run the system from health ministries with regional divisions, or establish regional authorities. To pursue the first option would have repudiated the advice of the high-level reports and appeared as an enormous repatriation of power from community to government. Such a move would have been both substantively and politically risky. The establishment of regional authorities was the only realistic approach to creating an integrated, upstream-oriented, responsive and participatory system.

Most goals of health reform were designed to increase the effectiveness and efficiency of the health system while others addressed broader political concerns – i.e., calls for increased accountability and public input. Some goals implied organizational changes, while others called for changes in provider and public perspective and behaviour. Regionalization addressed the organizational dimensions of the perceived problems. However, provincial governments added goals unrelated to structural change to regionalization's mandate.

As outlined in Table 1, the potential impact of these various health system goals depends on many factors, some related to regionalization and others not.

Table 1. Potential Impact of Regionalization on Health System Goal Attainment

1a GOAL: Aligning Needs and Resources; Potential Impact of Regionalization: High		
Factors Increasing Potential Impact	**Factors Decreasing Potential Impact**	**Current Canadian Circumstances**
Province genuinely committed to needs-based resource allocation and population health mandate RHA supports and prioritizes population health mandate RHA has authority to reallocate resources Good needs-assessment protocols Good performance measurement and reporting mechanisms Disadvantaged populations have effective voice and influence Elites support a needs-based allocation of resources Evidence-based policy and practice Adequate information base re: interventions as well as needs	Province only rhetorically committed to needs-based and pop. health approach and more traditional in practice RHA uncommitted to mandate Provincial funding rules rigid Constrained RHA autonomy to reallocate resources Province focuses on utilization targets, not impact or distribution Provincial government allows interest groups to end-run regions and have directions and decisions reversed RHAs responsive to interest groups and agenda derailed Provider resistance Poor needs-assessment protocols Poor performance measurement and reporting mechanisms	Restrictions on reallocation vary from some to significant Provinces struggling with population health mandate and accountability RHAs struggling with population health mandate and accountability Needs-assessments generally done but of varying quality Information systems still developing Performance measurement and reporting in early stages Some provincial governments more prone to end-runs and intervention in RHA affairs than others

1b GOAL: Integration of Services; Potential Impact of Regionalization: High		
Factors Increasing Potential Impact	**Factors Decreasing Potential Impact**	**Current Canadian Circumstances**
Wide scope of services falling within RHA mandate Consolidation of authority over various programs and sectors Provincial funding formulas aligned with goal RHA autonomy to reallocate resources Organizational charts that promote integrated planning and management	Important services (MDs, drugs) outside purview of RHAs Vestigial program autonomy (affiliation agreements, competitive and narrowly focused program boards) Provincial funding formulas misaligned with goal Constrained RHA autonomy to reallocate resources Organizational charts that promote "silo" thinking Historical program territoriality Resistance of providers	Generally wide range of services under RHA authority MDs and drugs not included in RHA mandates Regions have privately owned facilities and affiliation agreements Provincial funding often comes with conditions such as utilization targets Issues with provider contracts and morale

Table 1. Continued

1c GOAL: Service Quality and Evidence-Based Practice; Potential Impact of Regionalization: Low

Factors Increasing Potential Impact	Factors Decreasing Potential Impact	Current Canadian Circumstances
Rewarded by provincial funding and payment mechanisms Provincial health quality (HQ) and evidence-based practice (EBP) activities/resources An academic community committed to EBP Good information and performance measurement systems Provider culture well disposed to HQ and EBP RHA authority to allocate resources RHA control over number and distribution of MDs	Perverse incentives in provincial funding and payment mechanisms Absence of provincial HQ and EBP leadership Lack of emphasis in academic programs Lack of interest in HQ and EBP among opinion leaders and providers Poorly developed information and performance measurement systems Provincially set utilization targets as a condition of funding Excess capacity in some sectors Excess funding that papers over substandard practice Public opposition to changes in access, service configuration Provider opposition	Payment mechanisms generally indifferent to evidence-based performance Two provinces (Sask. and Ab.) have established a quality council; others, e.g., Manitoba, planning to do so Several provinces have centres that promote EBP but impact limited Academic programs vary in commitment to EBP Provider culture ambivalent toward HQ and EBP Some RHAs have invested considerably in EBP, and QI initiatives Information systems in early stages Fee-for-service generally rewards volume over efficiency Generally restricted ability to reallocate resources at RHA level RHAs have limited authority to create or close programs and facilities RHAs generally have little control over number and distribution of MDs though increasing in some provinces

1d GOAL: Health Promotion and Prevention; Potential Impact of Regionalization: Moderate

Factors Increasing Potential Impact	Factors Decreasing Potential Impact	Current Canadian Circumstances
Provincial and RHA commitment to these activities Explicit and high-profile mandate to pursue these activities Strong RHA leadership and buy-in from significant provider constituencies Accountability for performance in these areas Mechanisms to ensure voices of the dispossessed are heard	Public preoccupation with acute and medical care Weak provincial commitment Weak RHA commitment Lack of provider interest Impatience with long-term time frame for achievement of goals Lack of public and media interest	Public health on radar screen because of SARS, West Nile, flu epidemics Some RHAs very active in community development Many RHAs have pursued intersectoral partnerships and programs

1e GOAL: Improved Accountability; Potential Impact of Regionalization: Moderate		
Factors Increasing Potential Impact	**Factors Decreasing Potential Impact**	**Current Canadian Circumstances**
Substantial authority and autonomy truly devolved to RHA Sufficient RHA authority over the programs under its jurisdiction (i.e., clear and widespread consolidation of authority) Non-partisan board structures and behaviour Public confident in RHA and views it as legitimate decision-making body with a mandate to change Provincial government resistance to end-runs RHAs willing to make and take responsibility for tough decisions Opposition recognizes the devolution and legislative debate is altered Media create sense of legitimacy of RHA as decision-maker Good information used and available for prioritizing Good reporting mechanisms in place	RHA has little authority and autonomy Public regards only provincial government as accountable RHA boards partisan in nature Provincial government responds to end-runs and overrules RHA decisions RHAs attempt to offload tough decisions on government Opposition makes RHA-level decisions a constant political issue Poor information and reporting mechanisms	Devolution to RHAs incomplete and some power has been reconsolidated at the provincial level in recent years Government assumes ownership of major decisions even if RHA initiates them Consolidation of authority from local to the regional level has been partial Elections terminated in Sask., Alta., Quebec; exist in PEI since 1999 and initiated in NB in 2004 Performance reporting to public still in embryo Health remains a high-profile political issue among public Public holds provincial government accountable to greater extent than RHA Legislative debate for the most part traditional, partisan Media focuses on government behaviour more than RHAs

1f GOAL: Increased Public Participation; Potential Impact of Regionalization: Moderate		
Factors Increasing Potential Impact	**Factors Decreasing Potential Impact**	**Current Canadian Circumstances**
Explicit and high-profile mandate to pursue these activities Tradition of civic engagement in various sectors Public believes its participation will be valued and valuable Included in performance agreements and indicators as important measure	Weak RHA commitment Lack of public and media interest Not included in performance agreements and indicator sets	Some RHAs very active in experimenting with public participation Does not appear in most performance agreements and indicator sets

Increased effectiveness and efficiency from:

- *Aligning needs and resources:* The premise is the need for a transition to a population-based and needs-based service model. A fragmented model by its nature does not lend itself to assessing population needs comprehensively, nor to moving resources fluidly to respond to needs. As we discuss above, the transfer of authority to regions was explicitly intended to attain this goal (Table 1a).

- *Integration of services:* This proposed reform addresses a long-standing criticism of health services that they are silos unto themselves, and the gaps within and particularly across sectors (acute, continuing, community care, etc.) are barriers to optimal performance. A great deal of research and analysis suggested that "bed blockers" filled hospitals, too many elderly lived in nursing homes, there was underinvestment in community care and insufficient emphasis on prevention, tests were repeated, communication was substandard, etc. Integration of services was an explicit mandate of regionalization and its consolidation of authority over regionally based services (Table 1b).
- *Increased service quality and evidence-based practice:* Proposed innovations address concerns emerging in the 1990s that healthcare typically fails to adopt best practices supported by solid research evidence. More recently the focus has shifted to quality problems. These have led to calls for changes in provider behaviour and incentive structures, and in the prevailing health system culture. However, there is no explicit link to regionalization in these innovations (Table 1c).
- *Emphasizing health promotion and prevention:* The premise is that a reallocation of effort and resources to these "upstream" activities will improve health status, reduce disparities among groups and reduce the burden of illness in the future. (Table 1d).

Responses to greater demands for accountability and public input:

- *Improved accountability:* The idea is that increased reporting of health outcomes will increase accountability to the funder (government). In the regionalized context, the idea is that health regions with an explicit mandate to serve a wide range of population needs, a legitimate governance structure and an obligation to report health outcomes for a regional population will be more accountable to residents. An extension of this idea is that healthcare decision-making will be less conventionally partisan and less hostage to electoral cycles and interests if the system is more accountable for health outcomes (Table 1e).
- *Increased public participation:* This proposal is to respond to criticisms that the health system is dominated by providers and bureaucrats and should involve the public and users more in decision-making. Health regions were explicitly charged with increasing public participation, and also expected to be "closer" to the people by virtue of their smaller geographic size (Table 1f).
- Table 1 is obviously compressed, and there will be numerous exceptions and objections to its generalizations. If it is in the main a plausible depiction of both theory and current realities, the challenges become clear. Even where regionalization's impact is theoretically high, there are many practical limits to its effect. Although it can facilitate or impede change, in the end the will and actions of provincial governments, providers and other actors in the health system are fundamental to attaining more substantive goals. Many health reform goals require nothing less than a transformation of how society views health, and in the culture of healthcare delivery.

- It would take an extraordinary commitment and discipline on the part of many actors to allow regionalization to be the laboratory for large-scale change. Governments would have to accept the risks that invariably accompany experimentation and creativity. Providers would have to endorse and embrace goals that may appear to diminish the priority of what they do. The public – and the advantaged classes in particular – would have to endorse a focus on reducing health inequalities that requires a reallocation of resources. There may have to be trade-offs between short-term access to services, and investments in alternative strategies that will pay off only in the long run. All of these require a change in perspective and mindset, and a departure from traditional interest-based decision-making. Regionalization may be a necessary condition for even beginning these conversations, but it is hardly sufficient to rewire the thinking of the many constituencies involved.

Table 2. Changes in Regionalization from Time of Implementation to 2003, by Province

Province	Established	Restructured	Selected Changes
British Columbia	1997	2001	There are now five RHAs (covering 16 Health Service Delivery Areas) and one Provincial Health Service Authority. Board members are appointed. Before restructuring, there were 11 Regional Health Boards, 34 Community Health Councils and seven Community Health Services Societies.
Alberta	1994	2002 and 2003	As of April 2003 there are nine RHAs and all members are appointed. Before that there were 17 RHAs. In 2002 Alberta moved from an all-appointed board member structure to one that was two-thirds elected and one-third appointed. It reverted to an entirely appointed structure in 2003.
Saskatchewan	1992	2002	There are 12 RHAs and board members are appointed. Before that there were 32 health districts whose boards were initially all appointed. From 1995 to 2002, two-thirds of board members were elected and one-third appointed.
Manitoba	1997–1998	2002	There are 11 RHAs with appointed board members. Before restructuring, there were 12 RHAs.
Quebec	1989–1992	2001, and 2003–04	There are 18 RHAs, whose roles have been in transition since November 2003. Before 2001 board members were elected by a representative caucus of stakeholders and CEOs were appointed by the RHA board. Since then, board members and regional CEOs have been appointed by the province and CEOs are accountable jointly to the Deputy Minister and the regional board. In 2003 Quebec initiated a reorganization of its regional structures, which is currently in progress.
Nova Scotia	1996	2001	There are nine RHAs, with appointed boards. Before restructuring, there were four RHAs.

Table 2. Continued

New Brunswick	1992	2002	There are 8 RHAs, which had previously been Hospital Corporations. Board members are appointed. Since 2004, boards will consist of eight elected and seven appointed members.
Prince Edward Island	1993–1994	2002	There are four RHAs, with mixed elected and appointed members, and a Provincial Health Services Authority responsible for secondary and tertiary acute care services. Before restructuring, there were five RHAs.
Newfoundland	1994	-	There are six institutional health boards, four health and community services boards, two integrated boards, a Nursing Home Board and a Cancer Treatment and Research Board. Board members are appointed.

How Was Regionalization Implemented?

Thus, even a full-blown, authoritative version of regionalization could not in itself be expected to change a complex culture. But regionalization has not been full-blown in Canada. Devolution has typically been halting and provisional; there has been little stability (Table 2); in some provinces the regional CEOs are appointed wholly or partly by the Ministry of Health, and are wholly or partly accountable to them (see Newfoundland and Labrador Health and Community Services Association 1999; Office of the Auditor General of British Columbia 2003); and there have been constraints on the ability to act.

Recall that regionalization both consolidates and devolves authority. In almost all jurisdictions, there was real consolidation of authority in the sense that many boards disappeared, and others became advisory. But RHAs do not have exclusive authority over all services. They commonly enter into contractual or affiliation agreements with the owners and boards of non-profit, for-profit and religiously owned entities. Such boards may bring useful dimensions of community legitimacy, service quality and responsiveness, but they can also stand in the way of change. Particular interests and loyalties may conflict with the public interest, and parochial priorities may conflict with RHA mandates and aspirations. Thus, there have been historical, legal and practical limits to consolidation, especially where the public has strong allegiance to particular programs and facilities.

Similarly, the devolution of authority was in reality less than meets the eye. The notion of devolution suggests that the provinces have power to devolve. In a formal sense, this is of course true. But healthcare consists of millions of trans-actions negotiated between patients and providers. In a strict, authoritative sense no government or region actually "runs" healthcare. They control overall public spending levels, draw up organizational charts, set standards and regulate activities within a legislative framework. They can institute processes and rules that affect providers and recipients of care (e.g., the Coronary Care Network in Ontario, coordinated assessment and placement systems in long-term care, wait-list management systems, drug formularies). However, within these parameters clinical autonomy remains the norm; practitioners have the authority to make decisions that among other things drive expenditures; their credibility among the public is much higher than is politicians'; and many measures cannot successfully be implemented without their consent. Governance power is in some fundamental ways limited, and as a result, it is easy to overestimate the theoretical impact of devolving some of it.

Table 3: Opinions about the Clarity and Extent of Devolution of Authority

	Percent of Respondents in Agreement*		
	Boards	CEOs	Ministries
Clarity:			
The division of authority between RHAs and the Ministry of Health is clear.	50	31	32
If residents of a region do not support a board decision they take their complaints to the provincial ministry or government.	58	87	96
Extent of Devolution:			
Boards are legally responsible for things over which they have insufficient control.	77	80	59
Boards are too restricted by rules laid down by the provincial/territorial government.	71	70	30
Boards have less authority than I expected.	63	64	33

* The percentages of people agreeing with a particular item are based on the numbers who responded that they either "moderately" or "strongly agreed" versus those who "moderately" or "strongly disagreed." Those who did not respond or who had no opinion were excluded from the percentage calculation.

The ambiguity surrounding devolution has been documented. In a survey of board members and CEOs of RHAs and provincial government decision-makers in all provinces other than Ontario [2002], the majority of respondents indicated that the extent of devolution was unclear (Table 3) (Kouri et al. 2002). Most also felt that residents had a tendency to bypass RHA boards and present their concerns to the provincial government. All groups of respondents believed RHAs had responsibility without authority. Board and CEO respondents believed the government excessively restricts their decision-making latitude and that RHAs have less authority than they had anticipated; ministry officials tended to disagree on both counts.

Furthermore, the transfer of authority that did occur created new sets of problems. Consolidation at the regional level reduced for many a sense of ownership over local programs and services and connection to the system. Regionalization eliminated significant numbers of board members of local organizations. It was predictable that disenfranchising citizen-leaders or changing their roles would engender resentment, as will geographic shifts in power. Some provinces (e.g., British Columbia and Nova Scotia) created sub-regional community councils to enhance local influence and cushion the blow of eliminating local boards. This may have been advisable for political reasons, but such measures often created tensions between local and regional authorities and made it difficult for RHAs to earn the loyalty and respect of local communities.

As a result, it proved difficult to shift accountability. Regions are accountable to the governments to which they owe their existence and from which they derive whatever authority they possess, and also to their regional populations. Yet the public has a long and primary accountability relationship with its provincial government, and only a new and ill-defined connection to its RHAs. Citizens know how to call the government to account and may resist attempts to create a structural buffer that might make it more difficult to exercise their democratic authority. Or more prosaically, the public may continue to hold government accountable for regional decisions by virtue of the prominence of healthcare in provincial politics and a traditional focus on the legislature as the arena for debating and resolving health issues.

Nor was it clear whether RHAs should lead or follow public sentiment. Accountability for "doing the right thing" or advancing the goals of reform is distinct from accountability for doing what the public wants in every instance. In healthcare, most individuals relate to accountability in terms of satisfaction with discrete services in particular circumstances. There may in fact be no discernible "public" that would hold an RHA (or government) accountable for achieving certain population-based outcomes and overcoming disparities in health status, yet these are among the principal goals of reform. Interestingly, RHAs believe they will stand up to vested interests and majority views they believe to be wrong, while government officials believe that RHAs are more responsive to popular pressures (Table 4). This perception of RHA vulnerability may be one of the factors leading to the recent reconsolidation of authority at the provincial level in several provinces.

Table 4. Citizen and Stakeholder Influence on Board Decisions

	Percent of Respondents in Agreement*		
	Boards	CEOs	Ministries
Even if a decision is opposed by the majority of citizens in the community, board members support it if they believe it is the right decision.	83	90	57
Interest groups sometimes force boards to make decisions they would not otherwise make.	28	43	82
Vested interests have too big a say in board decisions.	25	27	71

* The percentages of people agreeing with a particular item are based on the numbers who responded that they either "moderately" or "strongly agreed" versus those who "moderately" or "strongly disagreed." Those who did not respond or who had no opinion were excluded from the percentage calculation.

Such tensions might be at least partially resolved by increased accountability for performance. However, performance measurement is still developing and remains an elusive concept in Canadian healthcare, particularly at a systemic level that attempts to transcend historical boundaries in the organization of healthcare delivery. Governments typically must approve RHA plans and budgets, and in some cases there are formal performance agreements that outline, to varying degrees, expectations and deliverables. A recent review in British Columbia found that the first generations of performance agreements had several defects. One was the peculiar combination of very specific deliverables – e.g., reducing the utilization of hospital-based mental health services by 2% – and vague commitments. A second was the confused lines of authority that made accountability difficult to locate. A third was the lack of recognition that RHAs could plausibly be held accountable for only a small fraction of goals such as health status improvement (Office of the Auditor General of British Columbia 2003). The answer to the question, "How are RHAs performing?" depends in part on whether performance expectations and agreements are reasonable, coherent and measurable, and whether there is a reasonable match between authority and accountability. The report of the Auditor General of British Columbia on RHA performance agreements nicely captured the gulf between the putative design of provincial–regional accountabilities and the actual implementation (Figure 1).

Figure 1. Governance Structure of Regionalization, British Columbia

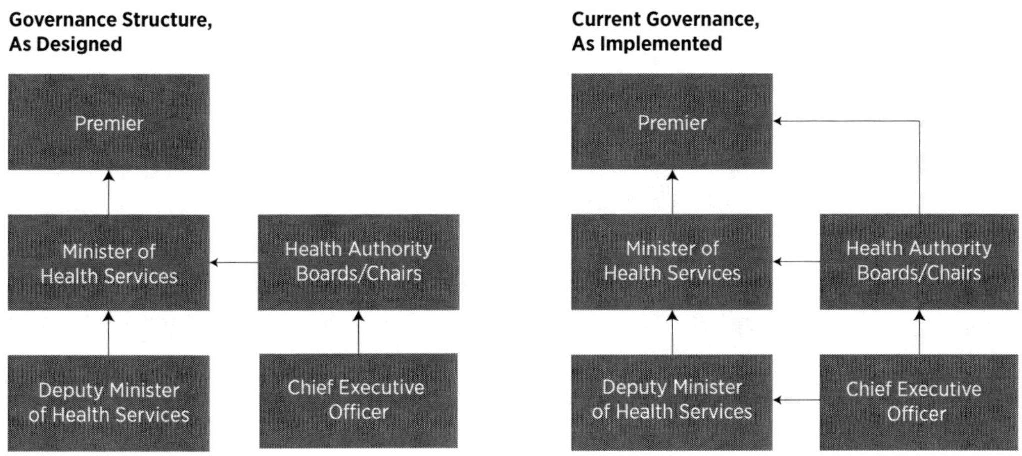

Source: Office of the Auditor General of British Columbia 2003: 22.

RHA legitimacy was compromised over the years by frequent changes in the method for selecting board members. Throughout the decade, some RHA members in Saskatchewan, Prince Edward Island (since 1999) and Alberta (very briefly) were elected by popular vote, and in Quebec there were elections by an assembly of stakeholders. However, in 2004 only Prince Edward Island and New Brunswick have elections. It is not clear whether this matters substantively – a 1997 survey of RHAs in Saskatchewan found that the views of appointed and elected members were similar, although it did not compare the mostly elected boards to all-appointed boards (Lewis et al. 2001). In addition, the dust rarely settles on a provincial or RHA organizational chart. Region size and boundaries change; opinion swings back and forth on the advisability of elected versus appointed boards; provinces alternately step back from and reinsert themselves into decision-making; CEOs often have formal or de facto divided reporting patterns.

A further source of instability has been funding. Throughout most of Canada, regionalization has not yet reached its teens, yet this child of reform has experienced long stretches of famine and feast. The move to regionalization was inherently destabilizing: the collecting up and devolving down of authority, the creation of new structures, the shift to population-based funding, etc. These changes alone created choppy waters for the healthcare ship, which was further buffeted by the fiscal downdraft of the mid-1990s, and the subsequent updraft ever since. Did regionalization make the navigation smoother, or did it remove the rudder just when the seas got rough?

Even with more complete devolution of authority, however, resource allocation issues would still need to be resolved. The principal financing mechanisms to achieve regionalization goals are (1) needs-based funding from the province to RHAs and (2) global funding to foster responsiveness to regional needs. All provinces have gone to some form of needs-based allocation, at least in theory. However, the actual practice is difficult to assess. Clearly, a number of provinces have done a great deal of sophisticated development and refinement of the methodologies of needs-based funding. But they are as yet imperfect, and their implementation is inconsistent across provinces. Unfortunately, we know little about within-region allocation of resources and whether RHAs have succeeded in fulfilling their mandates to respond appropriately to needs, to increase community-based care and to increase emphasis on upstream strategies.

Perhaps most significant is what wasn't regionalized. No province included physician services (or drugs outside hospitals) in regional design. Physicians are the gatekeepers of most of the healthcare system and in large measure establish its cultural norms. Regionalization was, among other things, intended to move beyond the volume-driven, piecework orientation of fee-for-service medicine toward a needs-based, outcomes-oriented metric. But regions are rarely physicians' employers and governments negotiate contracts independently with medical associations. Fee-for-service remains by far the dominant payment system. In recent years there has been a perceived physician shortage, which put medical associations in strong bargaining positions and resulted in large increases in fee schedules that made the status quo even more lucrative. RHAs have little control over the supply and distribution of physicians. Provincial governments have arguably made only modest progress in negotiating a new culture of healthcare, while RHAs are not well placed to drive key aspects of change.

Finally, there is some doubt that the visionary health goals developed in the early 1990s guide the system. A comprehensive study found that, in general, the goals are not central to provincial policy makers' activities and decisions, but interestingly, they seem to be more influential at the regional level (Williamson et al. 2003). This analysis tends to support the notion that regions may be more active incubators of innovation than provinces, at least under some circumstances. This is plausible in that, at the provincial level, political conditions change and it is difficult to sustain the energy to pursue goals whose realization does not conform to the electoral cycle. Conversely, "getting health right" is the only mission of RHAs, which, undistracted by either the immediacy of political conflict or competing priorities in other sectors, may be more likely to maintain their focus.

Increasing Regionalization's Contribution to Health Reform Goals

Health systems change slowly, and the impact of formal structures and policies can lose force given the highly localized and largely autonomous nature of most front-line health services. It is conceivable that regionalization is flawed in both theory and practice. Incontestably, many long-touted changes have been slow to see the light of day under both regionalized and non-regionalized regimes. The firmest conclusion we can reach is that only a limited form of regionalization has been implemented in Canada. There are nevertheless lessons to be learned from the experience, which in turn suggest future directions that may lead to greater success.

A More Stable and Transparent Provincial–RHA Relationship

Experience over the last decade suggests it may not be feasible for provinces to completely devolve authority because of the political dynamics of healthcare. Allowing RHAs to experiment, take risks, make mistakes and incur the wrath of their constituents will often have adverse political consequences for provincial governments. If government cannot devolve authority and accountability simultaneously, it will be reluctant to devolve authority, or at the very least it will retain the option to veto decisions or mandate certain initiatives.

However, the more frequently provincial governments change health authority structures and overrule their decisions, the more regionalization's potential for effectiveness is undermined. Regionalization cannot hope to succeed unless provincial governments provide more long-term stability to RHAs, and authority commensurate with accountability.

There will never be a perfect structure for regionalization. Logically, devolution should be clear and consistent, but government must recognize that it cannot devolve accountability along with authority by mere fiat. If it genuinely wishes to make regions more than just the instruments of provincial policy and management, it must recognize the extent to which this is a significant democratic reform and put in place the machinery to implement it successfully. Government cannot get out of the leadership business. As recent federal and provincial reviews have concluded, senior government leadership is essential for human resource strategies, health standards and policies to achieve health equity. Governments will have to decide whether they can and should get out of the management business. If the answer is yes, once principles and rules are established, provinces should avoid ad hoc interventions and micromanagement.

Information and Measures to Better Align Resources to Needs

One of health reform's most important goals, where regionalization has high potential impact, is to better align resources to needs, thereby increasing equity. This goal requires needs-assessment methodologies adequate to the task. In diverse communities, for example, it is no small accomplishment to obtain information about the needs of specific populations relevant to how healthcare interventions can respond. The goal also requires funding principles and mechanisms that facilitate reallocation of resources to meet needs: province-to-RHA funding formulas to respond to interegional inequities and RHA-level methods to respond to intraregional ones.

RHA-level resource allocation to increase equity, upstream strategies and quality of service cannot hope to succeed, however, unless the concepts are more widely understood and the corresponding standards accepted by providers and the public. There is reason to be skeptical about whether the public is willing to accept a vision of health and healthcare that is unconvincing to the providers with whom they deal on a daily basis. There is no groundswell of public demand for primary healthcare renewal, for example. The public remains focused on access and is just beginning to turn its attention to quality, but population health remains an elusive concept. RHAs and provinces require both the knowledge and at least public permission to move resources to meet needs.

Most important, performance measures for RHAs should create an accurate and complete portrait of need, service quality and health outcomes. These may be the only tools that will allow governors to recognize and reward improvements in performance and deal effectively with public and particularly provider interests and pressures.

Regional-Level System Integration

Critics have charged that regionalization has not been proven effective (MacKinnon 2002). But neither has it been shown to be ineffective. Often regionalization is mistaken as the "cause" of problems that originate elsewhere. Problems in rural areas of physician retention or facility rationalization, sometimes attributed to regionalization, are more a result of the larger secular trend of rural depopulation. Problems such as competition for specialized personnel and equipment are a reflection of the larger problems facing the entire system. An inability to adopt a more upstream, population-oriented approach may be due as much to government directives to spend new monies on, say, reducing waiting lists as to the particular failings of RHAs.

There is as yet no comprehensive evidence of the benefits of an integrated health system. One can point to individual studies, such as the evaluation of an integrated program of services for the elderly in a Quebec RHA, showing improved health outcomes for equivalent costs (Hebert et al. 2003), or the recently released policy synthesis that concluded that integrated community models provided the most effective and cost-effective bases for delivery of primary healthcare (Lamarche et al. 2003). However, some argue that geographic regionalization is not a prerequisite for service integration (Forest et al. 1999).

In fact, a previous issue of this journal posited integrated health organizations as superior alternatives to regionalization.

Perhaps not surprisingly, those working in regionalization attest to its value in facilitating integrative innovations. They argue that regionalization has reduced barriers, reduced duplication and increased the local responsiveness of services and programs. They also point to increased cross-sectoral planning and the beginning of a more balanced emphasis between individual clients and the population. Many had experienced the limited capacity of voluntary collaborations to break down territoriality. There are increasing calls for regionalization among healthcare leaders in Ontario, while no one in regionalized provinces argues for a return to the old way of doing business. In the 2003 Quebec election campaign the Liberals did promise to abolish RHAs, but have since proposed to retain a regional system, albeit changed in some of the relationships of authority at the regional level.

So what do we know about regionalization's achievements? Evidence is more anecdotal than systematic, but with experience comes a growing appreciation of the link between the consolidation of authority and the alignment of resources to needs. For example, the early vaccination of the elderly for flu in Edmonton has been widely touted as a value-added of regionalization. Because it governs public health programs, nursing homes and hospitals, the RHA is able to target higher-risk populations and deploy the staff effectively in reducing the risk. Negotiations and information gaps are reduced. In the SARS outbreak, the Vancouver Coastal Health Authority may have been lucky and Toronto the unfortunate victim of events. But the lines of authority, communication channels, ability to achieve inter-facility coordination and development of an authoritative strategy are undoubtedly more straightforward where the chain of command is self-evident.

Three factors appear instrumental to success. One is that RHAs are, other things equal, better able to respond quickly and strategically to challenges where there are fewer autonomous agencies and affiliation agreements to deal with. A second, and perhaps most crucial, reality is that physicians must be brought fully into the RHA fold, and paid in a manner that promotes rather than discourages coordinated care, spending time on complex cases, and ensuring that resources flow to areas in greatest need. They and other providers need some understanding of population health and the obligation of RHAs to address health disparities despite continuing pressures for more healthcare. Third, drug budgets should be integrated into RHA budgets. Drug expenditures now account for a greater proportion of health spending than physician services. Poor prescribing patterns, low adherence to prescribed regimens and financial barriers to optimal therapy result in health problems and, in many cases, hospitalization. Provincial governments have not been able to slow down drug budget increases, and proven innovations such as reference-based pricing have not been widely adopted. It would seem that the risk of bundling drug expenditures with RHA budgets is low, and the potential benefits are high – particularly if physicians also become genuine members of the RHA team instead of quasi-autonomous contractors.

Changes to Organizational Culture and Practice

Structural changes have changed the world of providers. Morale is low for complex reasons: the pace of change, a sense of distance between administrators and front-line providers, an aging workforce, the lingering aftershocks of the mid-1990s restraint. To confront resulting problems, RHAs are paying more attention to strategies for organizational and cultural change that both advance overall health goals and improve provider morale and productivity (see, for example, Casebeer and Hannah 1998; Casebeer et al. 2000). Among the unfinished business is the transition to a more evidence-based system based on comprehensive, accurate and timely information. RHAs need a licence and, better, a mandate to devote major resources to these foundations of quality improvement. Some, such as Calgary, spend close to 5% on these activities, but the national norm is closer to 2-3%. The best American non-profit HMOs – e.g., Kaiser Permanente, Group Health, Intermountain Health – spend up to 10% on information technology alone and additional amounts on research and analysis. Canadians tend to think that money spent on anything other than direct patient care is unproductive overhead; this mentality must change if regionalization or any other approach is to improve quality and efficiency.

> **Steven was a leader in arguing** for the need to evaluate regionalization, which had emerged in Canada a few years before. He brings an interdisciplinary and problem-solving perspective to issues ... it has made him a great contributor to healthcare decision-makers throughout the country.
>
> *Denise Kouri*

Change to organizational culture also speaks to RHA governance. Governance has always been a dilemma in healthcare regardless of organizational structure. It is extremely difficult to exert real authority over healthcare programs or systems given the knowledge and de facto power of providers. Canadian governors do not have access to the comprehensive and accurate information they require for assessing performance. They also lack adequate tools for effecting change. There is an art to governing a system where technical knowledge and interactions are highly decentralized and accountability is complex. That art must be mastered, and those charged with governance need appropriate tools as well as formal authority.

Governance entails more than a formal structure of authority. It also involves attention to practices, roles, rules and decision-making procedures. Governance approaches for devolved authorities that incorporate collaboration, citizen participation and longer-term social goals can be complementary to governments. They increase capacity to solve difficult problems by using place-specific approaches. They also foster civic virtue and engage citizens in community-building processes, encouraging them to look beyond self-interest to the larger public interest (Weber 2003).

The Canadian Comprehensive Audit Foundation has developed a list of attributes for information that is useful to governors (CCAF 1996). The attributes also apply to information used in accounting to the public. For performance information to be meaningful, it should link the processes of performance to outcomes, include appropriate comparators and clarify the implications – both human and financial. When RHAs report performance information meaningfully to the public at the regional level, this also serves to make the RHA role more transparent to the public.

Conclusion

At the end of the day regionalization is still mainly structural change. Attainment of health goals depends on provincial commitments and mandates. However, the record so far is that the provinces have wavered in their commitment to attaining health goals, partly because they realize that they are not meaningfully held accountable for them. Governments have proven vulnerable to pressures to slow down the pace of reform and paper over problems with money – hence the 42% growth in total spending between 1997 and 2003.

As implemented, regionalization is a quintessentially Canadian measure. At first glance it appears radical and bold, but on closer inspection it has been incremental and constrained. Local programs and in some cases communities lost some authority, while governments retained more than met the eye. Neither governments nor the public have seemed ready to fully embrace the new entities and give them free rein. The RHAs were barely out of the starting gate when saddled with the burden of carrying out the fiscal restraint of the mid-1990s, which arguably made it impossible to promote the wellness agenda and a population health perspective. Instability has been chronic. Evaluative data are hard to come by. Governments have repatriated some of the authority previously devolved.

On the other hand, there is far less fragmentation in the system, and there is now a large cohort of governors and senior managers attuned to the needs of the whole system, not just its constituent parts. There is less duplication of services in hospitals, and admission to long-term residential care is more streamlined and needs-based. There are intersectoral partnerships that probably could not have been developed without regionalization. Some regions are vigorously pursuing primary healthcare renewal. CCARH's national survey revealed that RHA board members and senior managers are highly committed to the wider, transformative goals of health reform. That regionalization has not in itself resculpted the landscape confirms that it is at most a necessary, but hardly a sufficient change agent. It can neither succeed nor fail on its own.

To succeed, regionalization needs a clear mandate, committed partners, outstanding leaders and a vision that will mobilize providers and the public. Government must decide, finally, what regionalization should be, and then leave the RHAs to get on with the job, fully accountable for performance.

Note

[1] There were health regions of various types well before the 1990s. Two examples are Saskatchewan's health regions established in 1945 (one of which, Swift Current, became the testing ground for what later became medicare), and Quebec's first round of regionalization begun in 1979. The 1944 report that recommended regionalization in Saskatchewan intended the regions to be comprehensive, but they ended up as essentially public health units geographically defined.

References

Canadian Centre for Analysis of Regionalization and Health. 2004. <http: www.regionalization.org/Regionalization/Regionalization.html>.

Canadian Comprehensive Audit Foundation (CCAF). 1996. *Governance Information – Strategies for Success.*

Casebeer, A.L. and K.J. Hannah. 1998. "The Process of Change Related to Health Policy Shift: Reforming a Health Care System." *International Journal of Public Sector Management* 11(7):566-82.

Casebeer, A., C. Scott and K. Hannah. 2000. "Transforming a Health Care System: Managing Change for Community Gain." *Canadian Journal of Public Health* 91(2): 89-93.

Church, J., and B. Barker. 2003. "Regionalization of Health Services in Canada: A Critical Perspective." *International Journal of Health Services* 28: 467-86.

Forest, P.G., D. Gagnon, J. Abelson, J.Turgeon and P. Lamarche. 1999. "Issues in the Governance of Integrated Health Systems." Ottawa: Canadian Health Services Research Foundation. <http://www.chsrf.ca>.

Hebert, R., P.J. Durand, N. Dubuc and A. Tourigny. PRISMA Group. 2003. "Frail Elderly Patients: New Model for Integrated Service Delivery." *Canadian Family Physician* 49: 992-97.

Kouri, D., K. Chessie and S. Lewis. 2002. "Regionalization: Where Has All the Power Gone? A Survey of Canadian Decision Makers in Health Care Regionalization." Saskatoon: Canadian Centre for Analysis of Regionalization and Health.

Lamarche, P.A., M.D. Beaulieu, R. Pinault et al. 2003. "The Path for Restructuring Primary Healthcare Services in Canada." Ottawa: Canadian Health Services Research Foundation. <http:www.chsrf.ca>.

Lewis, S. et al. 2001. "Devolution to Democratic Health Authorities in Saskatchewan: An Interim Report." *Canadian Medical Association Journal* 164(3): 343-47.

MacKinnon, D. 2002. "Regionalization: Is It the Answer for Ontario?" Speech delivered to the Ontario Hospital Association Conference, Ottawa, April 8.

Mhatre, S.L. and R.B. Deber. 1992. "From Equal Access to Health Care to Equitable Access to Health: A Review of Canadian Provincial Health Commissions and Reports." *International Journal of Health Services* 22: 645-68.

Newfoundland and Labrador Health and Community Services Association. 1999. "Framework of Accountability for Regional Health Boards: A Presentation to the Government of Newfoundland and Labrador." St. John's: The Association.

Office of the Auditor General of British Columbia. 2003. "A Review of Performance Agreements between the Ministry of Health Services and the Health Authorities." Victoria: Office of the Auditor General. <http://www.bcauditor.com/AuditorGeneral.htm>.

Weber, E. 2003. *Bringing Society Back In.* Cambridge, MA: MIT Press.

Williamson, D.L., C.D. Milligan, B. Kwan, C.J. Frankish and P.A. Ratner. 2003. "Implementation of Provincial/Territorial Health Goals in Canada." *Health Policy* 64: 173-91.

After the Sensible Reforms, What? The Next Big Issue in Wait-Time Management*

Steven Lewis

Baker and Schwartz[1] have outlined proven strategies for using resources more efficiently, among which are system redesign, such as eliminating unnecessary steps; defragmenting the entry portals into the system; and more flexible access to resources available to larger groups of people in need. These measures are intuitively sensible and, one would think, relatively straightforward to implement. But reengineering redeploys resources, and redeployment often affects providers' (notably physicians') incomes. In many hospitals and health regions, physician access to OR time has largely depended on the accumulation of large numbers of people on their personal wait lists. Those with the largest lists often get the most OR time; there is thus an incentive to maintain a large list. If the median or maximum waits for a physician's patients are long, the proposed solution is invariably more OR time; if this is the case across many physicians and patient categories, the proposed solution is invariably more resources. While the story does not play out in this manner everywhere at all times, it remains more the norm than the exception. These incentives are exacerbated by the vagaries of fee-for-service payment systems, which have always rewarded procedures over consultation.

* Originally published in *Longwoods Review* 2005, 3(2): 14-16, appearing in *Healthcare Quarterly* 2005, 8(3)

It is important to note that in such circumstances, neither the lists, nor the physicians' judgment about who needs what procedure are subject to meaningful peer or other scrutiny. Despite claims that medicare is highly regulated and severely managed, decisions about who needs and receives (particularly non-urgent) services are taken in a state of anarchy. This is more true of elective than urgent procedures, but there is a large body of Canadian research documenting huge variations in practice that persist even when known to administrators and practitioners.

The results are predictable: some patients will wait a very long time; some physicians will assemble large wait lists; there will be major variation in the indications for a procedure, and a general lowering of the threshold over time; and only energetic and savvy patients will be aware that wait times vary greatly by physician and institution. One would be hard pressed to design a system more likely to produce chaos, unfairness and constant pressure to expand.

There has been a more systematic approach where patients' lives are at stake. For heart surgery and cancer treatment, there is more monitoring of wait times and usually a reasonable attempt to serve people in order of need. Often there are standardized needs-assessment protocols and target wait times (some evidence-based, others not). Even here, though, there are unarticulated and unresolved dilemmas turning on the issue of need.

It is simple logic that if the need for services and the supply of services match, over time and in aggregate, wait time issues should disappear. At times there will be unforeseeable clusters of need and personnel shortages or maldistributions that create temporary or location-specific problems, but the basic principle holds. If, in a given time period, the number of people newly presenting with a need equals the number of people the system is able to serve, wait times should be trivial (assuming backlogs have been dealt with). But this basic equation depends on a crucial development: consensus on what constitutes a legitimate need that the healthcare system can address at an acceptable cost with a reasonable prospect of a positive outcome.

These are, of course, highly contentious issues. New Zealand faced them bravely by instituting a point count system to measure need, and setting thresholds for entitlement to service in the public system. Those falling below the threshold score were ineligible for publicly financed care. When the threshold is set too high in the eyes of the public and/or providers, two responses are predictable. One is a demand for a private option, so that people can pay for and get service regardless of their point count. The second is a loss of confidence in the public system as seemingly unjust decisions and pitiably ineligible cases make their way into the media and shape public perceptions. New Zealand does have a private, parallel system, and the public has on occasion expressed dissatisfaction with the thresholds set. There have also been reports of "gaming" the system by subtle and not-so-subtle cues that encourage patients to report higher levels of pain or disability, thereby inflating the point count above the crucial threshold. Regardless of these imperfections, we owe a debt to New Zealand for attempting to bell an elusive and sharp-clawed cat, just as we learned a great deal from Oregon's heroic effort at rank-ordering services.

The "What is a real need?" debates have generally featured so-called elective surgery, where quality of life, rather than life and death, hangs in the balance. But they apply equally to life-and-death situations as well, with a different twist. In such situations – cancer being a prime illustration - it is not the need that is in question, but the prospects for addressing it successfully. Science and medicine have not defeated most cancers: for many, interventions do little to alter outcomes, and in some instances the treatment diminishes quality of life without prolonging it appreciably. On a strictly utilitarian basis, one could convincingly argue that the costs of many healthcare interventions greatly exceed their benefits. Yet we are not strict utilitarians, and prosperous societies may thoughtfully decide to provide some costly and intensive treatments even when the odds against success are depressingly long. Rather than taking a New Zealand-type approach and draw a firm line that separates the eligible from the ineligible, in Canada we fudge the question in two ways. Either we make people wait (push them down the priority list), or we perpetually expand the eligibility pool by adding resources, in effect buying our way out of uncomfortable choices.

> **In your role as head of Saskatchewan** Health Services Utilization and Research Commission, you helped research, inform, and in some cases, resolve key health policy questions that I know had an effect on the actions of government and regional health authorities.
>
> *Glenda Yeates*

The "Canadian way" is not entirely an indefensible form of muddling through. Often it may be reasonable to lower thresholds for intervening – for example, if it proves safe to perform heart surgery on people over 80, adding years or quality of life, one would be hard pressed to argue against it. But some thresholds, particularly on the diagnostic side, have lowered dramatically without any evidence of improved management or outcome. Some of this utilization growth involves relatively inexpensive technologies, such as ultrasound, but much has occurred at the high end, particularly CT and MRI scanning. The threshold is not lowered as a result of transparent deliberation based on cost-benefit analysis and other measures of justice, effectiveness and efficiency. It is lowered by the collective but uncoordinated decisions of providers who find it almost irresistible to expand the use of technologies that pose no risk to patients and entail the marvels of human ingenuity.

Here is where flow optimization and system redesign successes meet their match, and in a sense sow the seeds of their own unravelling. Take the example of MRI. When practitioners knew that machines were few and capacity limited, they reserved referrals for cases where there was genuine diagnostic uncertainty and real urgency. Over time, the technology embedded itself into common practice and expectations, the referral criteria loosened and waits lengthened. Governments installed more machines. But adding capacity permanently solves the wait time problem only if indications for use remain roughly the same. They don't. If the new capacity is intended only to clear the backlog, the number served must exceed the number of newly presenting cases. This indeed clears the backlog, but also creates excess capacity, which in Canada is viewed as an embarrassment, if not a scandal. It is quickly absorbed by using the technology in new categories of cases, new line ups appear and the cycle repeats. So it is, *mutatis mutandis*, with cataract surgery, joint replacements, and so on.

I am not suggesting that there is no unmet legitimate need or that all thresholds are now "unreasonably" low. The point is that to solve wait times systemically and durably, there must be a serious discussion of need and its sister concept, appropriateness, in all their dimensions. This can be treacherous terrain, but there is no turning away from it. Otherwise, as the system successfully reduces wait times, "need" will be redefined downward – sometimes wisely, sometimes not – and avoidance of the central issue will be no more successful than Neville Chamberlain's policy of appeasement prior to World War II. Paradoxically, if we are not prepared to discuss needs and establish thresholds (on a principled and compassionate basis, with nuance and flexibility), leaving the wait time problem intact may be the best option. Vexing though they may be, long waits do discipline choices and behaviours, and the perception or reality of an overburdened system creates de facto thresholds – no doubt variable, unstudied and unfair.

In a just and well-ordered system, all waits should be insignificantly long, and medicare should serve all those with legitimate and addressable needs. The easy work is defining "insignificantly long"; the hard but important work is defining "legitimate and addressable need." We've circled the dilemma for too long; the prospects for a real solution to wait times depend on our confronting it.

Note

[1] Baker G.R. and F. Schwartz. 2005. "Innovation and Access to Cancer Care Services in Ontario." *Longwoods Review* appearing in *Healthcare Quaterly* 2005, 8(3)

Can a Learning-Disabled Nation Learn Healthcare Lessons from Abroad?*

Steven Lewis

Never ascribe to malice that which is adequately explained by incompetence.
— Napoleon Bonaparte

Napoleon was not renowned for his generous impulses, but this is surely one of them. Incompetence is a condition; malice is a motive. The presence of the former is hardly proof of the absence of the latter (indeed, the two often make a nice combo). Canada's healthcare system is, like everybody else's, large, complex, expensive and imperfect. We get many things right, we get some things wrong, and we aim to preserve what is right and remedy what is wrong. Yet our reforms seem timid and ineffective, and suffer enormous energy loss on the path from conception to outcome (e.g., physician payment systems; primary healthcare renewal; nurse practitioners; electronic health records; interprofessional education; patient safety and quality improvement, among others).

The connection between intention and action seems stronger and more immediate elsewhere. Other countries aren't Nirvana, but their errors are braver – sins of commission rather than omission. The United Kingdom exhausts its system with perpetual change; we exhaust ours with endless talk and death by a thousand demonstration projects.

* Originally published in *Healthcare Policy* 2007, 3(2): 19-28

Wherein lies the difference? Are we incompetent, maliciously hostile to large-scale improvement, gridlocked by federalism and vested interests, or too easily contented with what we have? We look to pockets of excellence for inspiration, but history and interest accommodation set policy. We accept great performance but never insist on it. If the status quo isn't good enough, we add money.

A perpetual question in Canada is what we can learn from other countries. Here we make two kinds of errors. Sometimes we claim we can learn nothing from other countries' experiences because they are so context-specific, culturally rooted, historically conditioned and structurally unique. Some are, but some aren't, and we need to know the difference. And sometimes we claim we can cherry-pick one feature – say, co-payments for physician visits in France – with no understanding of how it is connected to a broad and intricate policy regime. We obsess about the pathway to change while losing sight of the destination. Denmark hasn't built a nursing home bed in over a decade, and Kaiser Permanente patients use fewer than half as many hospital bed-days per capita as Canadian patients. Am I the only one who thinks it's odd that Canadians spend endless hours debating whether and how to organize a wait list and no time setting clear targets that match the best of elsewhere? What accounts for our innovation learning disability?

Canada's Strange Obsession with Sustainability

There are 30 countries in the Organisation for Economic Co-operation and Development. By my reckoning, 19 of them are, broadly speaking, Canada's economic peers, with a GDP per capita no more than 20% lower or higher than ours.[1] Here are some basic facts about their economies and healthcare spending (all data from OECD Principal Economic Indicators 2007 and OECD Health Data 2007).

- Canada's real per capita GDP grew by 16.6% between 2000 and 2006, about two percentage points more than the 20-country average, and four percentage points more than the G7 countries.[2]
- In 2005 all spent between 7.5% and 11.6% of their GDP on healthcare. Canada, at 9.8%, ranked sixth of 20.
- The government-financed share of total health spending ranged from 59% (Switzerland) to 87% (UK). Canada, at 70%, was next to last, and five countries exceeded 80%.
- Between 1970 and 2003, the average rate of real per capita spending increase in healthcare was 4%. Canada's rate was 3% – the sixth lowest of the 20 countries. On top of this, our governments are in excellent fiscal shape, with a long run of big federal surpluses, balanced budgets the norm among provinces, and all achieved while cutting taxes. Among the G7 countries our fiscal performance has been spectacular: our debt-to-GDP ratio has declined by two-thirds in a decade and continues downward, while others' are flat or rising.

In summary, governments have left a larger share of healthcare spending to the private sector than all but one of our peers; our cumulative rate of spending increases has been unexceptional; our fiscal houses are in order; and our economy is humming. It's hard to imagine a less daunting sustainability situation. Yet sustainability appears to be a uniquely Canadian preoccupation. How do I know? Google, of course.

In an earlier draft of this paper I included the results of a number of Google searches, such as "sustainable healthcare" AND "Canada OR Canadian". The numbers are unstable within very short time periods, and sometimes the results make no sense: "New Zealand" AND "sustainable healthcare" yields 884 hits, but the same search WITHOUT "Canada OR Canadian" yields 885, and the same search WITHOUT "Canadian OR Canada" yields 853. (This erratic behaviour is somewhat disconcerting from the genius search engine of all time and a company with market capitalization of $158 billion.)

So the exact numbers are not worth reproducing here, but there is a pattern. In a search for "country name" + "sustainable healthcare", Canada has slightly more hits than the United Kingdom, twice as many as Australia and 2.5 times as many as Sweden. But excluding references to Canada from searches for other countries reduces the UK total by half, and Australia's and Sweden's by 95%. Conversely, excluding references to the UK from the Canadian search reduces our hits by a quarter; to Australia, by 30%; and to Sweden, by 17%.

The overall picture starts to get pretty clear. Canada appears to drive a good deal of the worldwide talk on sustainability even though not a single objective economic indicator points to a Canadian problem. Needless to say, objective reality is not always the arbiter of conviction.

The sustainability crisis mantra is traceable to three sources of inspiration. One is ideology: those who want to privatize the system need to persuade the public and politicians that even if we think public healthcare is a good idea that serves us well, what we could afford then we can barely afford now, and certainly cannot afford in the future. Let's all pay our respects at the funeral and move on. A second is adherence to the contention that an aging population will bankrupt the system. And the third is concern about the growing proportion of provincial government spending consumed by healthcare. The first two have been refuted so well by so many that if you still believe either or both, your beliefs rely on other than fact and logic, and fact and logic are all that I have to offer, so I'll spend my words elsewhere.

The third claim is or has been factual, and merits examination. Governments have spent increasing proportions of their budgets on healthcare over the past decade. Bear with me here; how this occurs requires some parsing.[3] Following is a list of possible explanations for the increasing percentage of spending going to healthcare, and what has actually occurred.

1. *Governments can decide to increase the rate of healthcare spending faster than the rate of spending on other programs and services.* Over the past decade they have, and the percentage of the budget spent on healthcare has risen.
2. *Governments can slow the rate of increase, or outright reduce total spending in order to reduce or eliminate deficits, pay down debt, accumulate surpluses and/or build up a rainy-day fund (notably, the Alberta Heritage Fund).* This reduction can occur even while revenues are stable or increasing. If at the same time healthcare spending increases at the same rate or higher than before, its share of total spending will rise even if it is not taking a larger share of total revenues. This, too, was the case when provinces decided to get their fiscal houses in order. It is not generally the case now because provincial budgets are balanced or in surplus.
3. *Governments can limit the rate of growth in total revenues by cutting taxes.* They have done so dramatically. One result has been that the growth rate in healthcare spending has sometimes exceeded the growth rate in total government revenues.

None of these phenomena, either individually or in tandem, is cause for alarm. On top of this, healthcare spending rate changes are variable and controllable by governments. If healthcare spending is rising faster than some think it should, remember that governments formally have determined that this is good public policy – it is they who draw up the budget and decide on its component parts. Furthermore, since 2000 Ottawa has committed itself to huge and mostly unconditional additional cash transfers to the provinces for healthcare, with built-in escalator clauses, a situation that, among other things, sends signals to the sellers of labour and goods to increase their prices. (The rate of inflation in healthcare tends to be somewhat higher than the overall inflation rate.) Repeated polls suggest that the public in general supports higher healthcare spending, and governments occasionally do what the people want.

The key point is this: a proportion or percentage derives from a numerator (healthcare spending) and a denominator (the total pool of funds available to spend). Governments have deliberately determined the size of both; the deception is to claim that the changing proportion is an inexplicable act of nature, a fiscal crop circle drawn by aliens. If healthcare is eating others' lunch (as some, but not all, would concede), it does so by design, and government has a number of levers at its disposal to get some of it back if that's what's desired.

That said, there is nothing intrinsically unsustainable about gradually increasing the proportion of provincial budgets spent on healthcare. Relative expenditures change all the time. The important question is whether the redistribution produces good value for money. The percentage of household spending on computers and vacation properties has skyrocketed in the past generation, yet no one terms this a crisis. In a federal system like Canada's, the chances of at least one of 14 governments declaring a healthcare spending crisis at any given time are about the same as picking the winner if you bet on every horse in the race.

But let's put away the calculator and make the groundless concession that yes, healthcare has a sustainability crisis, we're spending too much, we're getting poor value for money (true) and we have to fix it. What can we learn from other countries? What measures hold some promise of improvement, and which are dead losers? Briefly, here's a buyer's guide to international healthcare innovation.

Is for-profit healthcare cheaper or better?

No. It is certainly more expensive (Devereaux et al. 2004), and in some cases – notably, dialysis in the US – it is of lower quality (Devereaux et al. 2002). In long-term care, for-profit institutions provide less direct and supportive care per resident (McGregor et al. 2006). Then-Senator Michael Kirby remained agnostic on the subject, but as a member of the board of directors of the for-profit nursing home chain Extendicare Ltd. and holder of over a million dollars' worth of company stock and options prior to releasing his report, his objectivity might reasonably be doubted.[4]

Are PPPs (public–private partnerships) cheaper?

No. They are more expensive. The government can borrow money more cheaply than private firms. Private firms expect, and almost always receive, a built-in, guaranteed profit, lucrative lease-back terms and so on. Pollock and colleagues (2002) have done the math in the UK. The verdict: the private partner makes off with huge returns, the public sector overpays and the risk stays with all of us.

Do user fees solve any problems?

No. They deter poor and sick people from seeking care, and have little effect on others. Where they are modest they raise little cash; where they are substantial – as for drugs – prices do not fall, utilization does not become more rational, but many people forgo effective treatment. Healthcare spending is highly concentrated – a mere 2% of people can account for over 40% of health spending in any given year. Nickel and diming – or even looneying and tooneying them – will accomplish nothing.

Is it better to have too few or too many healthcare workers?

For the workers, too few is better financially, but not necessarily for their overall well-being; for the public, a modest oversupply is better both financially and in terms of access. Europe has much higher physician-to-population ratios than Canada and, in some countries, significant physician unemployment (Rechl et al. 2006). It's just basic economics that if Canada tightly controls its workforce supply and guarantees every graduate a job, wages will rise and labour of all types will substantially control the agenda.

How many healthcare workers is enough?

No one knows. Canada is in constant turmoil about the doctor shortage. Many Canadians do not have a regular family physician. Curiously, the same physician-to-population ratio that was seen as a surplus 20 years ago became a serious and growing shortage by about 1995. It is still not clear why; per capita use of physicians' services has continued to grow throughout this time. But how does the physician-to-population ratio affect overall population health status? If you can figure out the connection from Figure 1 below, they'll name a statistical test after you. And remember that it's not all about doctors. Three dozen randomized, controlled trials have shown that nurse practitioners can deliver huge swaths of primary care as effectively as physicians (Horrocks et al. 2002), yet we continue to deploy them gingerly. At its August 2007 meeting, the Canadian Medical Association yet again attempted to turn back the clock on the sensible delegation of limited prescribing authority to pharmacists.

Figure 1. Life expectancy vs. physicians per capita

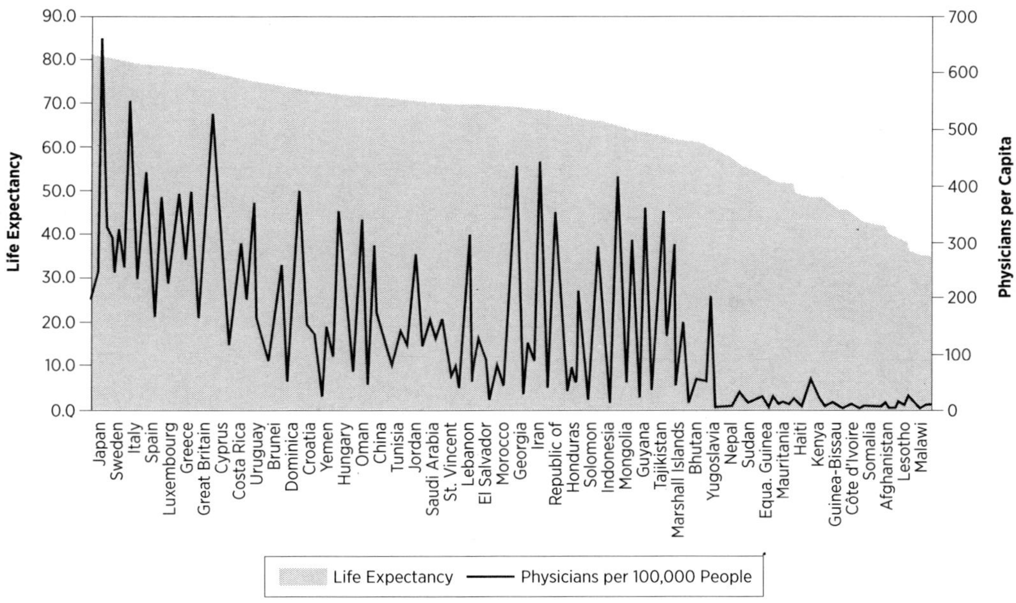

Source: Univ. of California Atlas of Global Inequality, http://ucatlas.ucsc.edu/spend.php

Left to their own devices, most healthcare professions want to maintain exclusive scope of practice over certain territory and move onto others' turf when it suits them. There has also been a marked trend towards increasing entry-to-practice credentials (e.g., to a baccalaureate degree for nursing, an added year of residency for family doctors, a master's degree for physiotherapy). Both the inflexibility of the workplace and the creation of barriers to entry into health professions contribute to shortages and inefficiencies.

Thus far the policy response has been to increase enrollments. Before doing so, we should have figured out how to allow healthcare workers to use all their knowledge and skills, acquire new capacities efficiently and replace a mainly credential-based framework to ensure safety and quality with a competency-based approach.

What's the key to controlling costs?

European countries with much older populations than Canada's appear to have better access, shorter wait times, as much or more high-end technology and similar or lower costs. How do they do it? They pay doctors less. They use more home care and less long-term residential care. They have more egalitarian societies and more extensive social programs. The government covers a larger share of health costs, particularly drugs.

That's all fine, but we're not Europe. What can we do?

Identify and shrink variations in costs. In Canada, three- and fourfold variations in intervention rates among identical populations are far from rare. South of the border, seniors in Miami use twice as much healthcare as seniors in Minneapolis, with poorer outcomes. We're terrified by underuse and oddly unconcerned about overuse. Pay attention to both and we'll save money.

What about information technology?

We're proven laggards. Denmark has a universal electronic health record accessible to patients on the Web. Its physicians estimate they save an hour a day previously spent chasing down test results and other information. The dramatic ascent of the Veterans Affairs health system in the United States from "worst to first" went hand in hand with major investment in and use of health information technology. We're haltingly building ground-up systems that may not be able to talk to one another, with different data definitions. In the move to alternative payment plans for physicians (a fine idea), we've actually lost data (a potential disaster). In the usual Canadian way, we don't invest enough, and we don't have a solid policy framework to ensure that the systems are useful for clinical care, management, governance, resource allocation and evaluation.

Sage ... provocateur ...
constructive agitator ...

Bonnie Brossart

What's the biggest lesson we can learn from other countries?

They think, they plan and they act, often decisively. Somehow, the risks of innovation and policy experimentation seem lower. They are less afraid to set meaningful targets and shoot at them. In Canada, the 2003 Health Accord promised that 50% of Canadians would have access to an undefined primary healthcare system on a 24/7/365 basis by 2011. England today offers you a physician's appointment within 48 hours, 99% of the time. We set vague and distant wait time targets and oil the squeaky wheels; England foresees that within two years the maximum wait time from first walking into a GP's office to completion of whatever procedure is necessary will be four months. I'm no fan of much of what New Zealand does, but it had the guts to set needs-based, measurable thresholds for surgical interventions, and it has bargained brilliantly to secure very low drug prices. You can raise or lower the bars in Figure 2 in accordance with your own perceptions of the healthcare world, but it is incontestable that many countries have lapped us in the race to reform.

Figure 2. Completely invalid inferred estimate of action-to-talk ratio in four countries

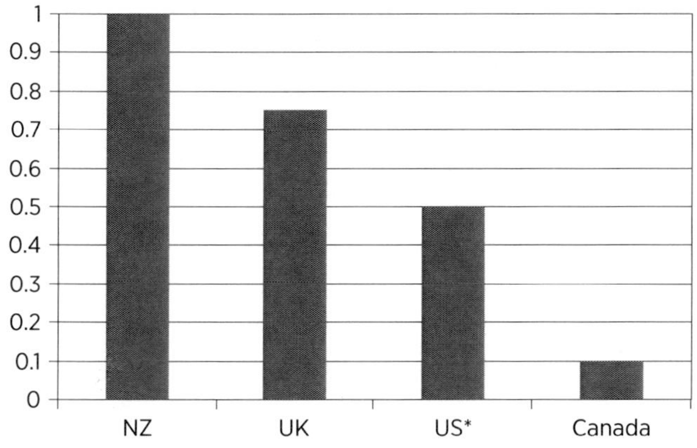

* In selected leading organizations

Which brings us back to sustainability. If we're going to get better at change, we need to declare a moratorium on the sustainability argument for at least five years. It is a monumental distraction that takes up too much deliberative time. Let's move on to more worthy preoccupations, such as quality improvement, aligning incentives with goals, making excellence mandatory and reducing health (and healthcare) disparities. Canada talks like other countries; now it's time to act like them. Only our refusal to embrace large-scale change that serves the public rather than private interests is unsustainable.

Notes

1 To illustrate, Greece is in, Hungary out (too poor); Luxembourg is out (too rich); the United States is out because its healthcare structure and data are real but absurd, and hence of no interest here.

2 Calculated using 2000 prices and exchange rates.

3 This version is highly truncated. For a much fuller explanation, see R.G. Evans, "Economic Myths and Political Realities: The Inequality Agenda and the Sustainability of Medicare," UBC Centre for Health Services and Policy Research, July 2007. <http://www.chspr.ubc.ca/node/791>.

4 Many, including newspaper editorialists, have doubted it – see http://www.healthcoalition.ca/kirby.html.

References

Devereaux, P.J., D. Heels-Ansdell, C. Lacchetti et al. 2004 (June 8). "Payments for Care at Private for-Profit and Private Not-for-Profit Hospitals: A Systematic Review and Meta-analysis." *Canadian Medical Association Journal* 170(12): 1817-24.

Devereaux, P.J., H.J. Schünemann, N. Ravindran et al. 2002. "Comparison of Mortality between Private for-Profit and Private Not-for-Profit Hemodialysis Centers: A Systematic Review and Meta-analysis." *Journal of the American Medical Association* 288(19): 2449-57.

Horrocks, S., E. Anderson and C. Salisbury. 2002. "Systematic Review of Whether Nurse Practitioners Working in Primary Care Can Provide Equivalent Care to Doctors." *British Medical Journal* 324(7341): 819-23.

McGregor, M.J., R.B. Tate, K.M. McGrail, L.A. Ronald, A-M. Broemeling and M. Cohen. 2006. "Care Outcomes in Long-Term Care Facilities in British Columbia, Canada: Does Ownership Matter?" *Medical Care* 44: 929-35.

OECD Principal Economic Indicators. 2007 (July). Data from OECD Annual National Accounts database. Retrieved September 22, 2007. <http://www.oecd.org/dataoecd/48/4/37867909.pdf>.

OECD Health Data. 2007 (July). Retrieved September 22, 2007. <http://www.oecd.org/dataoecd/46/33/38979719.pdf>.

Pollock, A., J. Shaoul and J. Vickers. 2002. "Private Finance and 'Value for Money' in NHS Hospitals: A Policy in Search of a Rationale?" *British Medical Journal* 324: 1205-9.

Rechl, B., C.-A. Dubois and M. McKee, eds. 2006. *The Health Care Workforce in Europe: Learning from Experience*. Copenhagen: WHO European Observatory on Health Systems and Policies. Retrieved September 22, 2007. <http://www.euro.who.int/document/E89156.pdf>.

Extreme Makeover: Can We Achieve Rapid Improvement in Canada's Healthcare System?*

Nandita Chaudhuri, Bonnie Brossart, Steven Lewis and Gill White

Extreme Makeover

Have you ever watched the wildly successful, reality TV show *Extreme Makeover: Home Edition?* If you haven't, here's the premise – each self-contained episode features a race against time on a home renovation project that would ordinarily take months to achieve, involving myriad designers, builders and volunteers who have just seven days to totally rebuild an entire house – every single room, plus the exterior and landscaping. In just one hour, the viewing audience sees how the deserving family's life – just like their house – is forever changed as a result (http://abc.go.com/primetime/xtremehome/show.html).

So what is the connection between this show and improving Canada's healthcare system? Actually, there is none – at least not yet. We do not believe, apparently, that the system needs an extreme makeover. Just some fine-tuning here, some wait-list management there, and all will be well. The reality revealed by some powerful evidence, however, suggests that we may be too sanguine: the quality of care in the middle of the curve is poor (McGlynn et al. 2003; Marshall et al. 2003; Katz et al. 2004). Furthermore, as Brown et al. note, Canada has been slow to connect performance improvement to tan-

* Originally published in *Healthcare Papers* 2005, 6(2): 28-34

gible reward systems. In such an environment, it is hardly surprising that performance reporting alone is unlikely to shift attitudes and behaviour. By contrast, in some other healthcare systems across the world, rapid and sustained improvements in healthcare performance have been taking place and with some very impressive results. In these instances, leadership has committed to transformative change and performance measurement is conceived as a tool to monitor and help the change process rather than acting as an independent catalytic agent.

Brown et al. have duly noted the relatively sparse evidence on the impact of performance measurement and reporting on health systems. However, they have only lightly touched upon the crucial assumption underlying change in Canada: that it is essentially a voluntary and incremental process based on a long and strong tradition of autonomous clinical practice operating with poorly developed information and communication systems. We can and should learn from other systems that are using performance measurement and reporting as part of their improvement strategy, and specifically delve into those systems that have gotten better faster. We should also learn from those systems in which change has been frustratingly slow, to better understand what not to do (Leape and Berwick 2005). For without such critical intelligence, our persistent attempts at making performance reports work will be of limited value because we might misconstrue the nature and source of the inertia.

Extreme Makeover Examples in the US and England: Elements for Achieving Large-Scale Change

In quality improvement circles, notable examples of large-scale, rapid change include the Veterans Affairs (VA) healthcare system in the United States and the primary-care and wait-time reduction initiatives in England's national health system. Both offer important insights into the factors that affect rapid change. Canada's current implicit change theory is very accommodating of the prevailing healthcare culture. Slow, primarily relying on voluntary uptake of evidence and innovation and largely peer-based, it fits with the well-entrenched traditions of individualism, professional fragmentation, hierarchical authority structures and diffuse accountability. However, as others attest, accepting this change theory will virtually by definition retard progress (Leape and Berwick 2005). Nor will it facilitate the success of performance management efforts (Smith 2002).

In the early 1990s, the Department of Veterans Affairs (VA) healthcare system was viewed as a large, ineffective and inefficient system (Jha et al. 2003). In 1995, the VA launched a major reengineering of its healthcare system including better use of information technology, measurement and reporting of performance, and integration of services and realigned payment policies (Jha et al. 2003). These changes, coupled with a system-wide commitment to quality improvement, have been instrumental in the VA's performance improvement. The VA is now widely recognized as a patient-centred, high-quality, highly valued healthcare system whose quality now surpasses that of Medicare and commercial Managed Care Organizations (MCOs). A similar dramatic transformation took place in the primary-care sector of England's national healthcare system in early 2000. Dr. John Oldham, a general practitioner with a passion for quality improvement tools and techniques, was appointed by the Minister of Health to lead a team of individuals to bring about rapid improvement in patient care. In a handful of years, over 5,000 practices covering 32.6 million patients achieved dramatic reductions in waiting times, significantly improving the quality of primary care.

Despite rather different approaches, what characterized these two rapid transformations was remarkably similar. Both included the presence of clear, measurable goals; ensured the infrastructure was there to support continuously measuring quality; and focused on clinical topics where the evidence was strong. Table 1 summarizes the appropriate factors behind large-scale change.

As is evident from the above list and confirmed by Brown et al., major change requires both recognition that it is necessary and tools and incentives to smooth its path. Simple logic suggests that if greatly improved performance is not an expectation, it will not occur. One would have to be remarkably optimistic to imagine that reporting on performance would on its own be a major change agent. In a world well disposed to continuous improvement, the reporting of indicators might seem sufficient to lubricate the process. But our world is not a smooth road. Misaligned incentives, deeply rooted cultural patterns and the assumption that the system's deficiencies are caused by a lack of money rather than indifference to quality create major barriers. This is a cultural reality whose aspects need to be better understood. How are these assumptions and reality of change unfolding in the Canadian healthcare scenario?

Table 1. Elements for rapidly achieving large-scale change

1	Widespread agreement (including the public) that the system needs changing
2	Commitment to change – both emotional and professional
3	Articulate a vision with specific, quantitative, well-tracked goals
4	Introduce change levers rather than a multiyear plan
5	Choose topics that make good clinical sense – start with focused, clearly defined areas
6	Implement an integrated, comprehensive electronic medical record system
7	Couple performance measurement with public reporting
8	Align resource allocation systems and incentives with performance
9	Unified policy framework and infrastructure for spread
10	Build relationships with key stakeholders including politicians
11	Train health professionals to work in teams
12	Systematically transfer knowledge
13	Create an environment that facilitates the uptake of ideas

Sources: Ken Kizer, "National Quality Forum," personal communication, November 2004; Leape and Berwick 2005; Oldham 2004.

Canadian Primary Healthcare Performance Measurement: Commitment and Challenges

In recent years, it is the primary healthcare setting where Canada has rhetorically committed to a significant makeover. In September 2000, the First Ministers, via the inaugural Health Accord, agreed that improvements in the primary healthcare were crucial to providing Canadians with a sustainable health system that provides timely access to quality health services. Since then, provinces and territories have been involved in primary healthcare renewal initiatives appropriate to their local contexts, and almost all the provinces and territories have attempted to partially or fully develop some kind of performance measures and tools appropriate for their own primary healthcare model.

This reform initiative has been guided by the premise that better accountability and transparent reporting on system performance can ultimately improve health status, increase equitable access to care, achieve a better fit between needs and services and help managers to allocate resources wisely. Several provinces have separately attempted to conceptually encapsulate their own universe and contexts of primary healthcare performance in the form of framework tools and logic models.[1] Recognizing these attempts, CIHI has recently identified British Columbia, Nova Scotia and Saskatchewan as provincial leaders in primary healthcare evaluation. While British Columbia and Nova Scotia have only developed the conceptual frameworks of primary healthcare evaluation, Saskatchewan has gone a step further to implement the evaluation framework tools.

In Saskatchewan, two levels of primary healthcare evaluation initiatives are simultaneously going on: (1) site-specific three-year interim and five-year evaluation of the primary healthcare demonstration sites and (2) implementation of an overarching provincial primary healthcare evaluation framework. The completed three-year interim evaluations of 10 primary healthcare demonstration sites in Saskatchewan primarily assess the expanded role of nurse practitioners, the impact of newly introduced primary healthcare programs on changing the style of practice, evidence of team development at the primary healthcare sites, patterns of care-seeking by catchment populations and satisfaction of patients with the services provided. The five-year evaluation of the sites has followed a more detailed process-oriented evaluation framework.[2] With various kinds of measurement tools such as program description forms, site narratives, client satisfaction surveys, team effectiveness tools and administrative data, this framework addresses specific process-oriented questions related to the various components of the team-based primary healthcare model in Saskatchewan. The province is currently engaged in gathering and analyzing data in accordance with this framework for eight sites slated for evaluation in 2005.

At a higher level, an overall provincial evaluation framework[3] has been designed to illustrate a logical flow beginning with broader goals of accessibility and quality and leading to the selection of specific relevant indicators and data sources. The indicators cover several primary healthcare areas such as access, improvement in prevention, acceptability, skill maximization, intersectoral partnership and community participation. The process, structure and outcome measures in this framework are similar to those developed elsewhere across the nation and in other significant international studies; speak to the short-term and long-term goals of primary healthcare in Saskatchewan; are improvable, doable and cost-effective; and meet various reporting requirements. Surveys and administrative data are the major data sources for this performance measurement tool. The primary healthcare managers from the province's 13 regional health authorities have prioritized an initial set of five indicators from this framework for implementation in 2005-06. While doing the groundwork for these measures, the province is waiting to see how the primary healthcare indicators initiative led by Health Canada unfolds at the national level.

Although Saskatchewan has tried to overcome methodological and conceptual challenges in performance evaluation that Brown et al. mention and has successfully identified and quantified measures of change, there have been several other key challenges in implementing evaluation for a relatively new reform initiative. Relying upon administrative datasets that are not research-ready has limited the scope of performance measurement. Other problems have been associated with the constrained capacity and resources for collection and analysis of data at the provincial level, absence of baseline data for comparison purposes, absence of a tangible reward system connected to quality improvement goals in the primary healthcare sector and adequately factoring in the political climate in prioritizing evaluation goals. Although the findings have identified significant successes and challenges,[4] a stable performance measurement culture has not yet emerged to utilize these for the purposes of facilitating change management. Rather, the findings have mainly been used to make a case for funding primary healthcare in the province and unfreezing Health Accord dollars.

In February 2005, Health Canada launched the Primary Healthcare National Evaluation Strategy at the national level. As part of this initiative, provinces and territories have been brought together through a series of workshops and meetings to formulate key primary healthcare evaluation questions, develop the right indicators associated with these questions for specific measurement purposes and frame appropriate tools for data collection. The indicator development work is being led by the Canadian Institute for Health Information (CIHI) while Howard Research Consulting in Calgary is leading the tools development work. The extent to which these efforts will be valuable in addressing evidentiary vacuums in the primary healthcare setting and impact overall quality improvement remains to be seen.

Even if these efforts come up with excellent performance measures, we must keep in mind that such measures by themselves will never be able to spur improvement. The Saskatchewan experience speaks to the fact that even perfect performance measures can never act as substitutes for appropriate actions in policy and practice. As Brown et al.

observe, performance measures need to positively stimulate quality measurement efforts and the evolution of performance measurement should not be seen as a policy option that can be pursued in a way distinct from the overall improvement of the healthcare system. Likewise, if evaluation of primary healthcare in Canada is to be central to progress and development of the healthcare delivery system, the huge disconnect between leadership commitments and performance reports needs to be overcome. These reports need to speak compellingly to managers, policy-makers and practitioners in primary healthcare in order to serve as catalysts to a major leap forward in quality and accountability.

Conclusion

Brown et al. have presented an overview of the concepts and applications of performance measurement in the current Canadian environment. In this commentary, we have explored a number of the various determinants of and barriers to major system change, and have explored Saskatchewan's primary healthcare evaluation framework and activities as an empirical test of these propositions. In our view, the Saskatchewan commitment to a grounded primary healthcare evaluation and performance measurement framework is a step forward towards a more intelligence-based and evidence-driven system. However, given the numerous barriers to system change and the challenges discussed, there are limits to how quickly a comprehensive set of indicators can be measured and utilized for purposes of change management.

The culture of quality improvement is still emerging, and historically the system has focused on access and volume rather than effectiveness, patient-centredness and outcome. The Saskatchewan evaluation initiatives are designed to enhance commitment to change and advance the culture of evidence-based decision-making. These, coupled with a province-wide quality improvement initiative focusing on coronary artery disease, diabetes and access to primary care bode well for large-scale change.[5] Since comparison is often a spur to improvement, the development of national-level indicators will also facilitate momentum. Yet optimism must be tempered by awareness of the strength of traditions and the paucity of change levers in Canadian healthcare in general, and primary healthcare in particular. A genuine commitment to new, performance-oriented models of primary healthcare will heighten interest in measurement and evaluation, just as report findings should strengthen the overall commitment to change. Each depends on the other, and it will be interesting to see whether Canada is genuinely up for a primary healthcare extreme makeover similar to that of US Veterans Affairs or England's primary-care sector, or will settle for the incremental and often isolated progress that defines our healthcare history. We need to remember that at the landmark first national Primary Healthcare conference in Winnipeg held in May 2004, a dominating theme among the 1,000 participants was frustration at the absence of significant change despite strong evidence and a history of successful pilot or demonstration sites throughout the nation.

Notes

[1] For example, from British Columbia, Watson et al., "A Results-Based Logic Model of Primary Healthcare: Laying an Evidence-Based Foundation to Performance Measurement, Monitoring and Evaluation" (September 2004). Nova Scotia, Saskatchewan and Newfoundland and Labrador have also developed their own evaluation frameworks for primary healthcare.

[2] Five-Year Evaluation Framework for Primary Healthcare Demonstration Sites, May 2004.

[3] Evaluating Primary Healthcare in Saskatchewan: A Proposed Rationale and Indicator Framework, June 2004.

[4] In diabetes management, there is an estimated combined lifetime cost savings of $88,618 in a single year (2002-03) through increased screening at a primary healthcare site over two comparable FFS control sites. From 1999 to 2002, the average cost of Ambulatory Care Sensitive Conditions (ACSCs)-related hospitalizations in one FFS control site is 44% more and in the second FFS control site is 16% more than the same PHC site that has been evaluated. Again, the first FFS control site has incurred 3.5 times higher recruitment costs compared to the PHC site because of the continuous revolving door of physicians. Similar findings on successes have emerged on various other components of primary healthcare in the province.

[5] In November 2005, the Health Quality Council in Saskatchewan is launching a Chronic Disease Management Collaborative starting with 20% of Saskatchewan primary-care practices.

References

Brown, A.D., H. Bhimani and H. MacLeod. 2005. Making Performance Reports Work. *HealthcarePapers* 2005, 6(2): 8-22.

Jha, A.K., J.B. Perlin, K.W. Kizer and R.A. Dudley. 2003. "Effect of the Transformation of the Veterans Affairs Healthcare System on the Quality of Care." *New England Journal of Medicine* 348: 2218-27.

Katz, A., C. DeCoster, B. Bogdanovic, R.-A. Soodeen and D. Chateau. 2004. *Using Administrative Data to Develop Indicators of Quality in Family Practice.* Winnipeg: Manitoba Centre for Health Policy. Retrieved August 24, 2005. <www.umanitoba.ca/centres/mchp/reports/pdfs/quality_wo.pdf>.

Leape, L.L. and D.M. Berwick. 2005." Five Years after To Err Is Human – What Have We Learned?" *Journal of the American Medical Association* 293: 2384-90.

Marshall, M.N., M. Roland, S. Campbell, S. Kirk, D. Reeves, R. Brook, E. McGlynn and P. Shekelle. 2003. *Measuring General Practice: A Demonstration Project to Develop and Test a Set of Primary Care Clinical Quality Indicators.* London: The Nuffield Trust.

McGlynn, E.A., S.M. Asch, J. Adams, J. Keesey, J. Hicks, A. DeCristofaro and E.A. Kerr. 2003. "The Quality of Health Care Delivered to Adults in the United States." *New England Journal of Medicine* 348: 2635-45.

Oldham, John. 2004. *Sic Evenit Ratio Ut Componitur: The Small Book about Large System Change.* West Sussex: St. Richard's Press.

Smith, P.C. 2002. "Performance Management in British Healthcare: Will It Deliver?" *Health Affairs* 21: 103-15.

Watson, D.E., A.-M. Broemeling, R. Reid and C. Black. 2004. "A Results-Based Logic Model for Primary Health Care: Laying an Evidence-Based Foundation to Guide Performance Measurement, Monitoring and Evaluation." Vancouver: Centre for Health Services and Policy Research.

Afterword: Delivering Quality by Design*

Steven Lewis

Reading these stories about high-performing health systems should make Canadians uncomfortable. From a small county in Sweden to a large, Canadian-style dispersed system in the United States; from a focus on primary healthcare to the pursuit of excellence in acute care; from implementing tools and techniques to the development of system-wide cultures – these narratives describe achievements to which Canada aspires but rarely achieves.

Our inability to make things right despite huge investments in healthcare is no longer a private failure. Chris Ham from the University of Birmingham, an astute international healthcare system observer, tells a revealing story. As the architects of the UK's National Health System (NHS) transformation charted their course at the beginning of this century, they looked, Ham recounts, elsewhere for inspiration and cautionary tales. The worst possible outcome, they concluded, would be to increase spending from 6% to 10% of GDP and end up looking like Canada. By this they meant it would be a travesty to spend so much and achieve so little.

* Originally published in *High Performing Healthcare Systems: Delivering Quality by Design* 2008. Toronto: Longwoods Publishing, p. 267-71.

Damn them for their prescience. In 1997 total Canadian healthcare spending was $79 billion. Ten years later the tab had reached $160 billion. Yet that decade of spending increases far above the rate of inflation did not fundamentally improve performance. In addition, public confidence has not been fully restored, and international rankings on measures such as public satisfaction and value for money, however controversial, do not flatter Canada. We support dozens of demonstration projects but rarely generalize proven success. We learn a lot about others' successes – everyone seems to know about the prerequisites for high performance and regiments of Canadian front-line workers, managers, board members and government officials have visited the UK, Intermountain Healthcare, Virginia Mason and their cousins. They all sing lustily from the Institute for Healthcare Improvement (IHI) hymnal. Whether we learn from them is another matter.

Why this apparent contradiction: on the one hand we are willing and able to learn, seem to want to change, sign up in droves to improve safety, succeed on a small scale, but on the other, we can't seem to close the deal system-wide? As careful comparative health systems analysts remind us, context is everything. What works in Sweden might not work here. So what is it about our context that holds us back? Are we in the end a learning-disabled nation, frozen by tradition, paralyzed by the power of vested interests, as complacent as Canadian hockey prior to the wake-up call of the 1972 summit series with the Soviets?

Peculiarly Canadian challenges

Our expensive mediocrity is not entirely an accident. Canada faces challenges that are less daunting elsewhere. They are not insurmountable, but we ignore them at our peril. Among the most prominent:

Mon pays, ce n'est pas un pays ...

Yes, the state of federalism holds us back. It is no secret that federal–provincial relations are at a low ebb. Canadians reliably support the involvement of both levels of government in policy making and direction, yet their governments do not share this view. Ottawa's role is to be a cash cow (see the accords of 2000, 2003 and 2004). With a guarantee of billions of new dollars coming down the pipeline for years to come, the predictable result is increased expectations for higher pay and plans to add capacity. The unintended (but inevitable) consequence is that our new money mainly buys the status quo while other countries' buys change. (We should have gone to the UK for counselling.)

Clinical autonomy rules

It is quite possible that clinical autonomy is more firmly entrenched in Canada than anywhere else. We know about and accept huge variations in practice with equanimity. Most physicians feel little attachment to health regions or larger systems, and medicine remains primarily a cottage industry. Autonomous judgment is a hallmark of professionalism and, properly applied, it is a fundamental building block of excellence. But autonomy without accountability is a recipe for huge variations in practice and an invitation to plunder public resources. It also makes managing wait times and achieving real equity of access extraordinarily difficult.

Perverse incentives breed cynicism

Everyone familiar with Canadian healthcare knows the following:

- It is more lucrative to practise bad medicine than good medicine, particularly in family practice. See 80 basically healthy patients a day for five minutes and you'll prosper. See 20 complex frail elderly patients and apply all of your learning and wisdom and you'll make a modest income at best. Medical associations by and large determine which specialities will make how much money and which practice patterns will be most lucrative – yet another example of a healthcare system designed to get the results we observe. Governments need to find ways to eliminate these perverse incentives.
- Governments send mixed signals about whether they wish to fund volumes or excellence and prudent use of resources. Their rhetoric supports needing and using less healthcare, but their behaviour rewards volumes. It is hard to take seriously their population health and prevention messages when they hold the system accountable for activity but not outcomes. Governments must commit to a population- and needs-based approach, and find ways to reward ingenuity that improves access and quality with less volume.
- Many professionals are woefully underused. Nurse practitioners are probably the best-studied occupational group in human history. Three dozen randomized controlled trials have confirmed that they can deliver a wide swath of effective primary care services. Lured by every imaginable form of incentive, family doctors still largely will not go to or stay in rural and remote Canada. Yet the juxtaposition of these two firmly established realities has not led to the obvious transformation. The guilds are powerful and it is instructive to observe how medicine has managed to change the focus to physicians' assistants (i.e., a hierarchical, doctor-controlled approach) from an expanded nurse practitioner model (i.e., collaborative and egalitarian approach). All health human resources stakeholders need to rethink the whole approach to education, credentialing and the division of labour.

Success notwithstanding

The barriers to improvement are real, but there are solutions – even in Canada. Most do not require wholesale rebuilding. They often rest merely on the removal of a few important barriers to improvement and on policies that encourage the behaviours to which we aspire.

Beyond pretend-management

Eight provinces have health regions, and Ontario has Local Health Integration Networks (LHINs). In theory, these structures have been established to decentralize authority, encourage experimentation and innovation, and set creativity free. Yet health ministries cannot resist looking over (even sitting on) the shoulders of health regions and LHINs, wading into mini-crises and generally letting the public know that they, and not the local authorities, are in charge when the going gets tough (and even when it doesn't). If ministries were brilliant micro-managers, with policies and incentives aligned, one might forgive them for their meddlesome and demoralizing hubris. Moreover, there is a lot of pretend-governance and pseudo-management. Costs are still heavily driven by independent and largely autonomous physician contractors. There is sufficient confusion about who really makes decisions to allow clever players several options for getting what they want. These are the elephants in the room, leaving scant room to pursue a truly needs-based, efficient and effective public interest mandate. The solution is to let organizations manage within sensible accountability frameworks and expand the concept of management into the domain in which it is needed most: clinical service.

Embrace the information revolution

When it comes to comprehensive, real-time health information, Canada exhibits all of the characteristics of a country that doesn't want to know and doesn't want to tell. Those responsible for the health information and information technology (IT) agenda have said over and over that it may take 10 times as much money as we have thus far been prepared to invest to produce real-time performance information accessible to providers, the public, managers and policy makers. Every high-performing health system story has electronic, standardized, widely used information at its centre. The next frontier is the office-based electronic medical record, which has to be standardized, interoperable, linkable and useful at multiple levels. Otherwise, we will end up with less analytical power than we had a decade ago.

Learn from the best – including ourselves

The key object lessons from the inspiring stories in this collection of case studies are:

1. Policy and leadership matter. Success cannot be optional. Accountability must be clear. Performance improvement is a serious business that requires steely commitment and a refusal to tolerate persistent failure.
2. Policy without tools is ineffective; tools without policy are highly limited.
3. It may take a village but it doesn't have to take a generation. Transformation is never complete, and in some areas progress can take a long time. But some transformations have been rapid – notably, at Veterans Affairs (VA) and in some aspects of the UK's healthcare system. Always aim for fast, even if sometimes slow is all you can get.
4. Integrating key providers fully into the system and engaging them in goal-setting and performance improvement are essential to success. Fostering a culture of cooperation and participation requires a dedicated strategy, resources and policy framework. In Canada, there are several competing cultures at play: hierarchical vs. egalitarian; primary care focused vs. intensive specialized care; a population focus vs. a patient

focus. Creating a unified approach to system improvement will not come about by osmosis. Great organizations invest a lot in building common cultures; healthcare must as well.

5. Let people experiment, fail, regroup and improve. Let them organize their own work. Once they have embraced the culture of performance, the need to instruct, cajole, persuade and intervene vanishes.
6. Be wary of narrow targets and paying for isolated successes. Incentives are important, but they must be carefully calibrated, and there is always the risk of unintended consequences. Healthcare is a public service with powerful ethical underpinnings. The greatest international successes seem to have abandoned flirtation with market concepts and pseudo-competition; instead, they have focused on cultural change supported by tools, relationships and a powerful sense of common purpose.
7. Successful transformers are fundamentally dissatisfied with the status quo. Canadians are slow to see the flames on the platform even when we feel the heat. Let's get constructively agitated and apply the resulting energy and sense of urgency to getting better. Every delay means that people will suffer needlessly.
8. Learn from Canadian success stories. There is hardly a species of excellence that cannot be found in Canada. From the Ontario provincial Cardiac Care Network to the Group Health Centre in Sault Ste. Marie to the Alberta Bone and Joint Institute, there have been triumphs of access and quality. Making excellence mandatory is the next step. That's what high-performing healthcare systems do, and that's what Canada ought to do.

CHAPTER TWO The Call for Professional Accountability

Degrees of Separation: Do Higher Credentials Make Healthcare Better?*

Steven Lewis

Sometime around 2050, the last registered nurse without a university degree will ride off into the sunset. Manitoba had gamely held out as the last province to retain the diploma option, but it too has thrown in the towel. Raising entry-to-practice credentials (ETPC) in health disciplines is the new pandemic. Among recent developments,

- nursing – a decades-long evolution from hospital-based to college-based diplomas, and then baccalaureate degree ETPC;
- medicine – family medicine residency lengthened to two years from one in the early 1990s, a major cause of the subsequent doctor shortage;
- physiotherapy (PT) – conversion to a master's-level ETPC almost complete;
- occupational therapy (OT) – ditto;
- pharmacy – talk of moving to a PharmD ETPC (the University of Toronto has pitched it to the government of Ontario, and Quebec has made similar noises); and
- various technologists and technicians – a regular push for a baccalaureate ETPC.

In a world that values education as an intrinsic good, these have to be admirable developments. Professions devoted to the public good and humbly aware of their limitations raise their ETPC as part of the journey to continuous improvement. Higher ETPC has to create

* Originally published in *Longwoods Essays*, October 2009

better-prepared graduates, improved system quality and a better patient experience. If a diploma is good, a degree is better; if a baccalaureate is adequate, a doctorate is superior.

Sounds sensible, right? Let's examine what we've learned about this phenomenon over the years. (Before I get into the analysis, full disclosure: As a public representative on the Canadian Nurses Association Board of Directors in the early 1990s, I cast the lone vote against what was then known as the BN 2000 resolution. For the past six years, I have sat on the federal–provincial/territorial Coordinating Committee on Entry to Practice Credentials [we have a gift for catchy titles]. So I have been around this topic for some time; and while it cannot compete with my obsession with baseball statistics, it ranks right up there among my day job preoccupations.) First, no one can pin down where raising the ETPC starts. Many have looked, and more knowledgeable and savvy people than I cannot trace such a change back to its origins. The best guess is that these movements begin in faculty lounges or around the board tables of professional associations. While we don't know how the credential upgrade begins, we know how it doesn't. Employers never demand increased ETPC; on occasion, they explicitly oppose it. No one has ever produced evidence that those practising with the about-to-be-abandoned credentials are harming the public. Governments never instigate the changes.

Second, increasing the credential does not necessarily mean more training. Take the therapies. Until recently, you got to be a physiotherapist by taking a four-year university degree in, sensibly, PT. Now you take a two-year master's program following an undergraduate degree in anything. Same with OT – my brilliant and talented niece got her MSc on top of her architecture degree, consisting of about a year in the classroom and a year of practical experience. We are to take it on faith that we get a more capable entry-level therapist in half the time it used to take, armed with a degree that sounds more advanced.

Nursing has been even more artful. First, it bid adieu to an intensive, roughly 23-month diploma program in favour of the four-year, but less jam-packed baccalaureate program. The degree students actually spend less time in practice settings during their training. The transition to a degree-only program predictably reduced the numbers of graduates. Employers and governments grew alarmed at forecasts of a 100,000-plus shortage of registered nurses (RNs) on the horizon.

No worries, responded the universities. We've got a solution. Presto – there are now 11 programs across the country that will give you a nursing degree on top of, say, a fine arts degree in two years! Follow the bouncing ball: two years wasn't sufficient to turn out a competent entry-level nurse 15 years ago, but now it is again. Excellent. (Advice to students: demand a master's degree for your troubles, just like the physiotherapists and occupational therapists. Of course, this would confuse regulators, irk nurses with four-year baccalaureate degrees and cause riots among nurses with real master's degrees. The physios and occupational therapists had the good sense to eliminate the undergraduate option altogether.)

Third, at least in some jurisdictions, universities, wielding their academic freedom, have acted with remarkable vigour to satisfy professions' aspirations for increased ETPC. The University of Saskatchewan – my alma mater and annual recipient of my donations, in case this essay prompts it to withdraw my degrees – decided on its own not to enrol a new class of PT students a couple of years ago, as part of its campaign to adopt the MSc as the ETPC. It somehow forgot to notify the government or obtain its permission, although it invoked the Cool Hand Luke defence. One might think the premier or minister of advanced education might have called up the president to inform him that this ringing exercise of institutional autonomy suddenly made a few million dollars vanish from the university's budget. Nah, bygones.

Fourth, the ETPC movement has created subtle changes in the meaning of advanced degrees. I believe the technical term is *phony baloney*. These so-called professional master's degrees and doctorates require none of the rigour, research or external scrutiny that used to be hallmarks of advanced education. While purveyors of these degrees acknowledge that they are different in important respects, they know full well that the public makes no such distinctions. The biggest assault on standards is where the advanced degree sits on top of an undergraduate degree in a different discipline. The master's-level PT and OT training has to be basic because no one has any grounding in the subject matter prior to entry into "graduate" studies.

Fifth, no one seems to know or care about the practical consequences of raising ETPC. People will disagree about the wisdom of the nursing conversion, but shouldn't we at least be curious about the consequences? (I'm not picking on nursing here; it's just that nurses outnumber the other professions combined, so the implications are huge.) Consider the following:

- How much did it cost? The transition reduced supply, which shifted bargaining power to nursing unions and led to bidding wars among the provinces. Every higher-than-normal contract settlement produced a domino effect across the country. I'm all for paying nurses well, but no one consciously decided that we ought to spend several billion dollars to make nursing more lucrative. Is it several billion? Well, if 200,000 nurses are getting 20% more than they would have, had the diploma option remained in place, and the average nursing salary is \$60,000, that amounts to \$12,000 more per nurse × 200,000 nurses = \$2.4 billion annually.
- Is nursing care better? We have no clue. There is some (largely American) research that attributes hospital care outcomes to RN staffing levels, but the studies have deliberately avoided comparing diploma- versus baccalaureate-degree nurses. Hint: You can read a ton of quality improvement literature without coming across any references to ETPC as a key factor.
- Are nurses happier? I hope not because they remind us weekly of their collective misery and plummeting morale, so it would be terrible if this reported malaise is

actually an improvement over their state of well-being prior to "degreeing up."
- Has the class structure of nursing education changed now that the profession is degree only? Are fewer working-class kids inclined to choose a career in nursing because it is much more expensive and time consuming to acquire the credential? What about Aboriginal people, recent immigrants and other minorities?

You would think that public policy makers might be interested in some case studies of the consequences of these decisions. Uh-uh. A number of us have proposed a research agenda to get to the bottom of these monumental changes and produce real evidence to resolve the ongoing debates. It might cost a few million dollars to do the work comprehensively, but we're dealing with multi-billion-dollar issues. The failure to commission the research betrays not just a stunning lack of curiosity; it is wilful ignorance that will condemn decision-makers to the same sort of ad hoc, ill-informed choices that have created the current mess.

But, one might counter, even if the ETPC changes were in a sense unnecessary, there are worse sins than overeducating the healthcare workforce. Not so fast. One of the reasons professions raise ETPC is to increase their status and credibility in the academy. They do this in part by developing complex theory and creating specialized identities. Merging these identities into unified inter-professional teams is a challenge under any circumstances; even stronger and more fragmented identities forged in longer education programs will hardly make this easier. Furthermore, graduates with higher credentials will expect to work at a higher level, and many will be disappointed and bored by the everyday but important work of patient care.

All that said, there is no definitive proof that increasing ETPC is a colossal mistake. I'm saying merely that it might be, but we know embarrassingly little about the consequences. And if we're going to require more education for healthcare newbies, we need to debate the form that education should take. Too many practitioners know nothing about the social determinants of health, health systems, policy, economics and the arts of citizenship. Maybe they need to broaden their educational horizons rather than deepen their discipline-specific identities. That nurse with a bachelor of fine arts degree and a two-year nursing degree may indeed turn out to be admirably educated for the challenges of working in a variety of contexts. But let's not confuse that prospect with the ETPC being essential to making healthcare better.

Primary Healthcare: The All-Too-Quiet Revolution in Waiting*

Steven Lewis and Jeanette Edwards

Remodelling the kitchen won't help the house with a weak foundation. The same holds true in healthcare. We cannot solve quality and access problems or deal effectively with wait times unless primary healthcare – the foundation of the system – is solid. That is why the First Ministers' 2003 Healthcare Renewal Accord identifies it as the cornerstone of tomorrow's healthcare system. But progress is slow, and the foundation is creaking under the strain of even greater pressures. Our healthcare system does a reasonable job providing acute care medical services. It is not very effective at prevention – witness the obesity epidemic and the rising number of people with diabetes. Nor does it do a great job of managing chronic conditions such as diabetes, heart disease and hypertension. The failures often end up in hospital, their quality of life diminished, with medicare picking up a hefty price tag. The comprehensive, multidisciplinary approach that defines primary healthcare is much better suited to addressing these complex and chronic problems.

Lately, primary healthcare has taken a back seat to other issues: wait times, pharmacare and funding. These are important, but attempts to address them will fail unless the primary healthcare revolution succeeds. Yet despite some notable successes, it is deeply mired in obsolete patterns of practice, turf battles and structural barriers to change. It is, quite simply, stuck. We continue to pour dollars into providing expensive treatments without giving enough support to strategies that help keep people well. It's like having a luxury car with a fabulous sound system and plush interior running on threadbare tires.

* Originally published in *Healthcare Quarterly* 2005, 8(1): 89-90

There are some hopeful initiatives, among them the federal government's $800 million Primary Healthcare Transition Fund, created in 2001 to seed primary healthcare projects around the country. Roy Romanow placed primary healthcare firmly at the centre of meaningful reform in both his report on Canada's healthcare system, and in his keynote address at the National Primary Healthcare Conference held in Winnipeg this past May. Good primary healthcare is, in his view, the foundation of a high quality, sustainable system. There has been a quiet revolution in primary healthcare in parts of Canada. However, as Romanow noted, the pace has been frustratingly slow.

Where it works creatively, the results are compelling. Consider the Youth Health Centres project in Halifax. Its goal is what a health system – as opposed to "sickness" system – is supposed to be about: keeping kids healthy and in school. The centres, a partnership between the Capital District Health Authority and the Halifax Regional School Board, address high-priority health issues such as sexuality, mental health, drugs and alcohol. Evaluations show that at-risk students are now less likely to drop out and persist in unhealthy behaviours. More graduates making sensible lifestyle choices means a stronger economy and reduced burdens on health and social services.

In Hamilton, mental health and nutrition services have been incorporated into the practices of 38 Health Service Organizations involving 77 physicians and170,000 patients. Depending on their needs, people are referred to dieticians, counsellors or psychiatrists. Among those with diabetes, 95% have decreased sugar consumption and 74% have lost weight. In-patient psychiatric admissions have dropped by a third and outpatient hospital visits by about 90%.

In British Columbia, the BC NurseLine has logged 560,000 calls in its first three years of service. The service has provided care and advice when people need it and has preempted 36,000 visits to physicians or emergency rooms.

Saskatchewan's 25 primary healthcare teams consist of a range of healthcare professionals that provide primary healthcare services.

As illustrated by these examples, primary healthcare goes beyond traditional healthcare services. It covers health promotion and healthcare; health and social services; individuals and communities. Both professionals and the public share responsibility for producing good health, and the approach breaks down traditional hierarchies within healthcare. These ideas are not new: Community centres such as the Mt. Carmel Clinic in Winnipeg have been practising primary healthcare for decades and have won awards for their innovative practices.

Primary healthcare is sound in theory and effective in practice. The status quo is plagued by problems of quality and access. Yet there is no stampede towards new primary healthcare models; rather there is a slow trickle of change, and many highly touted innovations are really minor modifications to the conventional practices ill-suited to contemporary needs. Resistance remains strong, and one wonders whether the system is so calcified that no rapid movement is possible.

Not so in the UK. John Bibby, a physician, and Ghislaine Young, a nurse practitioner, recently told the 1,000 delegates to the Winnipeg conference how they make primary healthcare work in northern England. Nurses manage almost all chronic conditions. Their electronic health record system allows them to monitor the effectiveness of care for both individuals and among population groups at the click of a mouse. A variety of providers respond to individual needs.

For some reason, change seems faster and more effective across the ocean. Maybe it's because they don't confront the complexities of federalism. Maybe it's because physicians are full and integrated partners in the National Health Service, while in Canada the norm remains the independent, fee-for-service contractual relationship. Maybe it's because UK governments are more decisive.

The delegates who attended the Winnipeg conference, mainly health practitioners and policy makers from across the country, expressed frustration over the lack of forward movement in primary healthcare. The newly released conference synthesis report "A Thousand Points of Light? Moving Forward on Primary Healthcare" captures both the energy and commitment of people in the vanguard of primary healthcare across the country, and their concern that their examples are too few.

They want more commitment from all healthcare disciplines to work together. They want more action and more political will to change.

What they don't want is to wait for yet more results, more pilot projects, more halting and compromised reforms. They already know primary healthcare works, and that the public needs it as the centrepiece of the health system. The barriers to change are clear and present dangers. The "Canadian way" is evolution, but primary healthcare needs a revolution. The quiet, voluntary, and incremental approach leaves too many Canadians underserved or badly served, and too many providers unable to use their talents to the fullest. The struggle to implement primary healthcare may prove just as important as the fight for medicare in 1962. If it is unsuccessful, there will be no healthcare fix for a generation, or ever.

Acknowledgment

To view the National Primary Healthcare Conference synthesis report in its entirety, go to www.phcconference.ca.

Spare the Policy, Spoil the Profession*

Steven Lewis

The jig is up: Canada's publicly financed healthcare system does not reliably deliver safe, high-quality, efficient care – and this after doubling spending in the past decade. Patient friendly it isn't; the convenience of providers comes first. Need primary care after 5:00 p.m.? Go to emergency. Got four complaints? Make four appointments. Every serious analysis comes to the same conclusion: the system needs a major refit to improve access, quality and value for money.

Yet, we remain a nation of demonstration projects, taking two steps backward for every step forward. Of the many obstacles to transformative change, one looms larger than all the others: organized medicine. For the better part of 40 years, organized medicine has more often than not stood in the way of efforts to re-engineer healthcare. It has pursued its own interests with brilliant success and passed them off as the public interest. It has secured more money, the right to saturate one jurisdiction or specialty with doctors

* Originally published in *Longwoods Essays*, December 16, 2008

and neglect others, largely autonomous and unaccountable practice, and separate and unequal access to the councils of state and the boardrooms of health organizations. Don't blame organized medicine for the way it behaves; blame us, meaning the citizenry and the governments we elect. We're the enablers.

Predictably, the system suffers: the documented shortcomings in safety, access and quality speak for themselves. More surprisingly, doctors are suffering too. Their own surveys unearth a litany of miseries, fantasies about leaving practice within a couple of years (they don't, even when they say they will), overwork, ennui. So, if it's not working for us, and it's not working for them, why does nothing change?

We owe the doctors of Canada a serious apology for spoiling a noble profession. By kowtowing to organized medicine, we end up with collective agreements and policies that entrench the status quo and keep Canadian healthcare in the dark ages. Doctors who have nothing to do with medical politics nonetheless bear the consequences of the positions taken by their representatives. The culture of self-centredness and privilege erodes idealism and produces generations of cynics who chafe under the rules of the game but lack the will to change them. Here are the main errors for which we need to atone:

First, we have erred in how we pay most doctors, and for letting medical politics determine what and who are worth more and worth less. Allowing organized medicine to divide up the pie has distorted care patterns, undercompensated many doctors, obscenely enriched others and pitted group against group. The doctors who use their hands out-earn those who use their brains. The ophthalmologist who does 20 cataract procedures in a day earns more than the one who figures out 20 complex eye disorders in a week. The dermatologist's pay leaves the rheumatologist's in the dust. We stand by in learned helplessness as the medical associations concoct a reward system that produces 10 times as many pediatricians as geriatricians, a steady abandonment of primary care and a generation of doctors practising at the low end of their capacities.

Second, we should apologize for letting doctors practice in the 21st century with the tools of Bob Cratchit. Governments sign collective agreements that condone quill pen medicine – we're at the bottom of the G7 pack in the adoption of the electronic medical record. Quality improvement (QI) tools and techniques are optional. There is no obligation to undergo practice profiling and recertification. Most doctors have no clue about the quality and effectiveness of what they deliver – and those who think they do are almost certainly wrong. The inevitable results: medical practice harms 10% of patients in hospitals; there is routine prescribing of dangerous dosages and drug combinations to the elderly; there is widespread failure to diagnose and effectively manage the most common and straightforward chronic diseases; primary healthcare patients get all of the evidence-based care they need only about half the time; and the list goes on.

Research shows that the longer doctors practise, the more they decline. We would never neglect the career development of our pilots, car mechanics or workers in fast-food restaurants the way we have neglected the professional competence of doctors. And instead of organized medicine imploring governments and health organizations to analyze patients' anonymized data, feed back the results and help doctors with QI, the Canadian Medical Association president makes ominous speeches about privacy.

Third, it's been a mistake to leave unchallenged the attribution of access problems to shortages of doctors and to inflate medical school enrolments by two-thirds in response. Instead, we should have mandated strategies that could dramatically improve access right now, such as advanced access scheduling. Millions of Canadians can't get to see their family doctor the same week they call for an appointment, while everyone in England can and does in 48 hours. Do the process re-engineering, optimize the division of labour among the professions and then assess whether there are shortages – and if so, of what? And recognize that expanding enrolments in medical school won't solve the shortage of specialists in the disciplines that internal medical politics has consigned to the bottom of the income ladder.

Fourth, we have erred in adopting organized medicine's view that all doctors' problems, dissatisfactions and anxieties are soluble in cash. When doctors tell us they can't be on call 24/7, 365 days a year in rural areas, we empathize and come to the table to help find a solution. Nurse practitioners? No thanks. Group-based practice? Can't sell it to the members. How about a hundred thousand bucks extra? Sounds good! So we inflate doctors' incomes to do the same things that sap their energy, ruin their home life and keep them on a treadmill to depression, substance abuse and burnout. Shame on us.

Fifth, we've blundered in letting medicine dwell in splendid isolation atop the heap of the health professions. We allow the guild to keep competent others out of the sandbox: nurse practitioners are threatening; let's go for physician assistants. The pharmacist who knows more than the doctor about pharmacotherapy remains a diffident subordinate instead of a true partner. The other guilds follow medicine's lead, and we wonder why inter-professional collaborative practice goes nowhere. If being separate and unequal were to make doctors happy and the system better, fine. But the job satisfaction survey data show the unhappy consequences of letting organized medicine get in the way of its own members' well-being.

Sixth, we owe a *mea culpa* for letting organized medicine's media grandstanding, government baiting, hyperbole and fear mongering go unchallenged. Because we do not hold organized medicine to a higher standard of discourse and accountability, its rhetoric becomes bolder and it comes to believe its own propaganda, that every misdeed or wait list is everyone's fault but doctors'. We've turned organized medicine into expert blackmailers: more money, more machinery, a bonus here, a new medical school there.

Attend a committee meeting? Pay us. Become true partners in the hard job of running the system? Nah, we like being independent contractors, not integrated team players. Staff the emergency room? Pay us fee-for-service, an hourly rate on top of that and a shift bonus on top of that. Set up shop in the poor part of town where the need is greatest and unmet? Charter of Rights! Freedom! We fed the beast and stood by as medical altruism and decency became entombed in a hard shell of self-serving cynicism. No one wins.

Our biggest mistake is failing to demand more of both organized medicine and individual doctors. We admit only superior students into medical school. We put them through intensive training (but not much education in citizenship and how systems work). We then turn a blind eye to huge variations in practice and never evaluate them seriously. And because this is a proven recipe for substandard quality, we let organized medicine persuade us that the remedy is to pay extra for mere competence – participating in chronic disease management collaboratives and following the occasional clinical practice guideline. This is our fault and our folly.

Lord Acton would have expected as much: power corrupts, and we have given organized medicine too much power. The dysfunction is intergenerational: we have not sufficiently protected and nurtured opportunities for new generations to chart a different path. We have given medicine autonomy without accountability and increased its allowance while its grades declined and it acted out at the table. Small wonder that practice is anarchic and error abounds. We didn't bring organized medicine up right, and we have only ourselves to blame for its values and behaviour.

Apology is a precursor to reconciliation and recovery. We need to recognize our mistakes and become the partners organized medicine deserves to restore its dignity as a profession that advances the public interest and justice for its members. Collectively, physicians are worse than the sum of their parts, and that harms all of them, and us. Our mistake has been to give organized medicine what it wants. It is time to give it what it needs, and to help it understand the difference.

Pay for Performance: The Wrong Time, the Wrong Place?*

Steven Lewis

It sounds like such a good idea: don't pay people to show up and scurry about, pay them for proven performance. It's the new Big Thing in healthcare financing. As usual, the Brits have pursued it most vigorously. Some Canadian healthcare executives get bonuses for achieving certain targets. The US Medicare plan has quit reimbursing hospitals for the costs of dealing with avoidable mishaps such as falls and bed sores. Healthcare cheques should come with performance strings attached. About time, right? Well, yes, if you overlook the pay for performance (P4P) track record. Renowned British health economist Alan Maynard found lots to be cautious about in his review of experiences to date. The Hay Group believes that even 5% to 10% of income at risk is insufficient to produce a significant effect, let alone the 1% to 2% typically on the table in such arrangements. In the UK, the vaunted GP bonus schemes – which can add tens of thousands of pounds to physician incomes – have turned into base pay. The average GP practice scores 95% of the bonus-triggering points available and virtually all get 90% or more. But the number of complaints per practice – one reasonable measure of satisfaction – varies considerably.

* Originally published in *Healthcare Quarterly* 2009, 12(3): 8-9

On examination, the very essence of P4P is troubling. It is a profoundly pessimistic concept of what makes people tick in healthcare: we can't rely on organizational culture, professionalism, devotion to public service, or commitment to excellence to get the desired results, so let's just concede that it's all about the money. Managers and practitioners are hardened cynics for whom *pecunia vincit omnia* - cash conquers all. So let's tell them what to accomplish, ring the economic bell and watch the Pavlovian throng stampede to improvement via the cash-stuffed trough.

Dishearteningly, P4P writ large becomes a self-fulfilling prophecy. Adopt its assumptions and fund or pay accordingly and you will indeed turn civilized people into econocentric shadows of their selves. Set up the game and people will learn the rules and play accordingly. Moreover, the game will inevitably lack sophistication, because to dole out the rewards, the goals must be clear and simple; the results easily measurable and immediate; and the reach modest (no one will play if it's too hard to win). All nuance and complexity are obliterated by the basic algebra of the payout. So it's hardly any wonder that British GPs are walking away with the dough. Ask not for what the bell tolls – it tolls for fee.

Incisive. In his research and his writing, he is direct and courageous. I often have learners read his work when I want to challenge their established notions, particularly the role of doctors in hindering reform.

Danielle Martin

But what if we're just learning, and eventually get it right, particularly if we learn from our masters in the private sector? You're doubtless as inspired as I am by the corporate CEOs with incomes almost entirely driven by the value of their (occasionally backdated) stock options and the quarterly earnings statements. They sure knew how to tally up the performance points. You get what you pay for, and the denizens of Wall Street decided to pay for scams so absurd that they make the Nigerian please-be-my-agent-for-millions howler look like Protestant-ethic capitalism at its sober best. IKEA CEO Anders Dahlvig refuses to take his company public precisely to avoid the tyranny of get-rich-quickism that makes a virtue of impatience and myopia and rewards Ponzi schemes over substance. But he never claimed to be as smart as the guys who ran Lehman Brothers.

For the hundredth time in a seemingly infinite series, the world is learning two key lessons: you don't get something for nothing, and appealing to baser instincts will improve neither humans nor their achievements. Healthcare is a uniquely fraught enterprise that deals with uncertainty, vulnerability, tragedy, hope, and trust. Of course it involves great amounts of money to which neither individuals nor organizations can be indifferent. Healthcare takes place in a messy world, not a monastery. But money is a resource for achieving other ends, and if it defines us or crowds out nobler preoccupations, the means become the end, the aperture narrows, and the golden calf beckons.

Doesn't it seem odd that we would have to coin the notion of "pay for performance" in the first place? What the hell else are we paying for? When did "doing one's job" uncouple from "doing one's job well"? Suggesting that ordinary performance – not spectacular, but merely satisfactory, like being nice to your patients or doing Pap tests at the recommended interval – deserves a bonus debases the entire enterprise. It creates a cultural norm in which lousy performance is the natural state and the passable is redefined as extraordinary. It dumbs performance down and leaves out the hard parts.

Show me a P4P system that rewards first class care of the frail elderly, life-enhancing management of multiple chronic conditions, reduced need for surgery 15 years from now, or ending one's career with sunny disposition and compassion intact, and I'm all ears. But in my preferred world, the first dollar and the last pay for excellence across the board, an ethos of care, devotion to the public good, and the perpetual search for knowledge. Pay individuals well and fund organizations fairly. Settle the money issues swiftly so all can focus on what the money is supposed to achieve. Do this well and we'll have pay for performance – not as cause-and-effect, but as a harmonious feature of a thriving culture.

Providers who practice to chase income targets and dangled bonuses are different from providers who want a reasonable income to pursue their callings out of love for what they do and a drive to serve people better. For those who crave the buzz of the financial transaction, there is a vast world beyond healthcare to explore. Healthcare that takes its cues from the rantings of the Chicago School and the MBA culture imperils its values and its practitioners. If those twin intellectual frauds can take down an economy, they can easily corrupt healthcare. Healthcare culture needs more than a behaviourist tweak and tuck. The worst imaginable outcome would be that P4P as currently conceived actually worked as intended, for that would prove just how far we have fallen.

A Man for All Sections: Physicians, Heed Thy Hobbes?*

Steven Lewis

I dunno, maybe it's the season, but I feel especially moved by the plight of doctors at the bottom of the medical politics food chain. Ontario emergency room (ER) docs are just the latest in a long line of disgruntled groups crying foul over the agreement negotiated by their medical association. That agreement got the support of 79% of Ontario doctors, but most ER docs said no. Now they're mobilizing to pursue distributive justice by other means.

Unfairness in the relative income distribution of physicians is not an occasional aberration, a minor side effect of an otherwise-exemplary allocation process. It is the inevitable outcome of a fierce competition within a guild that does most of its bare-knuckled work behind closed doors. Fee schedules are complex, and no well-intentioned amateurs – the kinds who sit at the table on behalf of their peers – can possibly master the game with equal panache. Over time, power shifts and accretes, some groups gain the upper hand and income disparities proliferate. There are winners and losers – all relative, of course, since every full-time physician's income is at least upper-middle class.

Provincial medical associations are the certified bargaining agents for all doctors, even for those who choose not to join. In general, the association and the government negotiate a total amount of money for physician compensation, and most of the details get

* Originally published in *Longwoods Essays*, December 23, 2008

worked out by the doctors themselves. Sometimes the government targets a top-up here, a fee code adjustment there; but overall, the physician categories, called sections, duke it out for shares of the booty. The mystery is not the injustices that follow but why habitually shafted specialties, from primary care to rheumatology to geriatrics, stay with the medical herd.

We outsiders don't really know. The doctors don't air their reasoning to outsiders. But we can speculate.

First, they are a profession, and professions love nothing more than self-regulation and self-management. They might prefer the irritations of internal decisions to the prospect of subjecting the guild to external scrutiny and meddlesome guidance. Who ya gonna trust: your peers or the bureaucrats? We are a band of brothers (and sisters), are we not? We look after our own – imperfectly, but we *get* you. Stay with us, and we'll try harder for you next time.

Second, they may sense that they are absolute winners, even while they are relative losers. Medical associations are sophisticated negotiators with vast accumulations of experience and corporate memory and a history of getting what they want. Incomes rise; occasionally the government ponies up money to redress the most egregious inequities, and all groups rise, to some extent, with the tide. No zero-sum games here. Hence, even the also-rans in the section wars might be better off than they would be on their own.

Third, governments may discourage rebellion and secession. It's hard enough bargaining with one agent; the migraines multiply when going head to head with three or four. Divide and conquer may be tempting theoretically, but that sword could cut both ways. At least there's some devolved discipline involved in tossing the pie to the medical association and letting it play Solomon with the slices.

Still, you would think that solidarity would eventually crumble sometime, somewhere. When the offended groups are large – notably, family practice – there is a lot of unexerted power. It is surely conceivable that they could do better on their own. And if the majority of physicians have a modicum of interest in overall fairness, there should be some appetite for blowing up a good deal of what is now done and starting over.

And, indeed, some have tried. A few provinces have explored the notion of a relative value approach that would rewrite the fee schedule to reflect, transparently, the education, skill, complexity and time required to perform various duties. These forays inevitably collapsed as some medical sections faced the spectre of income loss or unaccustomed parity with their hitherto poor cousins. The message to government was clear: you can buy prosperity for the undervalued, but not at the expense of the gilded-income set.

Alternative payment plans (APPs) are increasingly common, though fee-for-service still dominates. This holds some promise, especially if the new plans fall outside the overall compensation pool. If the APPs perpetuate the same distorted income patterns that fee-for-service generates, they will be partially effective at best (though they may be highly desirable on other grounds).

The solution to all of this is about 400 years old. Thomas Hobbes (1588–1679) coined the memorable phrase *bellum omnium contra omnes* – the war of all against all. To Hobbes, the state of nature was just such a war, resulting in a life that is nasty, solitary, brutish, short and poor – sort of how the Ontario ER doctors view their plight. (OK, it's not quite the same as a bunch of club-wielding guys in loin cloths, but stick with the metaphor.) And they're envious of family docs, for heaven's sake, who have sad tales of their own.

The interesting part is Hobbes's remedy. If the state of nature is a constant state of fear and conflict, the solution is to trade autonomy and power for security and order. Tom, Alice and Jim, left to their own devices, will thrash each other over whatever spoils are available, and even the winners will be battered. The solution: all agree to let Daphne rule (and Hobbes gave her a swell title, Leviathan, by which he meant the state). Daphne will dispense justice; it will not be perfect, but there will be peace and order, a damn site better than the *bellum omnium contra omnes.*

Where does the public interest lie here? If the only consequences of the medical sections' *bellum* were a few thousand doctors irked by the indignity of incomes south of $200,000, other matters might be more worthy of concern. But the effects are far more serious. Anticipated future income influences medical students' career choices. Increasingly, they eschew the categories needed to address Canada's immense and growing chronic disease burden: family medicine, geriatrics, rheumatology, psychiatry. It's not just income signals that create these imbalances, but money matters.

It is far too much to expect medical associations to get this right on their own. So why not try the hobbesian solution? Let someone else decide – a skilled tribunal that transparently takes into account all of the factors that should influence pay rates, including system needs. Some groups will and should get more, and others will and should get less. Those that get less will still get a lot, and everyone will do fine. The state of nature in medical agreement negotiations is not a happy place. Doctors and the public deserve better. In this case, the devil we don't know will almost certainly repair the damage more effectively than the devil we do.

CMA Emerges Dazed from Cave, Writes Report*

Steven Lewis

Remember the news stories from the 1960s and 1970s about Japanese soldiers emerging from island caves in full battle regalia, unaware that World War II had ended in 1945? For them, time had stopped. They were still at war and girded for combat. It appears they had some company: the authors of the recently released report of the Canadian Medical Association (CMA 2010), *Health Care Transformation in Canada.*

What a strange, atavistic confection, and what a missed opportunity. I had high hopes for the report – an updated perspective, some serious self-reflection. Surely CMA wouldn't recycle hoary old solutions and beguile us with policy legerdemain.

Surely it did. It is a remarkable document on many levels, both for what's in it and what isn't. Solutions based on unstated premises. More doctors, more services, more of everything – except restraint. Don't take my word for it – read it for yourself. Here's a sampler of the report's proposals:

* Originally published in *Longwoods Essays*, August 24, 2010

- More physician extenders (their term) but not a single reference to nurse practitioners. Handmaidens good; competitors with proven track records bad. Nurse practitioners are the loved that dare not speak their name. Physicians fought them off in the 1970s and 1980s, and they're fighting them off again. No surrender!
- Increased medical school enrolment and expanded residencies. Wake up, Rip Van Winkle! Medical school enrolments rose by 70% between 1999 and 2009, and residencies by even more. International medical graduates have easier paths to licensure. We're just beginning to see the bubble of new entrants to the workforce. Old docs aren't retiring as fast as predicted. Ontario has rostered huge numbers of new patients in family health teams with modest increases in supply. Can you spell g-l-u-t? Wait for it.
- Thousands of new nursing home beds, assuming current rates of institutionalization will be the norm for the future senior population. Memo to CMA: look around you. The middle class have abandoned nursing homes for private-sector assisted-living facilities that have left the medical model behind. Why not freeze bed numbers (like Denmark did by law 20 years ago) and pursue the alternatives that people actually want?
- Tax-deductible long-term care insurance, which manages to be both regressive and witless at the same time. Is CMA advocating full privatization of long-term care? Does it really want insurance to be cheaper for the rich than for the poor – the inevitable result of making it tax deductible? More perversely, insuring a certain form of care creates an incentive to use it, *which is exactly the opposite of what we should be doing.*
- Pay for performance, oblivious to (or maybe fully aware of, come to think of it) the UK experience that hugely inflates doctors' pay for performing to a level the public should expect routinely. Pay for performance isn't bad in theory, but too often it becomes a boondoggle because the targets have to be simple, measurable and achievable in the short run. In other words, no-brainers – which is why British general practitioners score 96% of the available bonus money.

If what's on the page is otherworldly, the omissions and subtexts are just as telling:

- Twice citing a report that ranks Canada 30th out of 30 on value-for-money, CMA still calls for more money. And it is utterly silent on doctors' contribution to the inefficiency, even though they drive two-thirds of the costs. There is no commitment to reduce variations in practice and no soul-searching about the over-medicalization of modern life.
- CMA applauds Quebec's regressive and inflationary policy shift (sequestered health saving accounts, "pre-funding" certain types of expenditures, utilization-based tax surcharges), guaranteed to feed the beast and exempt healthcare from competing with other public goods.
- In calling for expanded pharmacare (a good idea), there is not one word about shoddy prescribing patterns, doctors' penchant for getting their "education" from drug companies or the fee-for-service incentive to write a "scrip" and terminate the visit.

Here is a suggested preamble for every CMA report on the future of the healthcare system:

> Canada, we're in a mess, and we doctors are at the centre of it. We're the most powerful actors in the system. The system allows us to churn patients, mindlessly order CT scans, chop up consultations with complex patients into repeat fee-generating visits, saturate the cities and ignore the rural and remote areas with virtual impunity. And some of us do. We drive most of the costs and bear none of the financial risks. We're not responsible for all of the system's problems, but not much goes on without our say-so. We do some things well and some things badly. We are fully implicated in both the successes and failures.
>
> We must change, and we will change. We will no longer cry for more without delivering better quality, becoming good stewards of resources and calling each other out when needed. We will humbly acknowledge and learn from our imperfections and board the quality improvement train en masse. We will use electronic health records and welcome objective, publicly reported analyses of our performance to help us get better at what we do. We will get off the treadmill that ties our incomes to doing more and often doing it badly, because at times we need to do less and do it differently. We will cease hoarding practice turf and support efforts to make the division of labour more efficient. Only after we clean up our own house will we ask others to clean up theirs.

No such luck. Nothing sticks to this guild in this guild's world view. CMA is quick to lecture governments and the rest of us about what we need to do while spouting pious platitudes that exempt doctors from having to do anything. The report's authors include incoming CMA president Jeff Turnbull, a progressive keenly aware of the non-medical determinants of health and sharing none of the privatizing ambitions of his predecessors [Brian] Day and [Robert] Ouellet. Their fingerprints are all over this report; if Turnbull wants to make his mark, he would do well to hide it under a bushel.

Reference

Canadian Medical Association. 2010. *Health Care Transformation in Canada.* Ottawa, ON: Author.

Interview with Penny Ballem*

Steven Lewis

Steven Lewis talks with Penny Ballem[1] about the challenges of integrating physicians into health reform, federal-provincial relations and health information management.

SL: You've been a practising hematologist, a senior hospital executive and a deputy minister. Doctors are central to the system and they're very powerful – both collectively and individually. How successful have we been in Canada in aligning the physician agenda with the health reform agenda?

PB: We have a lot more work to do to make autonomous practitioners a more integrated part of our health system and for them to see this as an advantage rather than as one more way to make their life miserable. Most physicians see their role solely in regard to individual patients and not in relation to the broader needs of the public. Not surprisingly, our medical associations in Canada tend to support system change if it does not conflict with their members' economic interests. However, change in response to the public interest is more difficult.

That said, there's been a big shift from the old days where the only system leadership positions really available to doctors were to be a chief of staff in a hospital or the vice-president of medicine. Now we have doctors who are CEOs and deputy ministers, as well as serving in various senior leadership roles in healthcare organizations. In addi-

* Originally published in *Healthcare Policy* 2008, 4(2): 25-32

tion, it is encouraging that an increasing number of doctors are getting some formal training in management and business. Having physicians in leadership positions does make a difference as we work to continually reform our health system.

SL: Some have suggested that one way to get physicians more aligned with the broader agenda is to integrate them more fully into the regional health authorities. Do you think that's necessary, and if so, do you think that it's going to be feasible any time soon?

PB: Yes. Ideally, to really serve the public needs and interests, and get value for money from the huge taxpayer investment in our healthcare system, you have to have the physicians integrated and aligned at the regional level. If we were to follow the lead of most other international jurisdictions, the physicians' compensation should flow through the region, because their work is integral to the function and goals of regional healthcare structures.

But funding for physicians constitutes a large part of overall government spending, and the physician compensation file is a complex one. The risk is that some regions will manage the relationship – the labour relations, the compensation issues – well and others won't. To a certain extent, that's why governments have hung onto the physician file and manage it themselves, with variable amounts of input from the health sector.

Primary care physicians are a huge issue, because they tend to be the most isolated in the system, particularly if they're not involved in hospital work, which in the most populated parts of our country (the urban areas) they're not. They often experience the interface with the many parts of the system as an added burden versus something that should enable them to do a better job. To me, the first job of any health region should be to bring its primary care physicians into a more integrated role in the region, recognizing that they are a critical part of a high-quality healthcare system.

SL: In Canada we've begun, gingerly, to talk about pay for performance (P4P) to improve quality, effectiveness and efficiency in physician practice. The international literature seems mixed on the effectiveness of P4P. Do you think it is a major part of the quality and efficiency solution for Canada?

PB: Practising medicine is complex, and we've come to P4P so late – it's just not an integral part of our culture. Governments that also struggle with P4P in their own bureaucracies have begun to institute some P4P principles in physician agreements, with mixed success. I'm a big believer in the potential of P4P, and I hope we don't throw it out if early experience is mixed or even a failure. We should build on, and try to understand, the key elements that make for success and leapfrog over the failures. Canada still has a long way to go in terms of having compensation models that reward performance and incentive activities that benefit the public and are auditable to hold people accountable.

SL: Up to now, pay for performance schemes have mostly targeted activities that are easy to count and procedures that are easy to do.
PB: I think that's probably accurate.

SL: By contrast, we don't see P4P aimed at rewarding high-quality care for people with multiple chronic diseases or the complex frail elderly, where success is harder to define and it is difficult to say what ought to be done in all circumstances. So P4P can skew practices towards certain activities and away from others, and influence the choice of residencies among medical school graduates. And we end up a country with 10 times as many pediatricians as geriatricians.
PB: Exactly.

SL: So what do we do about that – how do we shift the focus of medicine, including prospective residents, towards the unmet needs and unsolved quality problems?
PB: If the governments continue to be the payer, they need to help push the profession to deal with these inequities, which in the end put the public at risk. They need to say, "We're not going to move everyone ahead at the same rate. We need to start to close the gap between the top of the pecking order and the bottom, and you medical associations need to support us on that." Some – to take your example of geriatricians – will have to move from the very bottom of the pecking order to somewhere closer to the middle or the mid-high range. P4P incentives that align with public need are certainly one way to accomplish the goal more effectively.

SL: Governments have known about these inequities and gaps for decades. Are they just incompetent negotiators? Have they ceded too much authority to decide what physician categories will earn for doing what, the result inevitably being the current mal-distributions? You're at the table. What are the two or three things that governments absolutely need to do to start turning this around?
PB: First of all, the government has to be clear about what it needs to serve the public interest. How many geriatricians, practising in what model of care, are going to meet the needs of the public? If there are twice the number of plastic surgeons in one province versus another, which one is the more efficient model of care, and how do you use a physician contract to get there? In Ontario, pediatricians are doing primary care. Does that make sense, and should a physician contract be designed to change this situation over time? When the only lever that you have with physicians is the fee-for-service payment schedule, it's tough. You have to have a plan, you have to know where you want to go and then you have to figure out the incentives to build into your negotiation strategy. That's a tough gig, and given the amount of money we are spending on physicians, we still have a long way to go. Interestingly, I think the public in Canada also needs to assist with a more informed approach, because ever since the 1960s and the great Saskatchewan

battle over the beginning of medicare, the public's general response in relation to physician negotiations has been, "Oh, for God's sake, whatever it takes, give it to my doctors because I want them to be there when I get sick."

Doctors in general in Canada are very well paid, but what is key is that the investment in our doctors and their models of compensation be designed to reward them for work patterns and activities that support the evolving needs of the public and of patients.

SL: That leads us back to primary care. The recommended movement towards a more interdisciplinary, comprehensive primary healthcare model doesn't appear to be catching hold in Canada. There are the early adopters, but no subsequent tidal wave. Physicians appear to prefer physician assistants working under their direction to the real partnership models alongside nurse practitioners, pharmacists and others. Do you think the interprofessional collaborative vision was pie-in-the-sky to begin with? What's the future of primary healthcare?

PB: I think we're making slow progress. There are some great examples of this working – the South Community Birth Program, started in 2003 in Vancouver, is a wonderful example. However, in general, this is one of the areas where there needs to be more overt leadership at the level of the College of Physicians and Surgeons, the medical associations and even the Canadian Medical Protective Association. Canada lags behind the rest of the world in the use of such professionals as midwives, nurse practitioners, pharmacists and other allied professionals to meet the growing needs of the public.

In some provinces, the medical regulatory colleges have dragged their feet in terms of working with other professional colleges to enable scope-of-practice changes that could improve access for the public, enhance quality of care and reduce physician burnout. There is also still tension about who leads the team, with a tendency of physicians to feel they must be in charge. I have a family member who is a speech pathologist. She works in the community with children with autism. She's overseeing teams working weekly with profoundly disabled children. She's far better trained to lead the team in providing care to these children than the family physician, the psychiatrist or the pediatrician, who may see these children only a few times a year. They are important members of the team, but just because they are doctors doesn't always make it appropriate, or even feasible, for them to be in charge.

SL: Students in all disciplines seem quite happy to collaborate and work in teams. There's a generational shift about workloads and preferred lifestyle. But yet again, most people say the movement towards collaborative practice is stalled. The primary healthcare revolution, if it ever got started, has been put down, and what we are getting are pretty conventional, traditional, hierarchical models.

PB: There are some excellent examples in Canada where we have moved on and have discovered the richness of an interdisciplinary model. For everywhere else, we've all got to get over ourselves and start to agree on and drive home some key messages. One is that interdisciplinary care is best practice. We're far behind the rest of the world on this point, to be honest. And I think the health sector in this country has tended to step aside and leave it to the government to carry the ball on moving the collaborative practice agenda ahead. I think that's unfair and an abdication of our responsibility.

SL: One of the dilemmas is that both federal–provincial relations and even interprovincial cooperation are at a low ebb in this country; there isn't very much common ground at the policy and governmental tables, and so medical associations and others can whipsaw provinces and territories to achieve their goals rather easily.
PB: Hmmm.

SL: You've been around those tables. Do you think there's a growing recognition that the jurisdictions need some common strategies that they stick to, or even some elements of negotiations that they can pursue in common across the country?
PB: I had the privilege to co-chair the Federal–Provincial, and chair the Provincial Conference of Deputies for a year. It was an amazing experience. Across all political lines, the provinces and territories did a lot of good work together, and usually were on the same page. They're all getting hammered in the media and their respective legislatures for the same things. The issues are just very tough problems to solve, and they require a lot of hard work and persistence.

> **He is a fervent believer that quality** must trump everything else in the health system ... Steven does have some critics who dismiss his views as too radical; however, not one of Steven's critics can mount a defence that equals his logic.
>
> *Ken Fyke*

To me, the most difficult dynamic was the federal–provincial–territorial relationship. There are tremendous opportunities for the federal government to be an enabling force that could help the provinces move ahead on their difficult health agendas – the creation of a national public drug plan, even if we start with expensive drugs for rare diseases, is an excellent example. This would end the chaos of the diverse plans currently in existence across the provinces and territories and would be a huge step forward for Canada. I feel quite discouraged about how ineffective we have been in convincing the federal government to play a role in an area such as this, which would enable progress but not require it to get entangled in the service delivery area.

SL: Let me put another perspective on the table. The provinces essentially got a huge amount of mainly unconditional money from Ottawa, just what they asked for. All they've done is entrench a pattern of very high healthcare spending growth, without getting many substantive results. So is there any way to get some negotiated, but cooperative, conditionality in the cash transfers so that at least the citizens of Canada – who don't really care which level of government is putting the cash on the table, it's all their money in the end – could say, à la Romanow, that the new money bought change?

PB: Yes, I do think that's possible. However, I think the process that leads to these agreements is quite unusual. Just think about this: a $40-billion transfer to deliver a very complex agenda and set of expectations is negotiated in three days by premiers and a small number of officials. The federal government comes in with an agenda and priorities that, in the case of British Columbia, were misaligned in at least two of the five areas they were investing in.

It was during the last Federal–Provincial First Ministers' Meeting that the provinces said, "Look, we're having a real struggle around public drug plans, and there's no reason why Canada shouldn't have a national pharmacare plan." At the end of the day, the federal government had no interest in that. So we said, let's start with expensive drugs for rare diseases, where it makes no sense for provinces to be acting on their own. No, they didn't want to do that.

To me, until the federal government is prepared to get involved in the delivery of a program where a national approach makes sense – resourcing the education of international medical graduates or funding comprehensive immunization programs are other great examples – it will be a struggle to know exactly what value the public got for its investment.

SL: Are provinces getting value for the doubling of costs in the past decade?

PB: I think we don't take enough time to celebrate where we have delivered real value for money. As an example, Ontario should be extremely proud of what it's done on wait times. They looked at the capacity of the system, they then drove it, and they made it work. They did invest more money, but they knew exactly what they got for it and everyone was held accountable - it was transparent.

Going back to federal investments in healthcare, it takes commitment and time to allow the building of a proper business case for agreed-upon priorities. Thrash it out and then let's talk about the money that it's going to take, and then everyone can get in front of the TV lights and write the cheques and all be heroes. You can't do it when you get a brown envelope on a Sunday night and by Tuesday morning, in front of TV cameras, the premiers are signing on.

SL: Let's turn to physicians and the health information agenda. Canada, again lamentably, is at the bottom of the G7 in adoption of IT – the EMR [electronic medical record], particularly. Some argue that you can solve a lot of problems with a health information system that can produce real-time data and reports at multiple levels, from clinical practice all the way to management and governance. Is this a key part of the solution, or do you think we are placing too much hope in it? Do you think we're prepared to invest the money that it's going to take to get there?

PB: Do I think it has the potential to deliver on the quality agenda? Absolutely. It is a vehicle, but it's not the only thing. Most practitioners have no real way to properly assess whether they're consistently delivering high-quality care to their patients. When we developed the online chronic disease tool kit in BC, it was an eye-opener for our practitioners. Once they started to use it (it was Web-enabled), it made a dramatic difference to them in terms of understanding how well they were doing in relation to best practice.

But while we have a group of physicians who absolutely buy into the need for a comprehensive, interoperable health information system, there is a nervousness about what will change in terms of accountability. I think our medical associations have seen what's happened in the National Health Service in the UK, where every primary care practice is being audited and compensation increases are tied to the quality of care delivered and, in some instances, patient outcomes. This is new territory, and we have lots to learn about how well it works.

Are we going to get productivity gains out of the EMR? That has been the business case used to convince government to invest. I think to achieve the promises will require a major shift in how governments do business. A lot of the return-on-investment estimates assume quality will get better, and we will get economies of scale and price reductions. I see those as being high expectations, particularly where physician fees are concerned. Ontario has probably had the best-documented success, where they were able to lower the hospital costs of hip and knee replacements – although not the physician costs. The obvious next step should be to negotiate the whole price, and have the institution and the providers figure out their roles in achieving the volume discount. Like any other sector, if we develop information systems that can enhance productivity, there should be a reduction in the unit cost – just how to achieve this is the challenge.

SL: What about capacity? We have ramped up medical school enrolments in this country by close to 60%, the effects of which will be felt in a few years. All in all, have we done the right thing, or might we find ourselves, a decade down the road, having made a big mistake by not taking the opportunity to change

the status quo, instead having opted mainly to make the status quo bigger?
PB: Well, I worry a lot about that. I think we did need to expand – certainly in some parts of the country. BC has never been remotely self-sufficient in educating its own physicians, so we did need to expand. Do we graduate physicians who have a completely different outlook on life and know they're going to practise in a different model and environment, as part of a system to which they're accountable? I think for sure their outlook and expectations are changing – however, there has been slow progress in the integration of opportunities for cross-disciplinary training. There are some very innovative programs – many of them involving rural rotations or opportunities to serve hard-to-reach populations, but there is a way to go before everyone, both at the undergraduate and postgraduate levels, has these new models as an integral part of their ongoing training. At UBC, where we created the College of Health Disciplines with great enthusiasm and hope for progress, there has been difficulty over the years in obtaining the appropriate support to have an impact on large numbers of health professional trainees.

If you look at high-performing health organizations in North America, such as Kaiser Permanente, the Veterans Affairs health system or Group Health Cooperative in Seattle, the environment drives you into interdisciplinary models, and there's an organizational culture that says, "This is the way we do business." But in the parts of Canada where the compensation model is primarily fee-for-service, we are going to struggle to move this agenda.

SL: As a last word, is there anything that makes you optimistic that we can actually start to fix some of these problems?
PB: One of the things that gives me hope is that we are starting to make better use of the information we collect in Canada – imperfect though it may be. As examples, we have seen the publishing of Hospital Standardized Mortality Rates for the first time in Canada; accountability agreements with clear patient-related outcome and access expectations are now standard with health regions; chronic disease management metrics at the provider level are now starting to be common across the country. This is all a shift from when I started practice. All of this provokes more awareness and transparency in regard to the quality of the service we are delivering, and drives an organized response to improve the results. I think we are learning that we don't have to spend a bazillion dollars and take 20 years to produce the perfect evidence to drive quality improvement. Lots of usable information is sitting right there; it's like a little gold mine we're sitting on. So, let's use it and make things better for Canadians.

Note

[1] Penny Ballem is a former Deputy Minister of Health for British Columbia and a Clinical Professor of Medicine at UBC. During her tenure as Deputy Minister of Health, Dr. Ballem served on a number of boards including Canadian Institute for Health Information, Canada Health Infoway, the Canadian Council for Donation and Transplantation and the Pan Canadian Public Health Surveillance Information System Project.

So Many Voices, So Little Voice*

Steven Lewis

There are four nurses in Canada for every physician. Public opinion polls confirm that Canadians greatly admire the profession. Nurses populate every health sector and every corner of the country. They are synonymous with healthcare, compassion and good works.

Medicare has always been and will always be about politics. Its core idea is distributive justice: the healthy and wealthy subsidize the care of the sick and the poor. How the system evolves is heavily influenced by its major players. Nursing's combination of numbers, reputation and reach should translate into power and influence over how healthcare is financed, organized and delivered. Yet politically, the profession punches below its weight. The country is the worse for it.

Organized nursing – regulatory bodies, professional associations and unions – has historically been a stalwart supporter of medicare. If any profession can claim to be in healthcare for largely altruistic reasons, it is nursing. Nurses are the backbone of hospitals and long-term care facilities. Their jobs are rarely glamorous. The pay is decent but not extravagant. They deal with every kind of unpretty frailty: cognitive impairment, incontinence, the ravages of cancer, fear, loss. They are embedded in the system's core, fully integrated into its structures. They are working and middle-class Canadians; we are they, and they are us.

* Originally published in *Canadian Nurse* October 2010, 106(8): 40, with the permission of the publisher

Yet among providers, the healthcare debate is largely framed by organized medicine. As a result, the debate is impoverished, both in substance and in ideology. Organized medicine opposed medicare at its inception and, rhetoric aside, rarely tires of chipping away at its foundations. Most recently, it has deployed the familiar tools of biased surveys, self-serving analyses and the recycling of myths to persuade us that the system is unsustainable. This predictable propaganda lands on the front pages of newspapers, and baseless arguments go largely unchallenged.

Neither the public nor nursing escapes the impact of this intellectual near-monopoly. The Canadian Medical Association and its provincial counterparts have spent the better part of the past decade pursuing policies that keep nurses in their place. The CMA's recent report on health system transformation praises physician assistants and cannot even bring itself to mention nurse practitioners; the Ontario family practice cartel labels NP-led clinics as grossly inefficient. NPs are a threat to the medical monopoly, and medical power has been dispatched to keep them off doctors' sacred territory.

Organized medicine is winning all the turf battles, and neither the public nor governments have offered up much resistance. Had nurses spoken with one voice, marched on legislatures and taken their campaign to the public – armed with 40 or so high-quality RCTs and observational studies demonstrating their primary healthcare capacity – the outcome might well have been different. Meanwhile, as organized medicine directs the public–private debate, conjures up the spectre of a silver tsunami of boomers about to bankrupt the system and ducks any responsibility for cost or quality failures, nursing seethes in silence, only rarely venturing a timid rejoinder and never mounting a sustained battle for the public mind.

Political space is finite, and there will always be a fight for the high ground. Organized medicine knows when and how to present a united front irrespective of the real divisions within its ranks. Nursing is far less politically accomplished and far less assertive. Nurses are not saints; I have seen and criticized their own brand of fear-mongering and indefensible turf protection. But their collective support of the principles and ideals of medicare has never been in doubt. That is why it is so essential for nursing to take centre stage in the debates about the health system's future. Doing so would benefit nursing, and it would be a great service to the rest of us.

CHAPTER THREE Research to Inform Policy

Creating Incentives to Improve Population Health*

Steven Lewis

Introduction

How do communities improve the health of their populations? For the past century, we have not been required to think deeply about the question because health status steadily improved. Life expectancy increased by 30 years in prosperous countries between 1900 and 2000. But now the question is emerging as one of the most important we face. The rate of "natural" improvement in health status appears to be slowing, and decline is not unthinkable if the sharp rise in the prevalence of chronic conditions such as obesity and type 2 diabetes continues unabated. Research identifying the nonmedical determinants of health has flourished in recent decades. The correlations are well understood, but the causes of health disparities and the extent to which they can be mitigated remain debatable. How do societies come to take population health improvement seriously? One potential pathway is incentives.

* Originally published in *Preventing Chronic Disease* 2010, 7(5): A 93

Some Sobering Realities

Improving health care is hard; improving population health is even harder, as the articles in this issue of *Preventing Chronic Disease* discuss. Decades of analysis and experimentation have confirmed the following:

1. Targets can be useful but also distracting and unintentionally destructive to the population health agenda.[1]
2. Little evidence supports the proposition that population health can be improved with resources freed up by making health care more effective and efficient.[2]
3. Pay for performance, so attractive in theory, is fraught with difficulties in practice, among them methodologic problems and moral hazard. As typically understood and deployed, the concept may be particularly inimical to a population health agenda.[3]
4. Health status variability is inevitable, but even people who are born with identical health status will have diverse outcomes over the life course because of circumstances and choices. Moreover, establishing causation is elusive because of the complexity of factors that affect the health of both people and communities and the danger of being seduced by ecological fallacies. Some also argue, more controversially, that if health is to improve, we must give up other social goods; the laws of scarcity apply, and there is no positive-sum scenario.[4]
5. Experiences in other sectors reveal the mixed and sometimes unforeseeable effect of incentives. In education they have worked in some instances but have also resulted in perverse behaviors (eg, gaming, adverse selection). Creating effective incentives for particular circumstances is challenging, ensuring that the incentives evolve as circumstances change even more so. Many jurisdictions have abandoned merit pay schemes for teachers, and the effect of teacher certification programs appears to have been modest. In health care, a combination of high-quality comparative evidence and incentives is insufficient to achieve the desired practices and outcomes.[5] Producing effective and durable reward systems is difficult in health care, and more difficult still in population health.[6]
6. Some policies could plausibly improve population health if applied more vigorously. Some effective programs fail not because of their inherent logic and structure but because of low uptake. For example, 67% of people who are eligible for food stamps are not enrolled in the program.[7] Performance measures and rankings can create awareness and a growing sense of responsibility for addressing population health needs and inequalities. However, it is important to sort out whether community health status is a dependent variable (based on how well systems and programs perform), an independent variable (based on need), or both.[8]

What Is to Be Done?

Notwithstanding these methodologic challenges, a thread of optimism runs through the incentives articles. Some authors propose that as the evidence gets stronger and more compelling, policy makers will eventually do the right thing. Knowledge about population health inequalities is deep and diverse, but links between policies or incentives and population health outcomes are not well documented. The implicit argument is that a critical mass of demonstration projects, evaluations, and case studies will ultimately have the intended effect on politics and society, and change will occur.

Unfortunately, there is reason for skepticism. If we conceive of population health improvement in terms of reduced disparities, benefits must increasingly concentrate on populations of low socioeconomic status. Experience suggests that narrowing disparities is extraordinarily difficult. We are limited in our understanding of the factors that produce better population health, but evidence suggests that societies with less inequality are healthier.[9] The problem is not that we have no clue about how to improve population health or that people oppose improving the health of disadvantaged populations in principle. The problem is that there is no strong political commitment to the pursuit of these aims, no political liability inherent in not achieving them, and no consensus that this goal should be pursued more ardently than other goals (that may actually exacerbate inequalities). The sciences of epidemiology and biostatistics explain the nature, extent, and consequences of population health inequalities, but we must look to the political arts to understand why they are so hard to mitigate.

At the heart of the political dilemma is the reality that population health improvement is but one of many competing values. Individuals and communities steeply discount future health benefits, and population health improvement is a long, winding process whose ultimate benefits may take decades to quantify. A similarly steep discount applies to saving or improving anonymous, aggregate lives compared with individual lives with names and faces. A third factor that steepens the discount rate is that society values health gains attributable to health care interventions more than those achieved through social and economic policies and interventions. In a political context, how health is improved matters as much as whether it is improved – or so it would seem, judging from our enormous investment in health care that delivers virtually zero at the margins, and from the beggaring of investment in nonmedical improvement strategies.

A large public has been persuaded of the value of increasingly specialized and sophisticated health care and health technology, despite the clear absence of effect on health status. This symbolic and empirical devotion to health care is a formidable challenge to a population health agenda. In Canada, we could eliminate poverty (as defined by Statistics Canada's low-income cutoff) for $25 billion annually[10] — about 20% of publicly financed health care spending. No one is in favor of poverty, but political sentiment does not favor reallocating any part of health care spending to its elimination.

If this analysis is plausible, it follows that generating broader political commitment to population health improvement has to appeal to democratically shared and expressed values that can be converted into a feasible political agenda. But should this case be cast in terms of population health and disparities reduction as the goal of policy, or as the happy effect of the pursuit of other objectives such as economic productivity, reduction in crime and social problems, international competitiveness, and general well-being? The Canadian Index of Wellbeing[11] has been developed to introduce concepts and measures of societal performance that are more meaningful and comprehensive than economically focused measures such as gross domestic product.

We should not overlook the potential contribution of accountants. The costs of disparities are enormous (eg, poorly educated and therefore unproductive citizens; crime, law enforcement, and incarceration; excessive use of health care that may be ineffective; safety surveillance systems). If voters, particularly the middle class, can be persuaded to endorse policies that enhance population health, governments may respond accordingly.

These reflections may lead to a sense of hopelessness and even nihilism, but we should not confuse a political dilemma with categorical impossibility. Suppose there were literally guns at the temples of senior policy makers, set to go off in 5 years in the absence of emerging evidence of population health improvement and in 10 years in the absence of concrete improvement. I, for one, have no doubt they would survive. If nearly $800 billion can be authorized in months to stimulate the economy[12], imagine the effect of a small fraction of that amount spent on universal child care, Head Start, micro-lending, tuition vouchers, subsidized fruits and vegetables, massive increases in supervised physical activity, and inner-city health clinic expansion.

Perhaps we should tailor our approach to the reality that population health is ultimately local, a function of community well-being and ingenuity. If communities are the mechanisms of action, we may need to let them figure it out for themselves, supported by community-level incentives. The California Endowment[13] has funded 14 communities to pursue goals such as reduced childhood obesity, increased school attendance, reduced youth violence, and a "health home" for all. Suppose the president or Congress offered municipalities large prizes for achieving concrete health gains in a decade – say, a check for $100 million for a community of 100,000, or $1,000 per capita, payable on January 1, 2022 (baseline data would be gathered in 2011, and the clock would start ticking 1 year later). Methodologic issues would have to be addressed, but these are not insurmountable. Such incentives might galvanize coalitions of leaders, business people, educators, and community groups to take population health seriously. If the whole country got the maximum bonus, the federal government would pay $300 billion (300 million people × $1,000), or $30 billion per year. That's barely the rounding error on the size of the 2009 US economic stimulus package, and the very structure of the investment would guarantee an excellent return on investment in terms of both health and productivity.

Acknowledgments

This manuscript was developed as part of the Mobilizing Action Toward Community Health (MATCH) project funded by the Robert Wood Johnson Foundation.

References

[1] Smith PC, Busse R. Learning from the European experience of using targets to improve population health. *Prev Chronic Dis* 2010;7(5). http://www.cdc.gov/pcd/issues/2010/sep/10_0041.htm.

[2] Fox DM. Realizing and allocating savings from improving health care quality and efficiency. *Prev Chronic Dis* 2010;7(5). http://www.cdc.gov/pcd/issues/2010/sep/10_0028.htm.

[3] Asch DA, Werner RM. Paying for performance in population health: lessons from health care settings. *Prev Chronic Dis* 2010;7(5). http://www.cdc.gov/pcd/issues/2010/sep/10_0038.htm.

[4] Mullahy J. Understanding the production of population health and the role of paying for population health. *Prev Chronic Dis* 2010;7(5). http://www.cdc.gov/pcd/issues/2010/sep/10_0024.htm.

[5] Haveman RH. Principles to guide the development of population health incentives. *Prev Chronic Dis* 2010;7(5). http://www.cdc.gov/pcd/issues/2010/sep/10_0044.htm.

[6] Witte JF. Accountability metrics and paying for performance in education and health care. *Prev Chronic Dis* 2010;7(5). http://www.cdc.gov/pcd/issues/2010/sep/10_0046.htm.

[7] Baxter RJ. Making better use of the policies and funding we already have. *Prev Chronic Dis* 2010;7(5). http://www.cdc.gov/pcd/issues/2010/sep/10_0055.htm.

[8] Oliver TR. Population health rankings as policy indicators and performance measures. *Prev Chronic Dis* 2010;7(5). http://www.cdc.gov/pcd/issues/2010/sep/10_0040.htm.

[9] Wilkinson R, Pickett K. *The spirit level: why more equal societies almost always do better.* London (GB): Allen Lane; 2009.

[10] The Subcommittee on Cities of the Standing Senate Committee on Social Affairs, Science and Technology: Evidence. June 13, 2008. http://www.parl.gc.ca/39/2/parlbus/commbus/senate/Com-e/citi-e/45505-e.htm?Language=E&Parl=39&Ses=2&comm_id=604. Accessed May 3, 2010.

[11] Canadian Index of Wellbeing. http://www.ciw.ca/en/Home.aspx. Accessed May 4, 2010.

[12] Recovery.Gov. *Tracking the money.* http://www.recovery.gov/Pages/home.aspx. Accessed May 4, 2010.

[13] Building Healthy Communities program. The California Endowment. http://www.calendow.org/healthycommunities/. Accessed May 3, 2010.

Toward a General Theory of Indifference to Research-Based Evidence*

Steven Lewis

Evidence-based medicine (EBM) and evidence-based decision-making (EBDM) were intended to revolutionize health care and health policy. Thus far they have not. A great deal of research has demonstrated the persistent ubiquity of error in health care, wide and unjustifiable variations in practice and the minimal impact of decision aids such as clinical practice guidelines. This paper attempts to explain why EBM and EBDM have remained largely unrealized ambitions. It advances 10 propositions that together constitute a general theory of indifference to research-based evidence. Some of these propositions are conceptual (e.g. the epistemic resistance to the randomized trial), some are empirical (e.g. the impact of the corruption of science by industry), some are cognitive (e.g. human problems are holistic while science is typically fragmented and narrative free) and some are normative (e.g. the primary goal is not adherence to methods, but to make better decisions with better outcomes, irrespective of their origins). EBM and EBDM over-reached, and their failure was, as a consequence, inevitable. However, with corrective action on a number of fronts, research-based evidence can and should be more influential. The first step is to reconceive EBM and EBDM as habits of mind rather than a toolbox and to recognize that the sociology of knowledge is as important as its technical content.

* Lewis, S. 2007. "Toward a general theory of indifference to research-based evidence." *Journal of Health Services Research & Policy* 2007, 12(3): 166-72, reproduced with permission

Introduction

Evidence-based decision-making (EBDM) and its progenitor, evidence-based medicine (EBM), once hailed as irresistible forces, have met immoveable objects – practitioners, managers and the public. How come? For some, EBDM affronts their belief that their work is impenetrably mysterious, artful and inspired, ungovernable by rules or protocols. A tiny minority of practitioners do not read and do not learn. These are not the subjects of this paper; there is little sport in clubbing fish that have washed up on the shore. The question is why EBDM has achieved little traction among people who are neither stupid nor hostile to science and rigour.

There are several serious conceptual challenges to the premise and promise of EBDM. Taken together, they constitute a general theory of indifference to research-based evidence. The theory is based on 10 propositions, each of which explores a distinct cause or rationale for EBDM fatigue and failure. Most deal with EBM rather than the realm of management and policy.

A convincing theory of indifference to EBM should be, all else equal, even more convincing with respect to EBDM. However, counter-intuitively, EBDM in the policy and managerial realms in some ways faces less daunting obstacles than EBM in the clinical.

'Evidence' here means research-based findings transparently compiled, analysed and interpreted according to rigorous methodological processes and standards. There are disputes about the appropriateness of the standards and the definition of rigour, but their resolution is not central to the theory advanced here. I use the term EBDM as the genus encompassing all forms of health care decision-making and EBM as the species describing clinical practice.

Proposition 1: The unbearable lightness of being statistically correct

Every datum can be evidence to someone. EBDM privileges data that are systematically gathered and rigorously analysed. It defines the world in probabilistic and collective terms. It explicitly discounts the importance of observations lying (typically) more than two standard deviations from the mean. The world of clinical and managerial decision-makers is personal and particular, where it is critical to know whether the here and now circumstance is a typical case or an exception.

There is no solace in a decision, based on rigorous evidence, that falls short because the patient under consideration is a rogue. Careful EBM proponents do not dispute this reality and often attach a disclaimer:

> External clinical evidence can inform, but can never replace, individual clinical expertise, and it is this expertise that decides whether the external evidence applies to the individual patient at all and, if so, how it should be integrated

> into a clinical decision. Similarly, any external guideline must be integrated with individual clinical expertise in deciding whether and how it matches the patient's clinical state, predicament, and preferences, and thus whether it should be applied. Clinicians who fear top down cookbooks will find the advocates of evidence based medicine joining them at the barricades.[1]

We have seen this before: the 'not responsible for stolen articles' sign hanging over even the toniest coatcheck facilities. The messages are mixed. On the one hand, individual reasoning is no match for the systematic review; set aside your hunches and biases in favour of the evidence. On the other, use your judgement – it is the ultimate trump card, an inalienable right, the hallmark of a professional. Well, which is it? If, when evidence and inclinations conflict, the counsel is to go with your judgement, what is the nature of the EBM claim? What about the obligation to take into account patient preferences? And how will the judgement tribunal (however configured) assess unorthodox decisions that result in poor outcomes: as reasonable in the face of uncertainty, defensible error or felonies? Is the test for using one's head one-tailed?

Another problem is that the producers and consumers of evidence operate under different accountabilities. The Cochrane authors are accountable for no single clinical decisions other than their own, if they happen to be clinicians. Miscalculating a confidence interval or shoehorning the wrong studies into the meta-analysis runs the risk only of scholarly rebuke. For researchers, EBDM methods are an unmitigated boon, conferring prestige, promotion and conference invitations. (Indeed, one may judge them by their conference intervals.) For practitioners, the consequence of error may be injury or death, personal humiliation or despair. For evidence producers, a rare event is often statistical noise; for practitioners, it is the Holy Grail whose detection and remedy is a major motivation and reward, and whose oft-concealed identity is a source of anxiety and doubt; and for the patient it is the only event that matters.

Proposition 2: Science is explicit, but important realities are tacit

Science is explicit: phenomena must be observable, replicable and describable. A theory is not scientific unless it is refutable by rigorous scrutiny or the appearance of incompatible data. Otherwise it is theology at best, dogma at worst. But much of what we know is tacit rather than explicit.

Tacit knowing underlies both a wide variety of human functions – from walking to recognizing one's friends – and to virtues such as good judgement. Invariably, 'we know more than we can tell'.[2] As the American baseball player Yogi Berra put it, 'I can't think and hit at the same time'. In the act of hitting a baseball, the senses and brain are processing thousands of data cues, yet the batter is not explicitly aware of any of them. Great clinical insight may come from complex pattern recognition, or inspired non-linear reasoning, rather than the orderly sequences of a decision tree.[3] This heuristic talent is especially useful in the substantial number of cases that must fall outside the so called normal distribution. In some instances, explicitness is feasible but undesirable. Euthanasia is widely practiced by excellent doctors and in first-rate facilities, almost always with the consent of patients' families.[4,5] Other than in jurisdictions such as The Netherlands, the rules are not codified and publicized. Some argue that this vagueness sends society hurtling down the slippery slope to moral bankruptcy; others disagree.[6] The preference for unarticulated rules is not mere squeamishness; it reflects the reality that formal criteria cannot account for all possible cases, and recognizes that the decisions are best left in the hands of trusted moral agents whose relationships to and interest in their loved ones are meaningful in ways ultimately inaccessible to third parties.

None of this devalues explicit knowledge and its pursuit. But where real uncertainty exists, tacit knowledge is often what divines the nuance that eludes the standard work-up. It may also be the inspiration for dramatic breakthroughs that break free from the advancing glacier of progress – the Kuhnian 'paradigm shifts' defined precisely by their departure from tradition.

Proposition 3: The epistemic resistance to the randomized controlled trial[7]

The randomized controlled trial (RCT) is an artifice; it does not occur in nature. Random assignment of subjects to the arms of a trial contradicts a fundamental orientation of health care, which is person centeredness. It is a wonder that patients voluntarily submit to such Kafkaesque arbitrariness, but we should be grateful that they do. RCTs have improved treatment and debunked innumerable useless and harmful practices.

So why are decision-makers sometimes persuaded by observational studies and sceptical of the findings of RCTs? It is partly because a messy, real-life cohort matches one's own experiences more closely. The clinical challenge is whether an intervention is likely to be successful in a patient with certain characteristics. The less those characteristics are represented in the trial populations, the less applicable the findings to one's patient. Most trials are too small to encompass a completely representative sample of human conditions. Some people refuse to participate; some drop out; often eligibility is restricted to a very narrow range of candidates. It is possible, even inevitable, that in some cases, important variables will be overlooked or be unavailable in sufficient numbers among the trial arms.

The devaluation of observational studies and the hegemony of the RCT places a great many topics of research beyond possibility for ethical and practical reasons, and conflicts with an almost universal and grounded perception of reality. Add to this, the growing literature on publication bias, non-random assignment and dubious meta-analyses, and one understands why the RCT is viewed as a flawed, if not humbled, deity. In methods, as in boxing, the bigger they are, the harder they fall.

Proposition 4: Evidence and methods are means, not ends

Evidence, even great evidence, is instrumental. We seek it to achieve something else: truth, justice, goodness, beauty and health. The wise would choose good decisions based on no apparent evidence over bad decisions with a first class evidentiary pedigree.

EBDM equates evidence-based with good. We should prefer EBDM because, and only because, it predictably produces better results than would be otherwise achievable. Here, too, the EBM advocates have acknowledged a problem: 'A fundamental assumption of EBM is that practitioners whose practice is based on an understanding of evidence from applied health care research will provide superior patient care compared with practitioners who rely on understanding of basic mechanisms and their own clinical experience. So far, no convincing direct evidence exists that shows that this assumption is correct.'[8]

The hegemony of EBM has a serious consequence: it skews our attempts to improve health toward conceptually neat and procedurally unambiguous interventions. EBM methods are eminently suitable to pharmaceutical research, which not coincidentally has become the dominant health care worldview. One does not need a conspiracy theory to observe that EBM methodologies (means) and the pursuit of profit (ends) constitute an ironic and fruitful marriage.

Proposition 5: Everyday life is normative, but there is no science of human values

To declare that decisions should be based on evidence is to declare that they should not be based on other things. In medicine, disagreements are frequently about the threshold for intervention or whether potential harm exceeds potential benefit. Many disagreements are technical while some reflect broader philosophical and social concerns (preserving the lives of very low birthweight babies). Research may unearth realities (e.g. that some groups' needs are better addressed than others) that force us into the nontechnical realm of distributive justice.

Deciding who gets what, where, when and how is political. Showing the comparative cost-effectiveness of an immunization programme versus adding hospital beds in winter to deal with elderly flu patients will not tell decision-makers what to do. But it may influence future planning and provide the means to justify decisions to the public. In some cases, evidence can prevent or reverse decisions by revealing them as formally incorrect (because they do not achieve the declared goals), but it cannot in itself produce better values or superior goals.

Proposition 6: Evidence often makes decision-making more difficult, not less

There is only one instance where evidence about a choice between two alternatives is utterly conclusive. That is where, and only where, the best outcome achievable by doing

A is inferior to the worst outcome by doing B. Where the outcome distributions overlap, there is a zone of uncertainty. That zone is the incubator of decision-making dilemmas.

Since there are very few 'pure type' logically determined choices, evidence provides little relief from choice. There are important debates about how much society ought to pay to achieve an added QALY, to extend life or to accommodate individual preferences that defy the evidence. Individual interests invariably run up against collective interests. Decisions and frameworks to guide them are the product of deliberation, not ratiocination, and sometimes justice demands exceptions to rules.

At the other end of the scale is a peculiar reticence to draw conclusions that appear to follow logically from highly persuasive evidence. 'Over a two-year period, we found no difference between aspirin and warfarin in the prevention of recurrent ischemic stroke or death or in the rate of major hemorrhage. Consequently, we regard both warfarin and aspirin as reasonable therapeutic alternatives.'[9] Far from being a simple refusal to draw normative conclusions from empirical data, the last sentence radically defines 'reasonable'. Moreover, it is profoundly at odds with the inferential logic of any decision-maker who confronts the daily realities of resource constraints. The authors doubtless know this.

Philosophers, political theorists and poets live and die by exhortation. Often their only evidence is their description of the human condition and their powers of observation and persuasion. By contrast, health care researchers armed with powerful data often fall over themselves to (appear to) avoid telling anyone what to do. What accounts for such reluctance to draw obvious conclusions from powerful evidence, while more ambiguous science (e.g. the costs and consequences of mammography screening) creates a tsunami of activity? Follow the money.

Proposition 7: Science is for sale

Deference to research evidence is an act of trust. It often entails the rejection of one's own experiences, creates conflict with peers, risks alienating patients and risks new forms of failure and disappointment. Only a research enterprise of redoubtable integrity and irreproachable transparency deserves the trust of the general community.

Unfortunately, the research enterprise is tainted. An enormous amount of incomplete and substandard science is published to serve various agendas and, most ominously, commercial gain. The presumption that science is conducted exclusively by disinterested investigators pursuing truth, immune to temptation and influence, has been thoroughly unmasked.

The relationship between industry (largely pharmaceutical) and academic researchers and institutions highlights the problem.[10] Industry has gone to inordinate lengths to suppress findings inimical to its financial interests.[11] Universities have been negligent in their duty to protect academic integrity and ensure that industry funding does not compromise the conduct of science.[12] More insidiously, subtle biases are built into study designs,[13] so that results from industry-funded trials show more positive therapeutic effect than those funded otherwise. Despite recently heightened vigilance, some of these deceptions escape detection and appear in the most prestigious journals. One can forgive practitioners for feeling betrayed and yielding to cynicism. It does not matter that most scientists are incorruptible, that others are unaware of (and in a sense innocent of) their corruption, and that most published work is unimpeachable. One does not license, let alone eat in, a restaurant where one in 20 meals will give you food poisoning.

Proposition 8: Gresham's law and the debasement of science

If counterfeit or debased currency circulates and is accepted at face value, soon there will be no gold coins and all currency will be suspect. So it is in science. There are about 20,000 medical journals in the world. Systematic reviews typically cull 80–90% of papers on a particular topic as unworthy of inclusion. Some winnowing is doubtless questionable, but most is perfectly defensible. The achievement of tenure and promotion depends more on quantity than quality; every manuscript therefore seeks a home in print. Given the huge ratio of chaff to wheat, small wonder that people are taken in by flawed science or are unable to reconcile the findings from different studies.

The exposure of most published research as valueless by Cochrane aficionados and EBM mavens cannot but arouse, however unintentionally, anti-science suspicions. Combined with the corruption of science by industry and undeclared bias, there is a disconcertingly strong case for wishing a plague on all their houses. Such wholesale rejection is of course ludicrous, but the fact that the scientific house is so vulnerable to attack on ethical and quality grounds is manna to the flatearthers.

Proposition 9: Humans seek narrative, science has expunged it

Narrative is anathema to contemporary scientific exposition. Top medical journals equate method with quality, and limit discussion and interpretation to a few hundred words. The main vehicle for discussing the broader significance of a study is the invited commentary or editorial. Results are held to be intrinsically meaningful.

But they are not. The human mind responds ascientifically to choice and risk: for example, the availability of multiple options superior to the status quo may reduce the likelihood that any of them will be chosen.[14] Science takes place in a confined, experimental environment, while clinical and policy decisions take place in a messy and turbulent world where stories count.

Humans are persuaded by narrative; that is why Plato proposed banning the artists, not scientists or bureaucrats. Totalitarian governments fear the abstract painting and the novel because they recognize their subversive and inspirational power. Patients and policymakers respond to stories, and outliers fascinate clinicians more than the phenomena falling within the 95% confidence interval. Brevity may be the soul of wit but not always of understanding.

Proposition 10: Science is fragmentary, decisions are holistic

Science is an increasingly refined and specialized enterprise. The dominance of the RCT has virtually forced investigations to be narrow and tight. Any given study conveys more and more about less and less. This is inevitable and a mark of progress, the consequence of having exhausted most of the possibilities for simple, inexpensive, whole-cloth triumphs of understanding and therapy. While there are widespread calls for programmatic research and interdisciplinary inquiry, the project remains the unit of activity and the compact article the badge of scientific honour. This is good for scientific production and a problem for research consumers, who confront a bewildering array of narrow and deep findings that are difficult to assimilate into a decision aid. Unassembled research findings almost never address the broad dilemmas confronting clinicians and policy-makers. A great deal of scientific inquiry and reporting has little or no concern for indirect effects or the context within which phenomena occur.

Even where basic, clinical and social scientists have had their say, their insights are buried in separate sites. Few will embark on a lengthy treasure hunt to chase down the parts and assemble them into a whole. Most will either rely on partial information, 'muddle through' to a decision, ignore the research evidence. Indifference to research-based evidence altogether, defer to tradition and habit or seek counsel from the wise without digging too deeply into their evidentiary toolbox. Reviews can be helpful, but these too are strictly bounded and prone to methodological controversy.

Clearly, these responses are not what EBDM theorists had in mind. But how else could it have turned out? Proponents of research evidence acknowledge that politics or values play major, even decisive roles in decisions. But they tend to regard these competing influences as forbidding territory fit only for the dark and beastly pèripheries of human nature. Their attitudes range from resignation – all we can do is lead the horse to water – to despair – why is democracy so disorderly, and why is the golden calf so popular? It may be that the highly specialized and fragmented approach to contemporary research is the root of the problem. Homer Dixon has identified an 'ingenuity gap', observing that despite the triumphs of science, humanity seems bereft of practical solutions to difficult problems that creatively incorporate diverse knowledge and perspectives.[15] Others have called for the application of complexity theory and methods to health care issues that defy traditional forms of evidence and analysis.[16]

From the cave to daylight

Indifference to research evidence is, then, the inevitable result of the fact that the theorists and producers of that evidence and its hoped-for audiences inhabit different cognitive and empirical worlds. The solution is to recognize the complexities of our epistemological and cognitive make-up, the asymmetries in estimates of risk and benefit, and the power of and human need for narrative enriched by historical, cultural, political, economic and organizational analysis.

In Plato's famous metaphor, humans are trapped in a cave and all they can see are shadows dancing on the wall in front of them. They take these shadows for reality and in a sense they are correct: they are the only reality they know. In health care, certainty about little is no match for provisional insights into much. A warehouse full of guidelines and clinical trials casts long and transfixing shadows. We work with what we have and infer as much as possible from the reality available to us. But the world of practice is complex and it appears as if practitioners 'regard clinical evidence as a square peg to fit in the round hole of the patient's life'.[17]

EBDM as a habit of mind

The realities that occasioned the development of EBDM remain firmly intact. The more we know about the quality of practice, the more sobering the findings. The medical error literature is abundant and growing.[18] Major and inexplicable variations in practice have not disappeared.[19] The standard of practice in the middle of the curve is alarmingly deficient, even where the research evidence is powerful.[20,21] Many physicians are unfamiliar with the basic tenets of EBM.[22] There is some evidence that clinicians value information they have actively acquired more than information produced by others – yet another cognitive twist to throw into the equation.[23] This seems like a recipe for nihilism.

Can we move the middle of the performance curve significantly to the right? The challenges are considerable in light of the huge expectations we place on practitioners. Most of the time, we want them to be confident, decisive, technically adept and sensitive to our individual needs, not overly reflective and bookish, insecure Hamlets unable to act, advise or reassure without a dozen qualifications. Yet, we also want them to be devotees of EBM, stewards of our and public resources, and appropriately sceptical of health care commerce. We demand multiple intellectual personalities, expertly deployed to suit the circumstance.

To Aristotle, virtue was a habit of the mind; so, too is EBDM. Whether such habits are innate or taught is an interesting question. Selecting candidates for entry to health science education programmes in today's highly competitive environment is a difficult challenge.[24] Admission standards are high, which makes the persistence of remarkably unscientific practice habits among so many bright and talented people doubly perplexing.

Should we attempt to create a new hybrid species of Renaissance Practitioner who dazzles the operating room team by quoting Dante and Rawls between incisions? Is there any reason to believe that broad learning would improve clinical performance?

How many more years could we add to the already lengthy education of the modern practitioner? Should we deny a license to the student who is excellent with patients, but vulnerable to the pitches of pharmaceutical sales representatives, inarticulate in explaining clinical choices, and weak in critical appraisal?

The reflex response is to reject radical proposals as impractical, misguided and naive. But there is too much health care failure to reject wholesale change categorically. A major American initiative to educate medical students in the nature of systems, health economics and policy, and the organization of services has produced more knowledgeable graduates, although its impact on practice is not yet known.[25]

At the beginning of this paper, I posited that EBDM is, somewhat counter-intuitively, less troublesome to implement than the apparently more research-based EBM. Policy, like contemporary clinical and social science, is preoccupied with groups rather than individuals, and probabilities rather than certainties. Policy-making is general and approximate. Policymakers are obliged to consider the decision-making context, opportunity costs and the broader public interest, while in the clinician–patient dyad, there are no utilitarians. Where the community or society is the unit of analysis, it can be quite straightforward to choose A over B in service of declared ends even if it is predictable that some will be harmed.

Both evidence-based policy and EBM are fraught with uncertainty, but of a different type. In the policy realm, values and objectives are contested, as are, at times, the means of their fulfillment. Unlike clinical practice, policy-making is supposed to be formally unconcerned with specific persons. In clinical practice, the values and objectives are usually unproblematic; the link between action and outcome is more direct; the locus of responsibility is narrower and clearer and all of the transactions are highly personal. The consequences are magnified for a few and unremarked by the many. In the policy world, context is everything; in the clinical encounter occasioned by a serious condition, the world becomes intensely small, and context is but a faint shadow of little consequence.

Beyond indifference: is there a way forward?

What, in the end, have EBM and EBDM contributed? After critiques and refinements, the principal message appears to be: read, learn, use your head, abandon what does not work, adopt what does and be prepared to justify what you do. This is good advice – hardly revolutionary, but cogent. Many clinical practices and health care policies are disturbingly at odds with both logic and evidence. That the creators of EBM and EBDM could promote them as a Kuhnian paradigm shift – however mistakenly[26] – reveals the worrisome state of affairs in health care at the beginning of the 21st century.

Will indifference to research evidence continue to be the norm? Very likely, until several conditions have been met. One is that the evidence must get stronger, less probabilistic, more patient-specific and less contested. Second, health care systems and practitioners must build decision-support technologies effortlessly into their activities. E-health holds great promise that must be harnessed and adapted to the realities of human cognition and preferences. Third, integrity in science must be restored – no easy task.[27] Fourth, research must be conceived and funded more programmatically to reflect the complex realities of communities, patients and the determinants of health. Fifth, there will have to be consequences for unjustifiable indifference; reward what you want and penalize what you do not want.

When things truly speak for themselves – when the evidence is definitive and the response follows invariably from it – they are tautologies. Our fondest hope should be to turn medicine into tautology, with computer-generated diagnoses, designer therapies tailored to our individual biological signatures and deliverance from probabilities that wallpaper over the cracks in our understanding. In those few domains where such success is even imaginable, health care will cease to be interesting to practitioners because their intelligence, wisdom and skill will have nothing to contribute. The art of medicine keeps the thoughtful practitioner interested in going to work every day, and scares the thoughtful patient. EBDM has different roles to play depending on where a decision lies along the continuum stretching from algorithm to art. Where knowledge is definitive, rely on the algorithm; where knowledge is provisional and incomplete, redouble the scientific effort; where uncertainty looms large, engage the right side of the brain. And above all, avoid category errors.

References

1 Sackett DL, Rosenberg WM, Gray JA, Haynes RB, Richardson WS. Evidence-based medicine: what it is and what it isn't. *BMJ* 1996;312:71-2

2 Polanyi M. *Personal Knowledge*. New York, NY: Harper and Row, 1957

3 Malterud K. The art and science of clinical knowledge: evidence beyond measures and numbers. *Lancet* 2001;358:397-400

4 Clark D, Dickinson G, Lancaster CJ, Noble TW, Ahmedai SH, Philp I. UK geriatricians' attitudes to active voluntary euthanasia and physician-assisted death. *Age Ageing* 2001;30:395-8

5 Baume P, O'Malley E. Euthanasia: attitudes and practices of medical practitioners. *Med J Aust* 1994;161:137, 140, 142-4

6 Ryan CJ. Pulling up the runaway: the effect of new evidence on euthanasia's slippery slope. *J Med Ethics* 1998;24:341-4

7 Ashcroft RE. Current epistemological problems in evidence-based medicine. *J Med Ethics* 2004;30:131-5

8 Haynes RB. What kind of evidence is it that evidence-based medicine advocates want health care providers and consumers to pay attention to? *BMC Health Serv Res* 2002;2:3. http://www.biomedcentral.com/1472-6963/2/3

[9] Mohr JP, Thompson JLP, Lazar RM, et al., for the Warfarin–Aspirin Recurrent Stroke Study Group. A comparison of warfarin and aspirin for the prevention of recurrent ischemic stroke. *N Engl J Med* 2001;345:1444-51

[10] Press E, Washburn J. The kept university. *Atlantic Monthly* 2000;285, online version. http://www.theatlantic.com/issues/2000/03/press.htm

[11] Hailey D. Scientific harassment by pharmaceutical companies: time to stop. *CMAJ* 2000;162:212-3

[12] Van McCrary S, Anderson CB, Jakovljevic J, et al. A national survey of policies on disclosure of conflicts of interest in biomedical research. *N Engl J Med* 2000;343:1621-6

[13] Dickersin K. The existence of publication bias and risk factors for its occurrence. *JAMA* 1990;263:1385-9

[14] Redelmeier DA, Shafir E. Medical decision making in situations that offer multiple alternatives. *JAMA* 1995;273: 302-5

[15] Homer-Dixon T. *The Ingenuity Gap: Facing the Economic, Environmental, and Other Challenges of an Increasingly Complex and Unpredictable World.* Toronto: Random House, 2000

[16] Martin CM, Sturmberg JP. General practice – chaos, complexity and innovation. *Med J Aust* 2005;183:106-9

[17] Freeman AC, Sweeney K. Why general practitioners do not implement evidence: qualitative study. *BMJ* 2001;323: 1100-4

[18] Baker GR, Norton PG, Flintoft V, et al. The Canadian Adverse Events Study: the incidence of adverse events among hospital patients in Canada. *CMAJ* 2004;170: 1678-86

[19] Honda K. Factors underlying variation in receipt of physician advice on diet and exercise: applications of the behavioral model of health care utilization. *Am J Health Promot* 2004;18:370-7

[20] McGlynn EA, Asch SM, Adams J, et al. The quality of health care delivered to adults in the United States. *N Engl J Med* 2003;348:2635-45

[21] Katz A, De Coster C, Bogdanovic B, Soodeen R-A, Chateau D. Using administrative data to develop indicators of quality in family practice. Manitoba Centre for Health Policy 2004. http://www.umanitoba.ca/centres/mchp/reports/pdfs/quality_wo.pdf

[22] Young JM, Glasziou P, Ward JE. General practitioners' self ratings of skills in evidence based medicine: validation study. *BMJ* 2002;324:950-1

[23] Redelmeier DA, Shafir E, Aujla PS. The beguiling pursuit of more information. *Med Decis Making* 2001;21:376-81

[24] Eva KW, Reiter HI. Where judgement fails: pitfalls in the selection process for medical personnel. *Adv Health Sci Educ Theory Pract* 2004;9:161-74

[25] Cox M, Pacala JT, Vercellotti GM, Shea JA. Health care economics, financing, organization, and delivery. *Fam Med* 2004;36:S20-30

[26] Sehon SR, Stanley DE. A philosophical analysis of the evidence-based medicine debate. *BMC Health Serv Res* 2003;3:14. http://www.biomedcentral.com/1472-6963/3/14

[27] Chalmers I. From optimism to disillusion about commitment to transparency in the medico-industrial complex. *J R Soc Med* 2006;99:337-41

How Has Health Services Research Made a Difference?*

Steven Lewis

Health services research (HSR),[1] like all research, is supposed to improve the human condition. Cultures that support and produce research tend to be more prosperous and free than those that don't. That research in general makes a difference is rarely disputed; in fact, the question is rarely asked. But it is asked of HSR for two main reasons. First, the discipline is only a few decades old, but there is already good evidence that the insights of comparative effectiveness studies and thousands of clinical practice guidelines are widely ignored. Second, HSR has come to advertise itself as a practical discipline that aims for tangible and fairly immediate impact (the very name of the Manitoba Centre for Health Policy implies that its primary activity – research – is instrumental). The public and governments tend to support basic science research as an intrinsic good that will pay off somewhere, some day, in unanticipated ways. They rarely cut HSR such slack: here, it's show me the impact.

Impact is not so easy to define. If only studies that result in a tangible change in the way health services are delivered, or the outcomes they achieve, can claim to have made a difference, HSR has almost always fallen short. But the definition is far too narrow. HSR can influence thinking, culture, policy, behaviour and practice. It takes place in an economic, social and political context, not in a linear, rationalist world where systemati-

* Originally published in *Healthcare Policy* 2011, 6(Special Issue): 74-79

cally acquired evidence explains all choices and results. Power, tradition, interests and uncertainty all affect what is done and what is achieved. Furthermore, health systems are riddled with perverse incentives and are principally organized for the convenience and profit of the supply side rather than the public or patients. Long-standing problems remain unresolved despite the efforts of managers, leaders and politicians, some of whom are genuinely interested in a more evidence-informed world.

The question is thus less whether HSR has made a difference, but what HSR should aspire to achieve. The argument here is that HSR should seek truth. It should shed light on phenomena inaccessible to common sense or intuition – the counterfactuals that confound simplistic analyses and glib prescriptions, and force a re-examination of the status quo. It should attempt to answer questions that are both broad and deep, mirroring the experience of people and organizations in complex adaptive systems. To be actionable, it should ask how and why things are as they are in addition to describing what they are. Producers of HSR are rarely decision-makers in the health system, but they can and should be attuned to how decisions are made and the vagaries of the political arts. The case here is not to exempt the choice of HSR topics or the design of studies from all considerations of relevance or potential use. It is to define "useful" and "important" in a more nuanced way.

A short paper cannot fully articulate the argument, but it can be illustrated by an examination of the impact of what are widely regarded as blockbuster HSR studies. Table 1 identifies examples of groundbreaking studies, their findings and, in very general terms, their impact.

Are there any patterns in this small sample of renowned research findings? It would appear that those with the greatest apparent impact – the HRT (Hormone Replacement Therapy) and hospital utilization studies – deal with discrete phenomena where behavioural change is relatively straightforward; where (in the case of HRT) users of services can act unilaterally; where findings evoke embarrassment, fear, hope, shame or other strong emotional response; and where the environment is more manageable (hospitals). Those with the least apparent concrete and tangible impact deal with complex phenomena; require concerted and multi-pronged initiatives to address; threaten traditional cultures, elites, egos and interests; and do not suggest an obvious blueprint for action.

Nothing, of course, is that simple, and experiences and research suggest further possible explanations for the presence or absence of a tangible and attributable response to research. People generally discount future, anonymous health benefits quite steeply in comparison to potential here-and-now health benefits that would accrue to identifiable people. (It is easier to raise money to send Alice Wilson to Loma Linda Hospital for a double-organ transplant than for programs that would help those under-achieving kids in poor Winnipeg neighbourhoods.) Hence population health studies are, other things

Table 1. Selected groundbreaking HSR studies

Body of Research	Main Findings	Impact
UK studies on gradients in health and the impact of inequality on health status	• Health status differs all along the SES gradient (Marmot et al. 1991) • The level of societal inequality is associated with both aggregate and group health status (Wilkinson and Pickett 2009)	• Shifted focus to non-medical determinants of health • Revived interest in class as an analytic construct in health • Broadened the nature of high-level reports on health • Led to major focus on inequalities in health in Europe, WHO • No reduction in health disparities in past three decades in almost all countries
Dartmouth studies on variations in healthcare use and costs	• Up to threefold variations in use controlled for health status, satisfaction and outcome (Wennberg and Gittelsohn 1982; Welch et al. 1993) • Explained by variations in supply-side behaviour (Gawande 2009)	• Broad recognition that healthcare use and results are poorly correlated • High-performing subsystems in US deliver better quality and lower cost • Work replicated in many jurisdictions • No reduction of variations in the US after 30 years of documentation
Women's Health Initiative Hormone Therapy Study	• Documented widespread use of HRT over decades (Rossouw et al. 2002) • Revealed major health risk factors that increase with duration of HRT	• Enormous publicity of findings immediately after publication • Virtually instantaneous reduction in HRT utilization
Acute care utilization studies in Canadian provinces in 1990s (BC, SK, MB, ON)	• Widespread use of hospitals for alternative levels of care (ALC) ("bedblockers"; up to 40% in urban hospitals and 80% of small rural hospitals) (Health Services Utilization and Research Commission 1994) • ALC needs ranged from none to nursing home beds	• Major, widespread focus on length of stay, discharge planning, utilization management • Changed conversation on rural healthcare in at least one province (SK) • *Methods and tools that formed basis for earlier studies no longer widely used*
Institute of Medicine *To Err Is Human* (Kohn et al. 2000) and related international studies	• Major iatrogenic death toll in hospitals in US, Canada, UK, Australia	• Sparked and accelerated the patient safety movement • Foundation of campaigns such as Safer Healthcare Now! • *Symposium held five years after IOM publication lamented lack of progress in saving lives*
RAND studies of primary care quality in US (McGlynn et al. 2003)	• Quality of care varies substantially from evidence-based guidelines • People commonly receive recommended care 50%–60% of the time	• Did not spawn major replications • Confirmed earlier findings about lack of impact of clinical practice guidelines • *No discernible acceleration of primary care reform or accountability*
MCHP study of high school graduation trends (Brownell et al. 2004)	• Huge neighbourhood-level variations in percentage of youth completing high school on time • Effect size exceeded intuitive estimates	• Major self-reported transformation in education policy makers' perspectives • A foundation of greater focus on intersectoral initiatives • *No claim of major impact on extent of disparities in performance*

being equal, less likely to engender a rapid, tangible response than some clinical studies (complexity is, of course, another major barrier to change).

But let's frame the question differently. Aside from natural disasters, intellectual insights and ideas have been responsible for all the great changes in human systems. The biggest ideas had no immediate and quantifiable impact. The Copernican and Newtonian revolutions did not change manufacturing, inspire armies or rearrange the means of production in any observable way. Yet, they changed the world and spawned an explosion of ingenuity in untold ways to enormous and irreversible effect. The new knowledge changed everything – but not in a mechanical, causal, transparently traceable fashion. Analogously, it is no longer possible to think that healthcare alone (or even mainly) determines health status; that need alone drives spending; or that regulation and licensure are sufficient to guarantee quality.

The health and healthcare conversation is vastly different today than it was 30 years ago, precisely because of the contributions of HSR writ large. Atul Gawande's (2009) compelling account of the Dartmouth studies in *The New Yorker* became required reading in the White House. As Clyde Hertzman has noted, some people are able to ignore convincing evidence in reaching their own conclusions about school performance but most, eventually, do not. In a world where there is a touted new cure, drug and technology every week, and where the media have an insatiable appetite for healthcare gadgetry and magic, there is nonetheless broad awareness that healthcare and health are conceptually distinct, and that the former explains rather little of the variance in the latter. HSR findings created this awareness, and the implications are potentially enormous.

All this suggests a paradox: the more concrete and obvious the relevance and impact of HSR, the less likely it is to be paradigm-altering. Typically, change happens because the antecedent conditions are already in place; research findings may be little more than confirmatory, or may provide a small additional tailwind to journeys already underway. Conversely, truly game-changing research is unlikely to change the game any time soon because it bumps up against the powerful forces of tradition, hierarchy, inertia, vested interests and complexity. Thus, the HSR that may make the biggest difference in the long run is highly unlikely to make any concrete difference in the short run because genuinely original and creative research is so difficult to absorb, let alone apply.

As a result, HSR would do well to resist selling itself as a purely responsive, relevant and useful service industry, its ear attuned to "Listening for Direction" and driven by the preoccupations of decision-makers faced with daily and vexing dilemmas. It has been clear for millennia that you cannot derive the ought from the is, and HSR is about the is. Often, decision-makers and other actors find the low-hanging fruit inedible, for whatever reason: there is a lesson in the widespread failure of healthcare workers to wash their hands in hospitals 160 years after Semmelweis's elegant and definitive research. There are no algorithms for estimating "knowledge demand," and not all wisdom lies in crowds (even crowds of talented decision-makers). You never know when that long-neglected research will emerge from the dusty shelf when the decision-making context changes.

Finally, this perspective suggests some reflection on another contemporary truism: you can't manage what you can't measure. That may be true in healthcare, but it is less true in estimating the worth of research. In my own efforts to assess the impact of HSR, it became clear that there are no reliable measures of the real or potential impact of the most interesting and relevant studies. It is easier (though not always easy) to recognize an important and original idea than to divine its likely impact in the foreseeable future. Researchers cannot control anything beyond the conception, design and execution of their research, and we do not live in a particularly evidence-seeking health culture. Before judging HSR on its utility, it would be helpful to learn how decision-makers perceive their role in leaving so much ostensibly useful research on the shelf. And before the wider community decides that putting itself in charge of the HSR agenda will yield a greater return on investment, it might profit from its own accounting of how it has used the research it has commissioned in the past. This would be a valuable complement to the work the Canadian research community has already done to advance the science of measuring return on investment (Panel on Return on Investment 2009).

Lest this argument be misconstrued, I should add that I have spent my own HSR career in an applied health research agency and as a consultant whose livelihood derives from doing others' bidding. It is my instinct to want to do things that will make a difference, but that presumes that those able to make a difference have the intention and the will to do so. There are infinitely more false negatives (not "using" research that should inform policy and practice) than false positives or true positives. That is the way of the world, and in such a world, it is ultimately more useful to attempt to enlighten than to steer. That is what the best HSR has always done, and when insights and ideas take hold, the world changes, and the return on the initial investment is immense, albeit unquantifiable – for now at least, and possibly for a very long time.

Notes

[1] HSR is defined here broadly, to include population health research as well as studies of the organization, financing and delivery of health services.

References

Brownell, M., N. Roos, R. Fransoo, A. Guevremont et al. 2004. *How Do Educational Outcomes Vary with Socioeconomic Status? Key Findings from the Manitoba Child Health Atlas*. Winnipeg: Manitoba Centre for Health Policy. Retrieved September 10, 2010. <http://mchp-appserv.cpe.umanitoba.ca/reference/ch.atlas.pdf>.

Gawande, A. 2009 (June 1). "The Cost Conundrum: What a Texas Town Can Teach Us about Health Care." *The New Yorker.* Retrieved September 10, 2010. <http://www.newyorker.com/reporting/2009/06/01/090601fa_fact_gawande>.

Health Services Utilization and Research Commission. 1994. *Barriers to Community Care.* Saskatoon: Author. Retrieved September 10, 2010. <http://www.hqc.sk.ca/download.jsp?LPEg0Lq2cW/rlf1Gd8ydgDBIzBf0QfLQkUwK4QBZaJsukoVcO+uniw==>.

Kohn, L.T., J.M. Corrigan and M. Donaldson, eds. 2000. *To Err Is Human: Building a Safer Healthcare System.* Washington: National Academies Press. Retrieved September 10, 2010. <http://www.nap.edu/openbook.php?record_id=9728&page=1>.

Marmot, M.G., G.D. Smith, S. Stansfeld, C. Patel, F. North, J. Head, I. White, E. Brunner and A. Feeney. 1991 (June 8). "Health Inequalities among British Civil Servants: The Whitehall II Study." *Lancet* 337(8754): 1387-93.

McGlynn, E.A., S.M. Asch, J. Adams et al. 2003. "The Quality of Health Care Delivered to Adults in the United States." *New England Journal of Medicine* 348: 2635-45.

Panel on Return on Investment in Health Research. 2009. *Making an Impact: A Preferred Framework and Indicators to Measure Returns on Investment in Health Research.* Ottawa: Canadian Academy of Health Sciences. Retrieved September 10, 2010. <http://www.cahs-acss.ca/e/assessments/completedprojects.php>.

Rossouw, J.E., G.L. Anderson, R.L. Prentice, A.Z. LaCroix, C. Kooperberg, M.L. Stefanick et al. 2002. "Risks and Benefits of Estrogen Plus Progestin in Healthy Postmenopausal Women: Principal Results from the Women's Health Initiative Randomized Controlled Trial." *Journal of the American Medical Association* 288(3): 321-33.

Welch, W.P., M.E. Miller, H.G. Welch, E.S. Fisher and J.E. Wennberg. 1993 (March 4). "Geographic Variation in Expenditures for Physicians' Services in the United States." *New England Journal of Medicine* 328(9): 621–27.

Wennberg, J. and A. Gittelsohn. 1982 (April). "Variations in Medical Care among Small Areas." *Scientific American* 246(4):120-34.

Wilkinson, R. and K. Pickett. 2009. *The Spirit Level: Why More Equal Societies Almost Always Do Better.* London: Allen Lane.

How Research Influences Policy Makers: Still Hazy after All These Years*

Steven Lewis

Libraries have been written about the theory and practice of public policy making. Yet, this enormous scholarship has proved insufficient to lift the veil of mystery and idiosyncrasy that shrouds the art of decision making. The heady ambition to turn both clinical practice and health policy into evidence-based bastions of rationalist decision making has been downgraded; the vocabulary is now "evidence-informed," and the realm of admissible evidence has been greatly expanded to include preferences, political contingencies, and psychology.[1] This newfound conceptual modesty and nuance does not suggest that we should abandon efforts to understand decision-making processes and to enhance the role of research-based evidence in policy. It merely confirms the complexity, contingency, and messiness of the terrain.

* Lewis, S. 2011. "How Research Influences Policy Makers: Still Hazy after All These Years." *Journal of the National Cancer Institute* 2011, 103(4): 306-16, by permission of Oxford University Press

In this issue of the *Journal*, Brownson et al.[2] have boldly entered this murky territory. They attempt to identify the potential impact of carefully crafted policy briefs on three groups of policy makers: legislators, legislative committee staffers, and public health executives. They reviewed a wide literature and created four policy briefs – data- or story-focused briefs that included state- or local-level data – on the topic of mammography screening. They persisted with recruitment efforts to engage hundreds of participants in six states, and given the topic and the terms of engagement, the 35% response rate is impressive. Their analytic objective was to identify which approaches are most effective in which circumstances and which characteristics of both the policy briefs and their recipients predict influence and uptake.

It is therefore a joyless duty to report that for all its creativity and effort, the study is less of an advance in our understanding of how evidence, mode of presentation, and policy making interact than one would have hoped. Its ambitions were not fully realized because of some critical design limitations that raise serious doubts about what the findings tell us, and whether they rest on a solid foundation.

> **Steven has insight – an extraordinary** ability to pierce the fog of well-meaning confusion and interested obfuscation that surrounds so many questions in the ever-contentious world of healthcare.
>
> *Kim McGrail, Bob Evans and Morris Barer*

The first serious design issue is the choice of subject matter. If one wants to perform an independent test of policy brief types among related but different audiences, it would be wise to choose a topic that respondents are unlikely to be informed about or invested in. It is unimaginable that a substantial proportion of respondents were unaware of mammography screening and/or neutral as to its utility. If the briefs had been designed to present the different perspectives on mammography, the study could have revealed how preexisting views and conclusions affect the reception of potentially countervailing information. Instead, all of the briefs promote the same entirely pro-mammography perspective, but nothing about the hazards of interventions occasioned by ambiguous screening results or any acknowledgment that while there may be policy consensus that screening women older than 50 years is a sound strategy, scientific controversy persists. One can counter that it is of no consequence whether the substantive content of the policy briefs is contestable – the study was designed to elicit views on clarity and use, not on scientific accuracy or comprehensiveness – but the very prominence of mammography in public discourse is an avoidable contaminant in a laboratory already fraught with uncertainty.

This leads to a second issue: the definition of "use." The questionnaires simply asked whether the respondents intended to use the brief. We do not know what "use" means. Does it mean that the brief created or altered either their understanding of the issue or their inclination to affect or create policy? Clear and persuasive information can confirm or change opinion about what to do and the urgency of doing it. Understanding how the policy brief "works" requires some understanding of respondents' baseline views and how the new or repackaged information affects them. It also requires knowledge of other sources of information and advocacy on the mammography issue. For some, the policy brief may be the first and only thing they have ever read on the subject; for others, it may be the first effective compilation of evidence in a single accessible format; and for others, it may be entirely redundant. Yet, the already well informed may report intention to use the briefs because they are already motivated to pursue policy in the area and are happy to have another platoon in the supporting army.

Some of the findings are counterintuitive and, as the authors note, inconsistent with previous research. Sometimes novel findings emerge from the ingenuity of the research and confirm why it is important to revisit supposedly settled issues. Sometimes, however, the new findings simply arouse suspicions that something is amiss. It is hard to believe that staffers are looking for stories and that legislators are looking for data. One wonders whether the staff championed the value of narrative in defiance of being typecast as politically naive and cloistered in data. Similarly, legislators may have been wary of appearing to be data-illiterate hostages to anecdote and interest brokering, indifferent to sound science, and overly swayed by the passions. To be clear, this is not to suggest that the respondents were deliberately untruthful; if doctors can genuinely believe that they are following clinical practice guidelines when they in fact are not[3], it is entirely plausible that policy makers are prone to the same unconscious or partly conscious misunderstandings of their own behaviors.

Finally, one wonders if the pathway to deeper understanding of the interaction between research-based evidence and public policy making is paved with qualitative rather than quantitative inquiry. Brownson et al.[2] aspired to breadth and achieved it admirably under the circumstances, but they may have sacrificed critical depth. To get an accurate understanding of how a policy brief might influence policy actors, one would want to know their preexisting knowledge and beliefs about the importance of the issue; their assessment of the policy making environment; whether they had formed a provisional or strong opinion on policy direction; the extent to which the brief changed their understanding and in which direction; and have a nuanced understanding of what they mean by "use." It would take a very long and complicated questionnaire to begin to get at these issues in any depth; moreover, one would want to look respondents in the eye when posing questions susceptible to producing a socially desirable response.

The study by Brownson et al.[2] is analogous to a clinical trial with ambiguous findings. Those interested in pursuing this important topic should carefully consider how to avoid the problems encountered in the current study, and perhaps go back to the methodological drawing board. Researchers need to be supremely sensitive to the possibility that the data they obtain might lend itself to multiple and even conflicting interpretations and be vigilant about the clarity of questions posed. The relationship between knowledge translation and policy making yields its mysteries grudgingly. It will never be possible to eliminate the chaos inherent in studies of real-world decision making, but we should redouble efforts to create order where we can.

References

[1] Bowen S, Zwi AB. Pathways to "evidence-informed" policy and practice: a framework for action. *PLoS Med.* 2005;2(7):e166.

[2] Brownson RC, Dodson EA, Stamatakis KA, et al. Communicating evidence-based information on cancer prevention to state-level policy makers. *J Natl Cancer Inst* 2011;103(4):306-316.

[3] Lomas J, Anderson GM, Domnick-Pierre K, Vayda E, Enkin MW, Hannah WJ. Do practice guidelines guide practice? The effect of a consensus statement on the practice of physicians. *N Engl J Med* 1989;321(19):1306-1311.

Health Services Research: Rethinking the Quest To Be Useful*

Steven Lewis

What health services research (including health care policy analysis) has made the biggest impact on the worlds of health and health care? A few examples immediately come to mind: the 40 or so high-quality studies showing that nurse practitioners can do most of what a general medical practitioner can do; the Dartmouth atlases showing variations in health care costs are unrelated to outcomes; the Institute of Medicine's *To Err Is Human* and replications around the world; the hormone replacement therapy study of the Women's Health Initiative. These studies are literally famous – they have been widely featured in mainstream media and a significant proportion of the general public knows of them. But only the last one can claim to have made an immediate, tangible and significant impact on behaviour and health.

Unaccountable and large differences in health spending on similar populations remain the norm in the USA. The progenitors of the Institute of Medicine study met five years later to lament why nothing had happened. Strictly speaking, one could argue that those studies were formally useless. Health services research (HSR) aims to be useful. It is a tautology to favour being useful rather than not useful. A health care world usefully

* Originally published in the *Journal of Health Services Research & Policy* 2011, 16(1): 59-61, with the permission of the publisher

informed by HSR would be better than one that isn't. Yet as anyone who has sat on an HSR grants review panel can attest, the assumption that curiosity alone invariably generates useful research is, to say the least, an optimistic view of how minds work. It is therefore understandable that funders of HSR from time to time want to steer the agenda towards research that actually matters. The question is whether a formal or implicit commitment to being useful ultimately produces research that is actually useful.

We must define useful. If it means that a study causes something – the allocation of resources, the rethinking of priorities – to be done, then almost no HSR is or can be useful. (Leave aside the research that does cause something, only to find that something turns out to be harmful.) The more clinical evaluative type of HSR does at times have causal effects – the HRT study being a prime example. But the broader scope of HSR offers few, if any such opportunities. Selecting priorities, responding to the needs and wants of interest groups, allocating resources, and reconfiguring programs are political activities – political in the sense of deciding who gets what, when, where, and why. There is no consensus on what the R-squared of research-based evidence can and should be, but it is far less than one. Policies in their best sense are far more than the sum of Cochrane-like reviews of every human endeavour. Virtually no research can meet utilitarian expectations narrowly defined, even if conceived, commissioned, and co-engineered by decision-makers.

A common temptation is to infer causation when a decision is consistent with good quality HSR findings. Sometimes there may indeed be causation, but sometimes the decision-makers have figured out what to do on their own, based on good sense or sound observations or just dumb luck eventually confirmed by the research. (If the decision is binary they have a 50% chance of getting it right by pure chance.) Or they may have made a good decision without much awareness of the research evidence that was in fact available and, as it turns out, supportive. It is possible to make good and even great decisions without high quality scientific evidence. Occasionally the most inspired decisions fly in the face of evidence that casts serious doubt on a particular course of action. A systematic appraisal of comparative naval power would not have encouraged England to take on the Spanish Armada in 1588. The political science community in 1988, in possession of a great deal of evidence about the state of the East Bloc, failed to anticipate the fall of the Iron Curtain in 1989. Research evidence that explains all decisional variance can only be addressing purely technical questions where context is unimportant and human attributes such as leadership and psychology play no role. HSR does not travel in such circles and is but one source of influence on individual, organizational and political behaviour.

A further confounding factor is the dimension of time. The interval between the genesis of a HSR topic and the completion of a reliably actionable (i.e. persuasively unambiguous) body of research is several years at a minimum. It is therefore virtually impossible to produce research that will answer today's pressing question posed by a decision-maker whose decision-making window is open for only a short time. The thing about decision-makers is that they decide. They are often forced or inclined to decide whether or not there is research evidence available to inform their decisions. Their preoccupation with a particular decision rarely lasts more than a few months, if that. It follows that the most influential research will have been conducted long before decision-makers have formulated or found themselves needing to address the question that it will help answer. Put differently, there is no point in ordering up most types of HSR if its perceived utility demands that it be ready in time to inform contemporary decision-making. The only research possible within those constraints is either secondary (a rapid systematic review) or a small-scale retrospective study for which data are readily available.

Then there is the issue of precision. HSR is much more a social than a natural science. It deals with a range of variables that are inherently less stable than the laws of physics or the beautiful logic of mathematics. Few HSR findings are utterly definitive; their main language is statistical and the most important adverb is 'probably'. Even where it is clear that a certain policy or practice results in certain outcomes, the mechanism of action remains elusive, and there are often baffling counterfactuals to the general rule. Such uncertainty is bound to disappoint decision-makers seeking 'the right answer'. And the more precise the data, the greater the likelihood that the research will have been deep but narrow, without analysis of important contextual variables – in short, rather artificial. Acting on such research, or relying on it too heavily, can be dangerous, misleading or both.

Finally there is the matter of originality and how it is typically received. The greatest research changes the way we view the world, be it the Copernican revolution or the Whitehall studies on the non-medical determinants of health. The extent to which research is truly novel and groundbreaking is inversely correlated with the likelihood that it will be put to immediate and practical use. The first reaction to genuine and valid originality is shock and loss – shock at the shattering of long-held truths and loss of stability as historical foundations crumble under the pressure of new evidence. Resistance invariably follows, especially strong among those whose material and/or psychological well-being will be compromised by the new order of things. Eventually the game-changing new (and also contingent) findings infiltrate the processes of discovery and application, but there is nothing straightforward and immediate about the journey. 'Eventually' can be decades, and sometimes we lack the means of practical application.

All well and good, but the reality is that governments, health care organizations, and charities fund HSR not as a fundamental science, like physics, but as an applied discipline judged on the basis of its concrete impact.

If great HSR is unlikely to be influential any time soon, and influential HSR is likely to be several years old, what, realistically, should the HSR community promise to its sponsors, and what should reasonable sponsors expect of HSR? I would suggest that the main adaptation required of researchers is in how they design their studies and present their results. Decision-makers weigh many variables in coming to a conclusion. It is of little service to them if HSR is carved up into narrow slivers and small studies are silent on factors that decision-makers consider important. Researchers cannot address every political and contextual variable but they can often address more than they do. Cost-effectiveness, acceptability of various service configurations and practice patterns, public views of fairness and equity – all of these and more matter. They are also researchable phenomena, and researchers who are able to empathize with the decision-maker's challenge and present findings that address the important questions he/she must consider may find themselves happily surprised at how their 'core' findings are miraculously more relevant.

A trickier adaptation is in how to present and interpret research with a view toward implementation. Many researchers are uncomfortable discussing whether and how findings can be generalized, which interpretations make the most sense, or what the policy and resource implications are. Sensible decision-makers are not interested in making policy advisors out of (most) researchers but, at times, they seek counsel on how probabilistic and partial findings should affect the decision-making agenda. They might value the advice precisely because the researchers are uniquely placed to fuse their scientific and citizenship roles. Researchers unwilling to discuss what the HSR might mean and how it might best be brought to bear on the issues of the day forego an opportunity to do some good. At the very least, those researchers willing and able to participate in such discourse ought to be praised rather than scorned by their more self-sequestering colleagues.

For their part, sponsors need to be realistic about what HSR can and cannot deliver, particularly in the short run. They should also recognize that HSR, like all forms of research, produces an inventory whose practical application cannot accurately be predicted. The most important HSR will challenge orthodoxies and turn attention to vexing problems that defy even the best efforts of public policy. A prime example is the accumulating body of evidence on mammography screening. Despite massive, multi-country studies with huge sample sizes and long-term follow-up, whether to screen and whom to screen remains controversial and fierce scientific, clinical and public debates persist. These tensions do not devalue the research; on the contrary they reaffirm the degree of uncertainty inherent in most good research, and the importance of replicating studies. And it is impossible not to reckon with the findings – a sure sign that the research matters.

Finally, if decision-makers welcome the proposed adaptations in researcher behaviour, they will have to do their part by funding bigger, more comprehensive studies that cross disciplines. Moreover they will have to support research infrastructure to sustain the capacity to produce the kinds of studies most likely to address truly important and enduring questions. The principal focus should be on importance, not immediate and practical impact. There is, to be sure, low-hanging fruit on the utility tree: comparative clinical effectiveness studies, program evaluations, small studies with local applications for which there is a ready and open-minded audience. By all means harvest it. But it would be a huge mistake to get out of the business of supporting HSR with no clear and linear pathway to impact.

It is, on balance, helpful for sponsors to take an interest in the formation and pursuit of larger questions but folly to expect answers to come easily, quickly or cheaply. Likewise it is imprudent to define the return on investment only in terms of foreseeable changes in health care delivery or health outcomes. The world remembers the important HSR long after it has forgotten the immediately useful HSR. What is truly important ends up changing the world but change is hard and never inevitable. Not promising to be useful immediately turns out to be immensely useful in diverse ways, over the long haul.

Weapons of Mass Seduction*

Steven Lewis

A government spending five dollars too much on a screwdriver brings charges of scandal. Spend billions extra on health care with little discernible result and the public smiles approvingly. In Canada, health care spending rose by a whopping 42% between 1997 and 2003, yet only 5% of Canadians identify cost as their principal health care concern (49% say it is access, 33% quality, and 13% the health of the population).[1] Health care already consumes 15% of gross domestic product in the US and will doubtless devour more as legislators draft 700-page laws to conceal their accommodations to the pharmaceutical and insurance industries while ostensibly improving the lot of seniors and the uninsured. In the UK, a centrepiece of the Blair government has been the systematic ramping up of health care spending.[2] By 1999, Japan had 23 MRI scanners for every million people, when the median in OECD countries was five.[3] The roads to the health care future seem paved with gold.

* Originally published in the *Journal of Health Services Research & Policy* 2004, 9(3): 130-1, with the permission of the publisher

By crude measures the return on investment is negligible. There is no correlation between life expectancy and health care spending beyond about US$500 per capita per year.[4] The extreme outlier is of course the US, which spends the most – within the advanced OECD countries – and achieves the least. But what the public values is more than crude measures and faceless statistics: the magic of diagnostic imaging, the statins that wrestle cholesterol, the drug-induced erection, and a panoply of analgesics and balms for the pains of mortality and sinful behaviour. For the persistent headache we seek reassurance from the MRI; entrepreneurs market the whole body scan as the 'next big thing'. Dylan Thomas urged us not to go gentle into that good night. Today we are restless by half past noon: rage, rage against the sagging of the flesh.

Such are the growing preoccupations of the well-to-do which, depending on your definition, includes the politically important third or half of the population in wealthy nations. Democratic governments resist such desires at their peril. Publicly financed health care set out to meet everyone's essential needs and collectivise risk. What used to be public funding of public goods is now public funding of an increasingly commodified set of transactions. 'Needs' are now both basic and manufactured, health care is seen as a major element of quality of life. The redistributive element remains: by and large, the low-income, sick person consumes more services than the stockbroker to the right and the teacher to the left. In a neoconservative age, health care stands out as the last, best exemplar of cross-subsidisation: the well-off pay many times the value of the services they use and, thus far, appear to feel good about supporting the public system; the poor pay only a fraction of what they use;[5] equity wins in a game without losers. Triples all around and if we're all drunks, does any of us have a problem?

Well, two, to be precise. One is that socio-economic health disparities are widening not shrinking. This is true not only where political sentiment champions inequality (most notably, the US), but also in famously egalitarian northern European nations.[6,7] The second is that health care designed for an articulate and assertive middle class, whose needs are typically episodic and self-limiting, often works less well for disadvantaged people with complex physical and mental health problems[8] and chronic diseases.[9] Even preventive measures work better among higher socio-economic groups.[10]

Certainly we continue to chirp in favour of 'health for all' and cleave rhetorically to the vision of Alma Ata. Such aspirations face a sobering reality: a seemingly limitless appetite for higher health care spending irrespective of its impact on health; public financing of a vast bazaar of consumer products; and persistent and even growing health disparities that health care cannot by itself do much about and may even exacerbate. Jobs, income support, free or low-cost education, good public transportation, publicly accessible green spaces and other infrastructure – such are the tools that create opportunity and quality of life for those of limited means. In a zero-sum public spending scenario, health care typically eats the lunch of these other sectors. The unintended consequence is that health status may decline relatively and perhaps even absolutely, among the very groups publicly financed health care was principally intended to help.

Defenders of health care spending point out, rightly, that its share of the gross domestic product has not risen alarmingly and people seem to want more, not less of it. But the other contemporary mantra is tax reduction. Governments have by and large committed themselves to capped or reduced revenue growth, higher health care spending and not spending more than they take in (the US being a notable current exception). The main casualties are (non-health care) social spending and their beneficiaries. Health care remains largely public, while improving the determinants of health is privatized by stealth or conviction. For addressing the symptoms of deprivation, behaviour, genes, luck and worry, there is more and better; for addressing (some of) their root causes, there is less and worse.

Some of this was predictable: the ingenuity of health research and entrepreneurship generates an impressive array of innovations, feeds on natural human insecurities and makes a mockery of attempts to hold the line on costs or the definition of 'medically necessary'. Thus far, the better-off don't seem to mind subsidizing their fellow citizens as long as the system serves them decently. The downside is that when public concerns about social equity focus so narrowly on the domain of health care, there is less appetite for more fundamental forms of health-enhancing redistribution.

Two questions emerge: should anything be done, and if so, can it be done? The 'should' question is ultimately democratic: let the public decide on how much health care it wants to consume and live with the consequences, even if the choices appear irrational to some or if their indirect effects actually widen disparities. To champion democracy is not to succumb to theories of historical inevitability. Societies may make choices under conditions of ignorance that they would modify under conditions of modest enlightenment. Enlightenment requires knowledge, such as the tricky work of estimating what health care at the margin actually produces in concrete terms, identifying who wins and who loses in the allocation of funds within and outside health care, and presenting alternative but realistic scenarios.

The public, and therefore governments, will continue to privilege health care until they are moved to privilege something else. A crucial step is to adopt a more comprehensive notion of performance. First, launch a sustained public discussion of the extent and consequences of health disparities and the impotence of health care to reduce them substantially. Second, look hard at the evidence on which approaches to social spending actually produce the intended benefits: not all hands out are hands up. Third, systematically work with the media to balance their shock and awe at every new invention and technique with a thirst to expose excessive and useless health care consumption (a side effect of which would be better health care quality). Fourth, create methods for cross-sectoral comparison, such as the costs and benefits of various therapies versus investments in other sectors. Possibly, even a well-informed public served by astute media would opt for essentially what it has now – only more of it. But as recent geopolitical events show, there is no escaping the effects of growing inequalities and its costs accrue to everyone. Both self-interest and altruism suggest a frontal assault on disparities and, in wealthy nations, resisting the seductions of health care may be the only realistic path to victory.

References

[1] EKOS Research Associates Inc. Romanow tracking poll. 24 November 2003. www.ekos.ca/admin/press_releases/romanow24nov2003.pdf

[2] Klein R. Britain's national health service revisited. *New England Journal of Medicine* 2004; 350: 937-942

[3] Canadian Institute for Health Information. *Medical Imaging in Canada.* Ottawa: CIHI, 2003

[4] Leon DA, Walt G, Gilson L. Recent advances: international perspectives on health inequalities and policy. *BMJ* 2001; 322: 591-594

[5] Mustard CA, Barer M, Evans RG, Horne J, Derksen S. Paying taxes and using health care services: the distributional consequences of taxed financed universal health insurance in a Canadian province. Conference on the state of living standards and quality of life in Canada. Ottawa, 30–31 October 1998. www.csls.ca/events/oct98/must1.pdf

[6] Cavelaars AE, Kunst AE, Geurts JJ, Crialesi R, Grotvedt L, Helmert U, et al. Differences in self reported morbidity by educational level: a comparison of 11 western European countries. *Journal of Epidemiology and Community Health* 1998; 52: 219-227

[7] Mackenbach JP, Bos V, Andersen O, Cardano M, Costa G, Harding S, et al. Widening socio-economic inequalities in mortality in six Western European countries. *International Journal of Epidemiology* 2003; 32: 830-837

[8] Menec VH, Roos NP, Black C, Bogdanovic B. Characteristics of patients with a regular source of care. *Canadian Journal of Public Health* 2001; 92: 299-303

[9] Booth GL, Hux J. Relationship between avoidable hospitalizations for diabetes mellitus and income level. *Archives of Internal Medicine* 2003; 163: 101-106

[10] van der Pal-de Bruin KM, de Walle HE, de Rover CM, Jeeninga W, Cornel MC, de Jong-van den Berg LT, et al. Influence of educational level on determinants of folic acid use. *Paediatric and Perinatal Epidemiology* 2003; 17:256-263

Categorical Nonsense, $p < .05$*

Steven Lewis and Denise Kouri

Efficient conversation has no place at lunch. On the surface, the Denise Kouri–Steven Lewis lunch of April 7, 2010, was pure *muda* (wasted time): too many topics, utter disorganization, innumerable tangents. Should we expect the young to memorize the multiplication tables? What percentage of the population has a passable grasp of statistics and calculus? (I didn't say we were fascinating, just inefficient.) This reminded D.K. that her daughter was reading a book on how research and scholarly publication have become tyrannized by a rigid notion of statistical significance – the .05 p value. If a phenomenon has less than one in 20 odds of occurring by chance, it's significant; if one in 19, it isn't. Rigour demands it, case closed.

It popped into S.L.'s head that the same categorical logic governs medicare coverage: services are either in or out, "medically necessary" or dispensable options. When money is tight, look for a province or two to search for healthcare services to delist. Maybe it's tattoo removal or sex change therapy; maybe it's chiropractic treatments or optometric visits. Oregon famously ranked 800 or so services in order of priority and drew a cut-off line where the money ran out. The goal is a clear choice: the service is either in or out. (It must be noted that the experiment, like so many, had mainly middle-class people ranking services to be delivered to the poor. That didn't make it stupid or evil; it just meant that those preparing the Kool-Aid weren't bound to drink it.)

* Originally published in *Healthcare Quarterly* 2010, 13(3): 6–7

It is important to understand the likelihood of a statistical finding occurring by chance, and likewise laudable to examine the usefulness of healthcare services. The error in both instances is making too much of minor differences and arbitrarily assigning nearly identical phenomena to different categories. Sometimes, as research grant review panels know only too well, arbitrariness is unavoidable. An application rated at 3.93 gets $400,000, and the next in line, rated 3.91, gets squat. Everyone knows this is conceptually absurd. When the National Institutes of Health in the United States sent out a batch of applications for a second round of review, about 20% of applications changed categories, from funded to unfunded and vice-versa. A score might have changed by a critical tenth of a point if reviewed by another committee, or three hours later in the day, or if one of the primary reviewers had a more soothing voice. But granting agencies exist to pick winners and losers, and there is no fence to sit on. (Well, not the way competitions are currently conducted, but one can conceive of options. A review committee could be given a pot of money and distribute the funds as it sees fit among all applications rated as worthy of support. Some might get all of the asked-for funding, and others might get less, proportionate to their relative merits.) Sometimes the molehill is a mountain, practically speaking.

Neither statistical practice nor medicare faces such stark imperatives, but both behave as though they do. It is not metaphysical truth but orthodoxy that has made the .05 *p* value a statistical icon. There is a reason for this, of course – the virtue of clarity has trumped the reality of nuance. However, many findings with a far lower *p* value (lower probability of occurring by chance) are utterly meaningless; when you have very large samples with dozens of variables, you can't help but generate statistically significant findings even if you have no plausible hypothesis for why X should be related to Y. Conversely, many findings with a higher *p* value (a higher probability of occurring by chance) can be truly groundbreaking. That is why some statisticians argue that the *p* values should be reported but not labelled.

The .05 convention is not just a sensible reminder to be cautious about jumping to conclusions. Academic journals often discourage long interpretive sections of papers – the data are supposed to speak for themselves. Some ruthlessly expunge discussion of the potential meaning of a finding outside the conventional significance range (occasionally authors are allowed to set a cut-off point at .1). This runs the risk of overlooking very promising results just over the border from the statistical promised land. But it does more: it narrows the interpretive lens, discourages free-ranging speculation, privileges research designs where large samples are easy to come by and produces far more correlations (X is associated with Y) than causations (X causes Y).

Regardless of where you stand on this debate, the point is that nothing – no Law of Nature, no externally imposed scarcity, no meta-evaluation – makes the convention unavoidable. It is widely adopted because it is easy to apply, transparent and, in a sense, disciplined. But as in all orthodoxies, true believers and others under their sway pay a price.

Likewise, consider how Canadian medicare – and most other health insurance schemes – define healthcare services as categorically worthy or unworthy of coverage. No healthcare services are useful in every circumstance, and few are always useless. Some services of no use to all but a few may be life saving for someone. A sex change operation could literally save the life of a person suicidally unhappy with his or her current identity. The removal of an ill-conceived tattoo from the face of a youth whose appearance would severely restrict employment opportunities could spell the difference between a productive life and dissolution. It is logically incoherent and inherently unjust to subject citizens to an insurance lottery whereby their coverage status depends not on their level of need and their prospects to benefit from an intervention, but on categorical coverage rules. If Harry needs a cataract operation to improve his vision, he's covered; if Sally needs eyeglasses, she's not. If Milton undergoes predictably useless back surgery, the state pays; yet Mary pays for the back relief she gets from a chiropractor.

The in-or-out decisions end debate precisely where it should begin. The biggest cost problem in healthcare is not an avalanche of voodoo treatments and fraudulent potions. It is the non-essential and sometimes harmful use of services that are effective when used appropriately, or that cost too much while delivering too little. Magnetic resonance imaging (MRI) and computed tomography (CT) scanning are wonderful imaging technologies, but the fivefold increase in their use over the past 15 years has created a culture of overuse that yields about zero at the margins. Good drugs used wisely produce health; the same drugs used unwisely can land you in the hospital.

So why do we play the delisting game over and over again? For one thing, it is easy. If the *Canada Health Act* doesn't mandate it, we can cut it. Saskatchewan just terminated public cost sharing of chiropractic services, and like many provinces delisted eye examinations provided by optometrists years ago (the poor remain covered). Second, it avoids the touchy subject of appropriateness because that would challenge the sacred ground of clinical autonomy, ask peers to narrow variations in practice, impose accountability where none now exists and demand investment in first-class information technology. Third, it betrays a lack of trust in the ability of providers – be they organizations or individuals – to make sensible and just decisions about the allocation of finite resources.

It is never easy to ration care, and providers may instinctively say no thanks to the more-freedom-and-more-accountability combo. But if the goals are justice and patient-centred care, providers must make context-specific decisions and be prepared to explain why another MRI or a $50,000 Hail Mary chemotherapy cocktail is neither good medicine nor sound public policy. The alternatives are profligacy and arbitrary third-party decisions – both simple and clear, but neither just.

In-or-out rule making inevitably harms some patients and creates unjustifiable inequities in entitlement. Even worse, it discourages organizations and clinicians from thinking hard about distributive justice and waste, and novel ways to help their patients. Someone has to manage public resources, and budgets must be finite. The question is whether clinicians and healthcare delivery organizations will be active stewards responsible for allocating resources and explaining their decisions. As things now stand, clinicians graze the common on behalf of their patients and wait to see if anyone – peers, administrators – calls them on it. This is a game with a predictable result: major variations in practice, conflict between managers and providers, game playing, grandstanding, the use of money to buy peace and questionable value for money. The squeaky wheels get the grease, and responsible stewards look like chumps.

Nothing good comes from exempting smart people from having to think about and account for their actions, or encouraging them to ignore the realities of limit and hard choices. In-or-out schemes fail the tests of logic and justice. Getting rid of them would signal a commitment to fairness and recognition that arbitrariness gets in the way of good and efficient care. It would broaden system stewardship and bring providers into the deliberative fold. It would require people to think more deeply about value for money, and to be more transparent in and accountable for their decisions. It would give providers the freedom to seek creative solutions to complex patient problems, along with the responsibility to give reasons for what they do. If we really want a more accountable, just and unified healthcare culture, it's a great place to begin.

Madame Minister, tear down this wall.[1]

Note

[1] As unrepentant social democrats, we rarely get to paraphrase Ronald Reagan approvingly.

CHAPTER FOUR The Reactionarian: On Privatization

Courting Trouble: The Supreme Court's Embrace of Private Health Insurance*

Colleen Flood and Steven Lewis

The Chaoulli decision is confusing and complex but to clarify there are three separate judgments:

1. The majority judgment, written by Justice Deschamps finding the Quebec legislation to be in breach of the Quebec Charter (which is similar to but not exactly the same as the Canadian Charter) ["the Deschamps judgment"] the result of which was concurred with by Chief Justice McLachlin and Justices Major and Bastarache ["the majority judgment"].
2. The judgment written by Chief Justice McLachlin and Justice Major on behalf of themselves and Justice Bastarache which finds the Quebec laws prohibiting private health insurance not only contravene the Quebec Charter but also are in contravention of section 7 of the Canadian Charter ["the McLachlin/Major judgment"]. The significance of this judgment is that it puts in question the constitutionality of measures taken in other provinces to prevent the flourishing of a two-tier system.
3. The minority judgment written by Justice Binne and LeBel on behalf of themselves and Justice Fish finding that Quebec's laws violated neither the Quebec nor Canadian Charter ["the minority judgment"].

*Originally published in *Healthcare Policy* 2005, 1(1): 26-35

In this brief review, we discuss the use and misuse of social science evidence by the court and consider how Canadian governments should respond to this decision.

One of the most concerning aspects of the Deschamps and McLachlin/Major judgments is their treatment of evidence presented by social scientists. The social scientists called all testified about the detrimental effects of allowing a two-tier system. All were dismissed in the harshest of terms and condemned for making arguments based on logic or theory rather than grounded in economic studies or upon the experience of other countries.[2] Indeed, McLachlin C.J. and Major J. conclude that governmental policy was "arbitrary," given in their view the lack of evidence supporting the contention that to allow parallel private insurance would undermine the operation of publicly funded medicare.

Writing for the majority on the Quebec Charter, Justice Deschamps states: "Some patients die as a result of long waits for treatment in the public system when they could have gained prompt access to care in the private sector."[3] This sweeping claim is based on anecdotal evidence from physician witnesses. If this is true, then surely the physicians in question, if they were not able to prioritize the needs of the desperately ill above others, would have brought this to the attention of relevant institutions and the relevant ministries of health. There would be lawsuits brought by the families of those who died.

The McLachlin/Major judgment is on a firmer evidentiary footing in discussing the psychological effects of dealing with anxiety and uncertainty irrespective of final outcome. But as the minority (Justices Binne, LeBel and Fish) succinctly point out, how much of a wait is too long from a constitutional perspective? The McLachlin/Major judgment speaks in such general terms here that there is the possibility that any waiting time could justify a s. 7 Canadian Charter challenge. The patient at the heart of this litigation, George Zelotis, waited a year for a hip operation but remarkably, given that waiting times was the seminal issue in the judgment, the majority does not discuss his case.

Having established that wait times are too long and that Canadians die and suffer harm as a result of a government-imposed monopoly in healthcare insurance, the Deschamps and McLachlin/Major judgments assume that the ability to purchase private insurance will remedy this problem. Moreover, the McLachlin/Major judgment concludes that allowing private insurance will benefit "ordinary" Canadians and not just the elite who can afford to fly to the United States and pay out of pocket for private care. Many will be familiar with the literature about the distributive consequences of private insurance and the cream-skimming and risk-rating behaviour of private insurers, and they will be surprised to learn of the benefits of private insurance that were heretofore unknown. The irony is that George Zelotis, the 73-year-old patient with hip and heart conditions, whose unsuccessful efforts to buy private insurance sparked these proceedings, would not, in all likelihood, qualify for private insurance if it were available.

The majority then considers whether or not allowing two-tier private insurance would detrimentally affect publicly funded medicare. Justice Deschamps superficially discusses the healthcare systems in Austria, Germany, the Netherlands, the United Kingdom, New Zealand, Australia and Sweden. Drawing on the Kirby report (Standing Committee on Social Affairs, Science and Technology 2002) the McLachlin/Major judgment provides a quick tour of the benefits of the healthcare systems of Sweden, Germany and the United Kingdom. There is also passing reference to Australia, Singapore and the United States. They conclude that "many western democracies that do not impose a monopoly on the delivery of healthcare have successfully delivered to their citizens medical services that are superior to and more affordable than the services that are presently available in Canada."[4]

The day of the announcement of the Castonguay Report, Steven organized an evening seminar for the fellows and CHSRF staff and faculty to discuss the policy implications of the document, especially how it related to the funding of health services in the province ... in less than six hours, Steven had read the report, described its context, explained its major findings, and commented on its recommendations ...

Jack Altman

Through their comparative analysis of healthcare systems, the Deschamps and McLachlin/Major judgments amply demonstrate why courts should be extremely cautious about wading into these difficult policy choices. The fundamental error is to conflate all healthcare systems with some role for private insurance into one group. In fact, there are at least four distinct ways of financing healthcare,[5] and European countries such as the Netherlands and Germany are better classified not as two-tier systems (which allow parallel private coverage for services ostensibly covered by the public system) but as group-based. In these systems, private insurance does not perform a duplicate role as would be allowed by the *Chaoulli* decision, permitting people to jump queues for treatment. Instead, private insurance is required to provide full coverage for certain segments of the population. For example, in the Netherlands, an individual earning less than $30,000 (Cdn$48,886) must contribute to and is eligible for social insurance (like medicare). All others must rely totally on private insurance (Wasem et al. 2004). Moreover, physicians don't have an incentive in the Netherlands to prefer patients with private insurance over those with social insurance, as the fees or tariffs paid are the same. In Germany, wealthier patients can opt to stay in the social insurance scheme or take out private insurance, but private insurance must cover all their needs, and one cannot easily opt back into the social insurance scheme. Private insurers in Europe are often heavily regulated to stop them from cream-skimming and risk-rating. To be clear, this kind of system will not evolve in Quebec as a result of striking down the ban on private health insurance.

Systems that have two-tier systems, such as is likely to emerge in Quebec post-*Chaoulli*, include New Zealand and the United Kingdom. In those countries, private insurance duplicates coverage of services that are provided publicly. Consideration of the specific experiences of these jurisdictions shows that historically, both countries have wrestled with waiting lists that are much longer than those within Canada (Tuohy et al. 2004). The length of waiting times in these two-tier systems strongly refutes the linkage made by the majority between long waiting lists and Canada's public monopoly on insurance. But neither the Deschamps or McLachlin/Major judgments consider evidence of long waiting times in these jurisdictions at all.

The McLachlin/Major judgment describes as merely "theoretical" the concern that a private-pay tier will undermine the public system. But the experiences of other jurisdictions demonstrate that this is a concern through the various measures they take to counteract it. For example, the McLachlin/Major judgment discusses how there is a small amount of private insurance in Sweden but fails to mention that physicians are prevented from working in both the public and the private sectors. Swedish physicians must choose one or the other, and the inability to operate largely in the public system with a top-up from the private sector provides a brake on the extent to which the private sector can develop at the expense of the public system. Similar measures are taken in other two-tier systems, namely those of Luxembourg, Greece and Italy (Colombo and Tapay 2004). This is also what many provinces in Canada do as well (Tuohy et al. 2004). Are all these governments misguided as to the problems of a parallel private sector? If not, then surely it is not "arbitrary" to take the next step and simply ban private insurance for essential hospital and physician services.

What went wrong, then? How could the majority of the Supreme Court have reached this outcome? There are, in our view, two reasons.

The first reason has to do with the quality of evidence about public and private interactions across healthcare systems. It is impossible to run a randomized, controlled trial to show irrefutably the effects of two-tier insurance. Indeed, it is a feature of systems with greater levels of private finance that they are more often in turmoil (Tuohy et al. 2004). Nonetheless, there is still a strong body of evidence about the distributive effects and inefficiencies of private insurance and clear evidence from countries such as the United Kingdom and New Zealand that eliminating a monopoly in public insurance will not eliminate waiting lists.

The second reason has to do with presentation of policy evidence in an adversarial environment. In an often-quoted essay, Lorne Fuller (in Winston 2002) argues that judges are good at determining bi-polar disputes and struggle much more with polycentric issues.[6] That is usually why, at least in theory, courts will be cautious about wading into complex policy areas. Indeed, on issues of resource allocation, courts have evinced a strongly deferential position, most notably on the part of the Supreme Court in the *Auton* decision concerning funding of a controversial treatment for autistic children.[7] But in a courtroom, a judge is as likely to be swayed by the direct testimony of physicians or patients as by systemic research, particularly where the research is neither clear nor overwhelming and has to counter a judge's own strongly held intuition or liberal values. In our society, there is a powerful presumption that competitive private markets are inherently efficient and virtuous. The intuition of many people, underscored by the liberal values enshrined in the Charter, is that allowing private markets will alleviate pressure on the public system. Those in health policy need to understand that judges will not necessarily share the presumption that healthcare is a public good rather than a market commodity. The court will start from the perspective of the rights of an individual, and although accepting that rights are not inviolable, will not easily be persuaded that government policy that treads on such rights is necessary.

Political and Legislative Responses

Now that the spectre of accelerated privatization looms large, provincial governments have several strategic options to pursue. The issues are by no means straightforward, and the battle is likely to be fought in three arenas, each with its own dynamics.

The first dimension is democratic. Medicare was forged in the political arena in Saskatchewan and prevailed over fierce opposition. The pro-medicare camp still commands the political high ground, and it should capitalize on this advantage. Though it is plausible to infer that some governments in Canada would be content to see medicare fade away as an icon and political litmus test, it is still risky in most parts of the country for a politician to declare that a tax-funded, single-tier system is a bad idea. Insisting that all candidates for provincial or federal office disclose their views would seem to be an important tactic. The central questions are:

- Should better-off Canadians be able to purchase faster service from doctors and hospitals?
- Would you support a two-tier system if the result is that waiting times in the public sector worsen?
- As a matter of principle, do you support the development of a private and parallel

system for physician and hospital services? Do we have too much or too little private care now?

Sorting out the politics is necessary, but not sufficient. The second dimension is to solve the problems of quality and access, the latter of which created the pretext for *Chaoulli* and which also portends future Charter challenges now that the court has left the door ajar. The purpose here is to improve the public system so that even well-heeled people lose interest in the private option.

First, the best defence to a s. 7 challenge will be to fix waiting lists and restore Canadians' confidence in the timeliness of medicare. Provinces must implement consolidated, standardized, province-wide wait list management systems: no more lists held in physicians' offices and opaque prioritization processes. Ottawa could and should insist on this as an addendum to the recent Accords. The next step will be to amend the *Canada Health Act* to mandate such measures (Flood and Choudhry 2004). Ironically, the Chaoulli decision now provides the leverage that governments need to implement such measures rapidly, regardless of the opposition they may face (Lewis 2005).

Second, the majority of the Supreme Court criticized the fact that there was no real appeal mechanism in Quebec for people languishing on waiting lists. Every province should establish highly accessible tribunals or patient commissioners to review cases swiftly and fairly (Pitfield 2003; Defining the Medicare Basket Project 2003). There should be some discretion to grant relief to individuals where the psychological effects of waiting are extreme, to head off further challenges under s. 7, or even to approve treatments that do not, strictly speaking, meet the usual eligibility criteria. Canada is a wealthy country, and erring on the side of generosity and compassion in delivering healthcare while pursuing reforms to eliminate waste and excess in the system, seems a reasonable compromise.

Third, there is great confusion about the evidence on public versus private, both in the minds of both the majority of Supreme Court justices and of Canadians. The *Chaoulli* decision makes inevitable further Charter challenges to similar laws in other provinces, but the question of whether they will or should succeed remains contested. The composition of the Supreme Court is changing with the addition of two new justices. A reconstituted court may come to a different conclusion. In anticipation, federal and provincial governments, in conjunction with health policy analysts, must marshall the best possible evidence on public–private financing and the detrimental effects on the public system of a second, private tier. At the very minimum, the forces in favour of privatization should not prevail because the best evidence was not presented to the relevant court.

Fourth, provincial governments need to create a thick firewall between the public and the private system. They should insist that providers choose one or the other, exclusively. It should also be made clear that public hospital capacity will be available to private patients on a purely discretionary basis, and that there will be no subsidization of this private option from the public purse. Ensure that they enforce the spirit and letter of the Alberta legislation that prohibits patients from getting faster public-sector service as a result of getting a private-sector diagnosis.

Fifth, if for whatever reason, the public system is compromised by a growing departure of doctors and other key personnel to the private sector, provinces should consider a two-tier tuition system to mirror the two-tier healthcare system. Currently, medical school tuition can run as high as $47,000 annually (at Dalhousie) for international students. All health sciences students should be given the option: commit to practising in the public system for a defined period of time and pay low tuition fees, or make no such commitment and pay the actual costs of the education. Public policy should not exclude students who want to retain the option of going private, but nor should it subsidize them.

Beyond these short-term measures, more systematic change is required. We need to revisit Canada's approach to health human resources (HHR). It is, we contend, wiser to produce a modest oversupply than a modest undersupply. Scarcity breeds wait times, tilts bargaining power heavily in favour of providers, leads to bidding wars among jurisdictions that drive up costs without adding service and tempts Canada to engage in the unseemly practice of raiding personnel from developing nations. Aside from physicians, it is relatively inexpensive to produce healthcare personnel. And even though educating physicians is costly, European countries have for years produced more than they needed, with an estimated 100,000 unemployed in 1995 (Orellana 2001) and more recent rates estimated at 3-4% in Sweden, 7-8% in Greece, 5-10% in Spain and as high as 20% in Italy (Avgerinos et al. 2004). Involuntary unemployment is unfortunate, and we are aware of the pitfalls inherent in merely adding more fee-for-service doctors to a system already vulnerable to supply-induced demand. On the other hand, shortages drive up salaries and compromise public confidence. Conceivably, a modest surplus combined with payment reforms, policies to prevent the over-concentration of personnel in large urban centres and other measures could create competition for quality, increase willingness to locate in underserviced areas and impose some semblance of market discipline on wages and salaries. As an initial step, economists and planners should undertake modelling exercises that project the costs and consequences of switching from a "just enough" approach to HHR to a "just a little too much."

Romanow (Commission on the Future of Health Care in Canada 2002), Kirby (Standing Committee on Social Affairs, Science and Technology 2002), Mazankowski (Alberta Premier's Advisory Council on Health 2002), Fyke (Commission on Medicare 2001) and Clair (Maioni 2001) have all emphasized the need to accelerate changes to the division of labour. Doctors are doing what nurses can ably do (Horrocks et al. 2002). Highly educated, high-priced surgeons are performing routine, high-volume procedures that technicians perform elsewhere - notably, cataract surgery - while their advanced knowledge and cognitive skills are underused. Primary healthcare reform is by common consensus moving at a glacial pace; even more discouragingly, ambitious, comprehensive models (Ontario Health Services Restructuring Commission 1999) have been diluted into physician-extender compromises. The result is a sub-optimal use of skills and often-demoralized personnel.

As many have also argued, we must tie funding to both organizational innovation and meeting performance standards. We must create incentives to speed up the adoption of comprehensive primary healthcare. We must withhold funding from jurisdictions and institutions that do not have wait time management systems or that fail to follow up with patients on the long wait time tail. We must also renegotiate agreements with medical associations and repatriate the power to establish comparative earning power among physician categories. If there is a shortage of family doctors, it is partly because new graduates are leaving family medicine residencies unfilled; the same holds true for geriatrics. Meanwhile, plastic surgery and dermatology residencies are oversubscribed, and there is already an oversupply of neurosurgeons. If the medical associations' internal collective bargaining process does not value what the public system needs, others must be at the table to bring about change.

Conclusion

The prime minister of Canada, among others, has downplayed the *Chaoulli* decision, arguing that it will not fundamentally affect medicare. It is true that technically the reach of the decision is confined to Quebec, but it will have repercussions far beyond those borders. First, because the court is split on the critical issue of the application of the *Canadian Charter of Rights and Freedoms* to laws prohibiting private insurance, the question will likely soon be tested in the provinces of Alberta, British Columbia and Prince Edward Island, which have similar laws. Second, there is the prospect that other provincial laws that effectively suppress a private-pay sector will be subject to a Charter challenge. Justice Deschamps, writing the majority judgment on the Quebec Charter, seemingly approves of legislative provisions in other provinces that stop short of expressly prohibiting private insurance. However, Chief Justice McLachlin with Justices Major and Bastarache, who find Quebec's insurance provision to be in breach of the Canadian Charter, do not comment on these other measures. This leaves open the possibility that provisions such as those that exist in Ontario, Nova Scotia and Manitoba (which prevent physicians' from charging privately more than they would receive from the public plan) may also be subjected to a Charter challenge.

More importantly, the *Chaoulli decision*, a ruling of the Supreme Court of Canada, will have a strong normative effect on the future tenor of the public–private debate. We are already starting to see the effects of this in editorials in the major newspapers. The ground has shifted, and the forces in favour of privatization have achieved a significant victory. They can now add an enormously strong plank to their heretofore rather weak arguments: they have been legitimated by the Supreme Court of Canada. The new role that the courts may play in healthcare is of crucial importance not only to the courts, but to the Canadian public and their governments. For years, health policy analysts have battled the "zombie" ideas of user-pays, private insurance and two-tiers (Evans et al. 1995). There is now a new venue for the debate, and health policy analysts cannot ignore it.

The Supreme Court decision, however misguided, has brought medicare to a new crossroads. We have proposed political, policy and legislative antidotes to the potential consequences of the *Chaoulli* judgment. Our preference is for politics and policy. Medicare's future should be deliberated in the political arena. Better that 32 million Canadians determine the structure and fate of medicare than seven (or nine) judges - a prescription shared by the dissenting minority.

Notes

[1] *Chaoulli v. Quebec* (Attorney General) 2005 SCC 35 (hereinafter Chaoulli). A copy of the judgment and various related materials is available at <http://www.law.utoronto.ca/healthlaw/>.

[2] *Chaoulli*, paragraph 136.

[3] *Chaoulli*, paragraph 37.

[4] *Chaoulli*, paragraph 140.

[5] Tuohy et al. (2004) identify four basic models of structuring the relationship between public and private financing: parallel public and private systems; co-payment; group-based; and sectoral.

[6] Also see L.A. Chayes (1976), «The Role of the Judge in Public Law Litigation,» in the *Harvard Law Review* 98: 1281.

[7] *Auton* (Guardian ad litem of) v. British Columbia (Attorney General), [2004] 3 SCR 657.

References

Alberta Premier's Advisory Council on Health. 2002. A Framework for Reform. Edmonton: Commission of Study on Health and Social Services. Retrieved August 3, 2005. <http://www.premiersadvisory.com/reform.html>.

Avgerinos, E.D., S.A. Koupidis and D.K. Filippou. 2004. "Impact of the European Union Enlargement on Health Professionals and Health Care Systems." *Health Policy* 69: 403-08.

Colombo, F. and N. Tapay. 2004. "Private Health Insurance in OECD Countries: The Benefits and Costs for Individuals and Health Systems." Working Paper No. 15 (p. 24, fn. 38). Retrieved August 3, 2005. <http://www.oecd.org/dataoecd/34/56/33698043.pdf>.

Commission on the Future of Health Care in Canada. 2002 (November). *Building on Values: The Future of Health Care in Canada.* Retrieved August 3, 2005. <http://www.hc-sc.gc.ca/english/care/romanow/hcc0086.html>.

Commission on Medicare. 2001. Caring for Medicare: Sustaining a Quality System. Retrieved August 3, 2005. <http://www.health.gov.sk.ca/mc_ dp_commission_on_medicare-bw.pdf>.

Defining the Medicare Basket Project. 2003. Retrieved August 3, 2005. <http://www.law.utoronto.ca/healthlaw/basket/index.html>.

Evans, R.G., M.L. Barer and G.L. Stoddart. 1995. "User Fees for Health Care: Why a Bad Idea Keeps Coming Back." *Canadian Journal on Aging* 14: 360-90.

Flood, C.M. and S. Choudhry. 2004. "Strengthening the Foundations: Securing the Modernity of the Canada Health Act." In T. McIntosh, P.G. Forest and G.P. Marchildon, eds., *The Governance of Health Care in Canada* (pp. 346-87). Toronto: University of Toronto Press.

Fuller, L. 2002. *The Principles of Social Order: Selected Essays of Lon L. Fuller* (K. Winston, ed.) (2nd ed.). Portland, OR: Hart Publishing.

Horrocks, E., C. Anderson and C. Salisbury. 2002. "Systematic Review of Whether Nurse Practitioners Working in Primary Care Can Provide Equivalent Care to Doctors." *British Medical Journal* 324: 819-23.

Lewis, S. 2005 (June). "Physicians, It's in Your Court Now." Canadian Medical Association Journal 173 (3): 275. Retrieved August 3, 2005. <http://www.cmaj.ca/cgi/reprint/173/3275?maxtoshow=&HITS=10&hits=10&RESULTFORMAT=&fulltext=lewis+s&andorexactfulltext=and&searchid=1123168972874_1324&stored_search=&FIRSTINDEX=0&sortspec=relevance&resourcetype=1&journalcode=cmaj>.

Maioni, A. 2001. "Emerging Solutions": Quebec Clair Commission Report and Health Care Reform. Retrieved August 3, 2005. <http://cprn.org/en/doc.cfm?doc=144>.

Ontario Health Services Restructuring Commission. 1999 (December). Primary Health Care Strategy. Advice and Recommendations to the Honourable Elizabeth Witmer. Retrieved August 33, 2005. <http://www.health.gov.on.ca/hsrc/home.htm>.

Orellana, C. 2001. "Is MD Unemployment in Europe Finally Coming to an End?" *Canadian Medical Association Journal* 165: 75.

Pitfield, C. 2003. Giving Patients a Louder Voice in the Health Care System. Unpublished master's thesis, University of Toronto Faculty of Law.

Standing Committee on Social Affairs, Science and Technology. 2002 (October). The Health of Canadians – The Federal Role. Final Report. Retrieved August 3, 2005. <http://www.parl.gc.ca/37/2/parlbus/commbus/senate/com-e/soci-e/rep-e/repoct02vol6-e.htm>.

Tuohy, C., C. Flood and M. Stabile. 2004. "How Does Private Finance Affect Public Health Care Systems? Marshalling the Evidence from OECD Nations." *Journal of Health Politics, Policy and Law* 3: 359-96.

Wasem, J., S. Greb and K.G.H. Okma. 2004. "The Role of Private Health Insurance in Social Health Insurance Countries." In R. Saltman, R. Busse and J. Figueras, eds., *Social Health Insurance in Western Europe* (pp. 227-47). London, UK: Open University Press.

Medicare's Fate: Are We Fiddlers or Firefighters?*

Steven Lewis

If you never read another Supreme Court judgment in your life, read this one. The court was heatedly divided. The four justices in the majority didn't even agree on all of their findings, while the three dissenters were united in their reasoning. The language in some parts borders on bitchy – the majority scorning the dissenters as letting their emotions interfere with judicial reasoning, the dissenters snorting that the majority played fast and loose with the evidence and ran roughshod over the entitlement of society and governments to define the public interest.

I'd rather hear the tapes of those discussions over Grewal-Murphy-Dosanjh any day. I'm no lawyer, but it's bad law. The majority's use of health-systems research was facile at best, glibly accepting that Canadians routinely die while waiting for treatment while,

* Originally written for the *Winnipeg Free Press*: The View From the West - a forum of ideas and opinions. Sunday June 12, 2005

apparently, people elsewhere in the world do not by dint of the availability of private insurance. The decision also roamed far from the facts of the case – Montreal chemical salesman George Zeliotis' year-long wait for a hip operation – and essentially turned it into a class-action suit for all Canadians. Instead of presiding over virtual anarchy, the court could have considered many other remedies, such as insisting that provinces establish and monitor wait-time standards, set up rapid appeals tribunals for aggrieved patients, and actively manage their wait lists.

But it didn't, and here we are. So what's next?

There will be at least a short-term burst of private-clinic expansion, financed by investors offering lucrative salaries and spiffy quarters to physicians. It won't be cataclysmic because it's been going on for years, but it could create troublesome shortages in some public practices and institutions for awhile. Later on, the effect may diminish as expanded classes of doctors and nurses graduate.

Some clinics will want status as private hospitals, offering not just day procedures but overnight stays. Some governments will balk and stall. Others, such as Alberta, given Premier Klein's thumbs-up to the SCOC decision, may sign on quickly. If such hospitals emerge in large cities, private insurance will become more attractive in that it would secure a paying patient's access not only to physician care, but to at least some forms of hospitalization.

Blessed by their governments, some hospitals will be tempted to rent their facilities to privately insured doctors and patients to make a buck. They will tell their communities that the money they make will be used to enhance public care. They will assure the public that access will not suffer, and that everyone will win. Should this happen, the realities of two-tier service will be more visible.

Insurance executives are already surveying the market and plotting their strategies but, more importantly, businesses are also plotting theirs. Most private health insurance is employer-based (some is cost-shared). Employee health benefits are already big business in some parts of Canada, but insuring core doctor and hospital services is a major step up in cost and complexity. Canadian corporations, particularly the auto industry, have long recognized the economic advantage of medicare. They will be dragged kicking and screaming, if at all, into the private-insurance morass. But let's take a deep breath. The decision, however perverse, is a wake-up call for governments and citizens devoted to the idea of a single-payer, universal public system. All that is lost for certain is the legal crutch that politicians have leaned on to keep the privatization tide at bay.

Here are some options:

- Make the public system better by doing all the things the quality-improvement gurus have told us to do for years. Manage wait lists properly and make sure waiting patients are followed up regularly. Give pharmacists a greater role in prescribing to reduce the errors and illness caused by doctors. Use nurse practitioners more effectively. It doesn't take more money. It may even take less.
- Refuse to subsidize private care and personnel. Charge medical students $5,000 tuition if they sign contracts to practise exclusively in the public system, and $60,000 (more like the real cost) if they want the option to go private. Do the same for nurses and therapists.
- Strike public-interest bargains with physician unions. It's doctors, not governments, who insist on underpaying primary-care physicians and geriatricians and overpaying ophthalmologists (who do cataracts by the thousand) and gastroenterologists (who earn huge incomes by scoping every available orifice).
- We have, up to now, let the doctors sort out their relative incomes, and it has been a disaster. Enough already.
- Create incentives to provide quality service. Fine doctors who close their office doors at 4 p.m., refuse to provide after-hours service, and punt their patients to emergency rooms. Withhold payments to hospitals and health regions that don't have systems to ensure that wait times are reasonable and that the neediest patients get served first. Educate the public about how to use a health system effectively and prudently. The privateers treat health care as a commodity and prosper, in part, by ministering to the "worried well". "Care for a full-body CT scan, sir? A few more tests just to be sure, ma'am?" The hawking of services will get worse before it gets better. Governments should deal with it aggressively. Hold media conferences about the dangers and uselessness of over-service. Meet with editorial boards to alert them to scams and shams.
- Publish honest and thorough performance reports about the public system. Be honest about mistakes and limits. Treat the public like adults. Pay attention to complaints and public satisfaction surveys.
- Enlist an unlikely ally – corporate Canada (minus the insurance companies). Their prosperity is linked to good public health care. Get them involved in the political battle.

And let's get the medicare questions right: How did such a rich and admired system fall prey to an impish display of jurisprudence? Why is primary health care in disarray? How come a 60-per-cent increase in spending since 1997 hasn't bought solutions? Why is the health-care system a non-system, better described as anarchy than orderly and fair?

It's because we mistook a quality problem for a money problem. We allowed too many foxes to guard too many henhouses. We funded but did not really manage. And we expected legions of smart people to do a 21st-century job with 19th-century tools.

There is nothing irretrievably wrong with medicare, but there is no assurance that it will be fixed either. For decades we have shrunk from battles with vested interests that now need to be joined. We have rightly made an icon of the basic structure of the system, but have wrongly taken our eye off its tangible performance. Politicians have found it easier to shovel money and avoid conflict, proving yet again that hope triumphs over experience.

So perhaps a questionable court decision has done us all a favour by conscripting us into the fray. Every provider, every citizen and every politician needs to take a hard look in the mirror. We have all been complicit in the events that have played into the hands of that ever-chirping minority of enemies of public health care. Our values and our tough-mindedness have been put on notice. If we screw this up, the private ship will leave the dock fully booked, and over time there will be an even wider gulf between those that have and those that don't.

The choice is ours: We can be fiddlers or firefighters as Rome is set ablaze.

Physicians: It's in Your Court Now*

Steven Lewis

The Supreme Court decision of June 9, 2005 clarifies the political choice facing organized medicine in Canada.[1] Many of Canada's doctors are strong and eloquent supporters of single-tier health care. Many are not, and never have been. A mere decade ago, at the CMA's annual General Council meeting, a motion declaring that citizens "must have the right to choose regulated private insurance for all medical services" fell on a vote of 88 to 68.[2] Focus groups conducted by the CMA in 1996 revealed a wide chasm between the strong public support for public health care and the then 78% of physicians who believed stronger private-sector participation in health care was either very or somewhat acceptable.[3] And, of course, organized medicine was heatedly opposed to the introduction of medicare in Saskatchewan in 1962. More often than not, doctors' organizations have strongly opposed measures that they have subsequently embraced. In this they are no different from any other privileged group – whatever their virtues, attunement to the will of the demos is not among them. The profession's support for single-tier health care has always been provisional, and it has been largely silent – one must infer approvingly so – on the growth of for-profit clinics. Some physicians have contracted out to the public system, others have plied their trade on both sides of the street and a few have abandoned medicare altogether. Until June 9, the debates among doctors were not central to the future

* Originally published in the *Canadian Medical Association Journal* 2005, 173(3): 275-77, with the permission of the publisher

of the system. Proponents of a private and parallel option had to chip away at medicare's edges, abetted by a federal government that has been castigated by the Auditor General for refusing to enforce the *Canada Health Act*. Now "private and parallel" has the high court's blessing, with a new twist: the legal buying and selling of insurance for medically necessary services. The court has tasered medicare; the question is now whether the system is temporarily stunned, or mortally wounded.

CMA President Albert Schumacher declared the Supreme Court judgment "a stinging indictment of the failure of governments to respond to the mountains of studies that show we need real action on our health care system." That we need real action on our health care system is incontestable. That government should be the exclusive or even principal target of indictment is the question on the table. The evidence suggests we should look elsewhere.

Governments fund health care and establish its general legislative and regulatory framework. Beyond that, the system is largely in the hands of physicians, who make the day-to-day decisions, prioritize patients, prescribe drugs, admit patients to and discharge them from hospital, order tests and carry out innumerable interventions with a remarkable degree of autonomy. They are not held accountable in any meaningful way for performance. They are indifferent, apparently, to the clinical practice guidelines produced by their own colleagues. There are huge variations in their practices that go unchecked, despite the obvious implications for quality and access.[4-7]

The "real action" needed on our health care system includes primary health care reform, a more rational division of labour, quality improvement and a remedy for inequities in pay scales that overvalue day-surgery assembly lines and undervalue geriatricians and rheumatologists. The call for these reforms has come largely from governments, and it has been thwarted or delayed not by governments but by doctors.[8] Both Romanow and Kirby noted the glacial advance of primary care reform. It is medical associations, not governments, that allocate incomes among specialties. Nurse practitioners, pharmacists and therapists are anxious to expand their scope of practice and to use their expertise fully. Try to find a government that disagrees. Try to find a medical association fully on board.

According to organized medicine, system failings are always someone else's fault. Somehow Mr. Zeliotis' hip surgery delay was caused by the nature and stinginess of the single-payer system. Nothing, apparently, is attributable to physicians retaining control over their individual wait lists and refusing to standardize criteria for assessing and prioritizing patients.[9] The failure to look for doctors with shorter wait times, to share responsibility for fairness and to participate in the kinds of process improvements that by 2003 got 88% of UK citizens into primary care within 48 hours of picking up the phone[10] is – government's. If it's government's fault, it's because government didn't follow Whitehall's lead and just say no to chaos.

Given its anarchic characteristics, it is bordering on miraculous that the system by and large serves most people well most of the time. The median wait time for cardiac surgery in Manitoba is 23 days.[11] Median wait times in British Columbia are well under three months for every surgical category except for corneal transplants (17 weeks), hip replacements (22 weeks) and knee replacements (28 weeks).[12] In Saskatchewan in 2004, 82% of surgeries were completed within six months, but 5% had wait times longer than 18 months.[13] And here is where the problem comes home to roost: if even as few as half of the 5% were waiting involuntarily, great harm was done.

Who is responsible? Governments don't manage the wait lists. Governments are not responsible for following up, or not, with patients waiting for procedures. Governments do not decide that patient A will get served in two months while patient B, with identical needs, will wait 20 months. Doctors do. The Canadian long waits are not a capacity problem: simple arithmetic demonstrates that no one has to wait 18 months in a system where 4 out of 5 (or more) patients wait well under six months. But until recently the only response of organized medicine to these long waits was to cry poverty and enlist the public in government bashing. One would have thought the Hippocratic oath would have diverted some of this energy toward looking after the long-suffering. It does not take a cynic to observe that the long queues admirably served the purpose of extracting more money for health care – both public and private. And they also provided the pretext for Chaoulli, and here we are.

> **On a day in 1996 ... our mission was** supposedly simple, scripted by Steven ... to speak truth to power. We confronted them [Federal Finance Minister and DM] with the prickly issue of the federal cash floor and support for Medicare ... We lost ... I was mortified but Steven was philosophical ... Steven has never lost his passion to make Medicare better.
>
> *Tom Noseworthy*

The history of medicare is a clash between the state's goals of equity, order and efficiency with medicine's goals of autonomy, growth and control. Society has made enormous concessions to organized medicine, such as the right of doctors to set up practice anywhere, the right to remain independent contractors rather than full partners in a complex system, freedom from the measurement, scrutiny and accountability of US-style managed care, and pay scales that vastly exceed those extant in the European systems the court and medicare's critics selectively admire from afar. It has also encouraged governments to increase public spending by an astonishing 60% in the past eight years, an ongoing mea culpa for the four-year period in the last 35 when spending modestly declined. All the public expects in return is a shared commitment to single-tier equity, a willingness to participate in reforms and decent performance. Apparently this has been too much to ask.

Now, thanks to the Supreme Court, the legal underpinnings of the system have been dealt a blow, and the choices are starker for doctors. They can now openly abandon the public system and get in on the ground level of an emerging private insurance system catering to people with money. They can market the virtues of commodified medicine and concentrate on the sexy diagnostics and high-volume procedures under the guise of enhancing Canadians' Charter rights. No more unlucrative sessions with the complex geriatric case. No more dealing with intractable chronic diseases. No more unrewarding encounters with the underclass. It's an easy and pleasant $275,000 a year for family doctors at a clinic that bundles core services with the extras, charging $1,700 up front and $2,300 annually.

No doubt surgeons in the orthopedic and cataract centres can easily double and triple that income.

The Supreme Court has raised the stakes, and the public needs to know where official medicine stands. Will it accelerate public-system reforms, improve its performance and effectively preempt the market for private insurance? Or will it decant more care to the private sector, which, according to recent evidence from Australia's hybrid system, increases public sector wait times?[15] Will it promote a fair income distribution so that graduating doctors no longer leave family medicine and geriatrics residencies unfilled while they flock to dermatology and orthopedics? Will it propose and participate in comprehensive wait-list management systems, like Saskatchewan's, to ensure that no patient's health is endangered by unmonitored waits and that those with greater needs get served first? Will it leap to the fore of the quality revolution, or continue to provide an endless source of material for the small-area-variation research industry?[16]

Perhaps, in its testily divided decision, the court has done the country a favour. We have not had a national, focused debate on where to draw the line on two-tier health care for decades, resorting to fictions about medically unnecessary services and ignoring the evidence under our very noses – most recently that for-profit long-term care facilities provide significantly less direct and support care to residents than their nonprofit counterparts.[17] Nor have we carefully and conclusively debated Tommy Douglas's unrealized vision of a genuinely balanced continuum of care. Physicians have fought long and successfully to remain at arm's length from the system. You wouldn't get on a plane built by engineers who decided independently what parts to make and whether and how to fit them together. Why would anyone expect excellence from a health care system that is largely ungoverned and where mistakes and overuse trigger an avalanche of funding and income while prudent, efficient practice has the bracing effect of lowering one's income?

This is not a time for hysteria or fear-mongering, but for self-examination, reflection and choice. How governments respond to the challenge is of course vitally important, and the political exchanges promise to be lively. But citizens and governments delude themselves if they imagine that a public system can succeed without a medical profession that is widely and officially committed to its values and more often than not promotes rather than resists constructive change.

For too long the rule of the game has been to spend more or lose physician support. We've spent more – a lot more – and the return on investment has been low. Canada is a country governed by elites. Will the medical profession rise to the challenge of creating a new and improved medicare, or will it, like so many elites, talk about the public interest but act in the interests of the few?

References

[1] *Chaoulli v. Quebec* (Attorney General). 2005 SCC 35.

[2] Sullivan P. Private health care dominates meeting as General Council calls for national debate. *CMAJ* 1995;153(6):801-3.

[3] Sullivan P. Focus groups confirm that MDs, public differ on role of private health care. *CMAJ* 1996;154(8):1247-9.

[4] Kennedy J, Quan H, Ghali WA, Feasby TE. Variations in rates of appropriate and inappropriate carotid endarterectomy for stroke prevention in 4 Canadian provinces. *CMAJ* 2004;171(5):455-9.

[5] Jaglal SB, Carroll J, Hawker G, McIsaac WJ, Jaakkimainen L, Cadarette SM, et al. How are family physicians managing osteoporosis? Qualitative study of their experiences and educational needs. *Can Fam Physician* 2003;49:462-8.

[6] Brownell M. Tonsillectomy rates for Manitoba children: temporal and spatial variations. *Healthc Manage Forum* 2002;Suppl:21-6.

[7] Katz A, DeCoster C, Bogdanovic B, Soodeen RA, Chateau D. Using administrative data to develop indicators of quality in family practice. Winnipeg: Manitoba Centre for Health Policy; 2004. Available: www.umanitoba.ca/centres/mchp/reports/pdfs/quality_wo.pdf (accessed 2005 Jun 20).

[8] Medical Reform Group. Nearsighted physicians reject deal with government [media release]. Toronto: The Group; 2004 Nov 21. Available: www.hwcn.org/link/mrg/press.release.html #Nearsighted_Physicians_Reject_Deal_With (accessed 2005 Jun 20).

[9] Sanmartin C, Shortt SED, Barer ML, Sheps S, Lewis S, McDonald PW. Waiting for medical services in Canada: lots of heat, but little light. *CMAJ* 2000;162(9):1305-10.

[10] Department of Health. Achieving shorter waits: the PPF promises shorter waiting times across the service. London (UK): The Department; 2005. Available: www.dh.gov.uk/PolicyAndGuidance/PatientChoice/WaitingBookingChoice/WaitingBookingChoiceArticle/fs/en?CONTENT_ID=4066038&chk=ZurIX5 (accessed 2005 Jun 20).

[11] Winnipeg Regional Health Authority. Health services wait time information: cardiac surgery. Winnipeg: Manitoba Health. Available: www.gov.mb.ca/health/waitlist/cardiac.html (accessed 2005 Jun 20).

[12] Median wait times and wait lists. Victoria: Government of British Columbia; 2005 Mar 31. Available: www.healthservices.gov.bc.ca/cpa/mediasite/waittime/median.html (revised 2005 May 17, accessed 2005 Jun 20).

[13] Wait time information. Regina: Saskatchewan Surgical Care Network. Available: www.sasksurgery.ca/wait-list-info.html (accessed 2005 Jun 20).

[15] Duckett SJ. Private care and public waiting. *Aust Health Rev* 2005;29:87-93.

[16] Tu JV, Pinfold SP, McColgan P, Laupacis A. April 2005. Access to health services in Ontario: ICES Atlas. Toronto: Institute for Clinical Evaluative Sciences; 2005. Available: www.ices.on.ca/webpage.cfm?site_id=1&org_id=67&morg_id=0&gsec_id=0&item_id=2862&type=atlas (accessed 2005 Jun 20).

[17] McGregor MJ, Cohen M, McGrail K, Broemeling AM, Adler RN, Schulzer M, et al. Staffing levels in not-for-profit and for-profit long-term care facilities: Does type of ownership matter? *CMAJ* 2005;172(5):645-9.

Chaoulli, Truly: A Supreme Irony*

Steven Lewis

On January 11, 2008, 77-year-old Jacques Sauvageau went to a private medical clinic in Montreal that advertised itself as capable of delivering emergency care. Despite being in obvious acute respiratory distress, Mr. Sauvageau was told to wait. He fell unconscious, and his dentures tumbled out. After other waiting patients raised the alarm, a physician emerged, pronounced the man dead and told the nurse to call 9-1-1 to report the death. The 9-1-1 operator pleaded with the nurse to try to revive the man; another patient and, later, the paramedics vainly intervened. A coroner's report revealed that Mr. Sauvageau had died of a pulmonary embolism and nothing could have saved him. But the physician who refused to attempt to revive him could not have known this to be the case.

Lo and behold, that physician was none other than Jacques Chaoulli, the great champion of two-tier medicine who persuaded the Supreme Court to strike down Quebec's prohibition of private insurance for medically necessary services. A confession: when the *Globe and Mail* article describing his behaviour came to my attention, it made my day. Is my pleasure guilty, and is it *schadenfreude* – taking pleasure in others' misfortune?

I'm not sure. Chaoulli has not to my knowledge suffered any misfortune. He is missing the humiliation gene. Confronted with a waiting room full of aghast patients in a state

* Originally published in *Longwoods Essays*, May 5, 2008

of insurrection about the disregard for Mr. Sauvageau's welfare, he refused to humanize. Nothing in his history suggests he gives a tinker's damn about what the media or the public think of him. Neither self-doubt nor shame inhabits his psyche.

That doesn't make him unique, and elementary failures of human decency are too common to be newsworthy. Chaoulli's transgression is of interest because a Supreme Court decision bears his name. This is a man who argued to the highest court in the land that the public system makes people wait too long and therefore harms them. So when the private clinic in which he was working makes a blue-faced old man wait unattended until he dies, we are treated to a spectacular irony.

We all screw up, and it's usually bad form to pile on. Is it fair game to raise questions about Chaoulli's character and motives from this story? Yes it is, because he has for years cast himself as the conscience of the country with a burning desire to make people's lives better. He has compared himself to Gandhi and claimed he and Tommy Douglas have a lot in common. He has publicly mused about "playing the role of safeguard for the Canadian people as to quality healthcare ... Since I was the one to lead this legal challenge, I believe I'm in the best position to know what Canadian people need in terms of healthcare quality". He sees a communist under every healthcare bed. In a report for the libertarian Cato Institute in the United States, he blames the US Congress for the plight of 6,000 Americans awaiting transplants because the country prohibits the selling of organs.

No one forced him to portray his quest as a righteous crusade. Since he speaks and writes in moral language, he invites scrutiny as to whether he walks his own talk. My reaction to his current plight may be *schadenfreude*, but explanation requires Sigmund Freud. The public record suggests that he has a messianic view of himself, invoking not just Gandhi but Martin Luther King in a speech to the right-wing Heritage Foundation in the United States: "I have a dream. My dream is to show the world how to get rid of a new and subtle form of tyranny hidden under the cover of a Welfare State's compulsory health care program." He went on a four-week hunger strike in 1996 to protest the government's refusal to allow him to charge patients directly for his services.

Good people can make bad policy, and bad people can make good policy – Nixon in China and all that. Not every doctor tempted by the riches afforded by two-tier medicine would pull a Chaoulli on a patient at risk. And lots of medicare-loving doctors treat their patients and colleagues abysmally. Everyone has a breaking point, and no one behaves impeccably 100% of the time.

Nothing in the public record suggests that Chaoulli is a sympathetic character. He had his wife put the touch on her Japanese, non–English-speaking father for the $500,000 to fund his court challenges. I wonder if that's starting to smell like week-old sushi. Assuming the membership screening committee has booted him out of the Gandhi and

Douglas club, it is only natural to speculate on the company that shares his values. Elmer Gantry? Jim Bakker? Investment bankers? Gary Hart, the 1988 Democratic presidential aspirant who dared the press to catch him *in flagrante*? They did, and he was done.

Chaoulli has his place in history, thanks to the four Supreme Court justices whose disturbingly flawed decision misread the evidence and failed to discern the real agenda. But now, that history has a footnote that is sure to follow him around the speaking circuit. The Quebec College is investigating the clinic. Chaoulli brought it all on himself. I suspect the right-wing think tanks who fawned over him will find the coroner's report and newspaper coverage in their in-boxes. Will they stand by their man, or discreetly distance themselves from St. Jacques?

CHAPTER FOUR The Reactionarian: Conflict of Interest

Where There's Smoke, There's Pfizer: Sparks Fly Over Recent CIHR Appointment*

Steven Lewis

The Canadian Institutes of Health Research (CIHR) Governing Council (GC) has a new member: Dr. Bernard Prigent, the vice-president of medical affairs for Pfizer Canada. CIHR president Alain Beaudet warmly welcomed Dr. Prigent's appointment as a sign of commitment to the agency's commercialization mandate. When the (Liberal) government created the CIHR to replace the Medical Research Council, it pointed to Canada's indifferent record of translating scientific knowledge and discovery into commercial products that would benefit the Canadian economy. Hence the implicit quid pro quo: government will give CIHR more money but will in turn expect that the grant-generated science will translate into patents, products and sales – the sooner the better.

Who better than a drug company executive to help shape CIHR commercialization policy? Pharma is the poster child of commercialized health. It is multinational capitalism incarnate: mega-firms, blockbuster products, massive revenues, huge marketing campaigns (from 24 to 40% of revenues). With multi-billion research and development (R&D) budgets, drug companies scour the basic science laboratories and journals in search of the next big thing. They partner with scientists and universities, buy up intel-

* Originally published in *Longwoods Essays*, December 2009

lectual property, invest in clinical trials and go through years of testing and regulatory approval; and, if it all works out, boom goes the GDP. If anyone can provide expert counsel on how to ensure that the D follows the R, it's a pharma exec.

The GC certainly thinks so – every last member signed a letter to the House of Commons Standing Committee on Health supporting the appointment to its ranks. But is this marriage made in heaven?

The merit of the appointment rests on the answers to four questions:

1. Is the commercialization mandate potentially in conflict with CIHR's fundamental mandate to support excellence in all the health sciences (including health services research and population health) in service of the public interest?
2. Are there other ways for CIHR to get commercialization advice and guidance than by appointing representatives of commercial corporations to the GC?
3. Is it appropriate and fair to appoint a representative of a particular commercial interest from a particular sector to the GC, given the inevitable exclusion of competitors?
4. Do we know anything about Pfizer that would make it an especially worthy or unworthy corporate presence at the CIHR governing table?

Many public policy and ethics questions are fraught with complexity and highly nuanced. Fortunately, for fans of short essays, these are not. In sequence:

First, of course the commercialization mandate on occasion conflicts with CIHR's fundamental mandate. A great deal of health services and independent clinical research – much of which is supported by CIHR – reveals the unhappy truth that many commercial successes produce little or no health value. Billions of dollars have been made hawking needlessly expensive me-too drugs, duping physicians into mis-prescribing and convincing otherwise-sane people to medicalize and medicate the normal vagaries of the human condition. These commercial successes are public interest failures. Furthermore, one of CIHR's core functions is to create and terminate institutes. How does a Pfizer vice-president remain agnostic about whether the Institute of Health Services and Policy Research should be renewed if it supports research that shows a Pfizer drug is dangerous or identifies the massive public subsidies that flow to drug companies?

Second, is the GC table the only or best place to get commercialization advice? There are innumerable alternatives, all of them cleaner and more transparent. CIHR staff can talk to Dr. Prigent and his peers daily if they want. CIHR can set up a commercialization committee to advocate for the cause within and outside the confines of CIHR. All universities have technology transfer offices whose job is to promote the commercialization of research. There are legions of former or retired executives who have commercialization expertise but no active loyalties to corporate entities.

Third, Dr. Prigent's fundamental allegiance is to Pfizer. Pfizer competes with other drug companies; and pharma competes with other commercial sectors in health. As a member of the GC, he will from time to time have access to information that his competitors do not, and he can exert a steering effect where they cannot. Yes, there are ethical guidelines in place, and honourable people will absent themselves from decisions where conflict of interest is possible, even where there is room for creative interpretation of the rules. If Dr. Prigent's ethics are unimpeachable, he will recuse himself from both discussions and voting a great deal of the time. That's of no benefit either to him or to the GC.

Fourth, over the past decade or so, the seemingly countless systematic transgressions of pharma against scientific integrity and honest marketing have been documented in grisly detail. The industry's greatest innovations have occurred outside the laboratory: expensive junkets for docs-for-hire to shill for their products to their peers; the purchase of previously distinguished academics to affix their names to ghostwritten papers; the suppression of unfriendly clinical trials and adverse effects data; the publication of the same data in different journals to bias systematic reviews and meta-analyses; etc. ad infinitum.

The very first time I heard a presentation by Steven Lewis at a symposium 30 years ago, I was challenged to rethink my positions on the organization, financing and delivery of healthcare services in Canada.

Dennis Kendel

It is hardly irrelevant that the company to which Dr. Prigent owes his livelihood and his allegiance has owned up to sleaze that stands out even among its shady peers (Evans 2009, November 9). Since 2004, it has paid US$2.75 billion in criminal fines and penalties, most recently a whopping US$2.3 billion for fraudulently marketing Bextra (valdecoxib), a painkiller withdrawn from the market in 2005, and three other drugs. Dr. Prigent's signature adorns the confessional letter that alerted Canadian practitioners to the company's malfeasance. Given these facts, one is hard pressed to view the appointment as anything other than a deliberate provocation.

There are excellent reasons to exclude people actively engaged in healthcare commerce from the GC table, to save the institution, and themselves, from the appearance and reality of conflict of interest. Canada would do well to take a lesson from the United States, which is moving in the opposite direction by removing registered lobbyists from advisory boards ("No Place for [Registered) Lobbyists" 2009, December 3). Some will counter that Dr. Prigent is but one of 17 GC members, so what's the harm and where's the risk? A single person can exert influence in many ways, not just by voting. Would you approve of a jury where "only one of 12" jurors has an obvious interest in one outcome over another?

How this plays out is now in the political arena. The House of Commons Standing Committee on Health held hearings to review the appointment on November 30 and December 7. As I write this, over 3,300 people have signed a petition protesting the appointment (http://www.gopetition.com/petition/32371/signatures.html), many of them prominent researchers, ethicists and public policy experts. If you're concerned about commercial interests steering Canada's scientific agenda, sign the petition, write to your MP or write an op-ed for your local newspaper. The government and CIHR want this to go away; their biggest allies are silence and resignation.

References

Evans, D. 2009, November 9. *Pfizer Broke the Law by Promoting Drugs for Unapproved Uses.* Bloomberg. <http://www.bloomberg.com/apps/news?pid=newsarchive&sid=a4yV1nYxCGoA>.

"No Place for (Registered) Lobbyists." 2009, December 3. *The New York Times.* <http://www.nytimes.com/2009/12/04/opinion/04fri4.html?_r=1&th&emc=th>.

Well I Declare: The Emasculation of Conflict-of-Interest*

Steven Lewis

Science and public policy thrive when thoughtful people debate the issues. That Dr. Sharma has entered the debate about the Prigent appointment to the CIHR Governing Council is commendable. He has marshalled a number of arguments in defence of the appointment. I am certain that many scientists (but few ethicists) share his perspective. Let me explain why I do not. Dr. Sharma's case has 6 essential elements:

1. *Scientific inquiry is riddled with ethical transgressions* (e.g., "climategate"), so why hold the CIHR GC to a higher standard? Scoundrels abound, so we might as well resign ourselves to this reality and invite them into the deliberative tent where we can look into their eyes. This view is logically coherent – an endorsement of the race to the bottom in ethical conduct. But the decline has consequences, not least of which is growing public scepticism of all science.
2. *Dr. Sharma dismisses my reference of the "seemingly countless systematic transgressions of pharma against scientific integrity and honest marketing"* as irrelevant to whether a pharma official ought to sit on the GC. It is precisely the frequency and reach of pharma's malfeasance, some of which is criminal, that casts doubt on fitness to serve. Disbarred lawyers or defrocked physicians don't get to make regulatory policy. Members of Hell's Angels do not sit on parole boards even if they have not personally been convicted.
3. *Everyone has an angle on the GC; parochialism and special pleading are inevitable*. Dr. Sharma's proposed remedy is to balance out the interests in the hope that the collectivity will broker a reasonable approximation of the public interest. But there is a

* Originally published in *Longwoods Essays*, December 2009

profound difference between an academic with a particular disciplinary background whose career is devoted to discovery and free intellectual inquiry and a drug company executive accountable to shareholders. The CIHR is mandated to support excellence in basic, clinical, health services, and population health research. It is not mandated to serve pharmaceutical industry shareholders. That some CIHR-supported science may one day serve those ends is an indirect consequence. An interest in an expanded health services research agenda is quite different from a shareholder-driven interest in creating institutes committed to pharmaceutical research or terminating support for institutes that fund research that casts doubt on the value of certain drugs.

4. *If we exclude pharma, we should have no commercial representatives on GC.* Here I agree with Dr. Sharma. CIHR can get commercial advice from hundreds of sources. Parliamentarians and public servants can and do talk to registered lobbyists pursuing their interests but it would be ethically indefensible to put active lobbyists in the Cabinet. There should be no active commercial health sector officials on GC because their fiduciary obligation to private interests conflicts with the GC obligation to the public interest.
5. *Pharma pays taxes, and taxes fund CIHR.* Dr. Sharma speculates that pharma deserves a privileged place at the GC table on the principle of "no taxation without representation". Paying corporate taxes does not buy you a share in a national research granting agency any more than it entitles you to a percentage of seats in Parliament. Pharma taxes are not earmarked for health research any more than yours or mine are. Selling Indulgences went out of fashion with the Reformation.
6. *The declaration of conflict of interest is sufficient to guarantee that it will not occur.* This is, I believe, the heart of the matter: it is an all-too-commonly accepted norm in public life. We no longer seek to avoid conflict of interest; we take the fox's word that he will become a vegetarian when given the keys to the henhouse. No robust understanding of conflict-of-interest legitimizes this view.

It must be said that Dr. Sharma takes his own theory seriously and walks his own talk. He has received funding from eight drug companies, including Dr. Prigent's employer Pfizer – a fact undisclosed in his essay. Dr. Sharma may sincerely believe his long history of drug company funding for research, speaking, consulting, and travel has no influence on his opinion about the suitability of Dr. Prigent's appointment to the CIHR GC. He may think reasonable people will agree that the Sharma-pharma connection does not put him in a conflict-of-interest position as an objective commentator on the suitability of the appointment. Readers can decide for themselves whether this is a case of plausible deniability.

I would simply pose three questions to Dr. Sharma. First, would he have felt moved to write the article defending the appointment if he had never received drug company funding? Second, does he think it's possible that pharma will be more inclined to support his work and fund his talks now that he has come out in favour of the GC appointment? Third, if he felt the appointment violated conflict-of-interest principles, would he have published an essay opposing it?

Neoliberalism, Conflict of Interest, and the Governance of Health Research in Canada*

Steven Lewis

In late 2009, controversy arose over the appointment of Dr. Bernard Prigent, vice-president of medical affairs for Pfizer Canada, to the Governing Council (GC) of the Canadian Institutes of Health Research (CIHR). As of 25 January 2010, 4411 people had signed a petition for the appointment to be rescinded on grounds of conflict of interest. The story attracted considerable national media attention[1] and generated debate between critics and defenders of the appointment.[2-7] The appointment was referred to the Standing Committee on Health of the House of Commons, which convened two hearings to review it.[7] A motion to recommend the withdrawal of the appointment was defeated in a split vote.

Conflict of interest has many definitions applicable in diverse settings but, in essence, a conflict is present when a person is obliged or inclined to pursue interests that compete with one another in fundamental ways. I should not sit on a committee selecting a literary award winner if my best friend is one of the nominees. I cannot simultaneously be a governor of the Toronto Maple Leafs and the Montreal Canadiens. The test is not whether my interest in X invariably conflicts with my interest in Y; it is that there is a reasonable likelihood of the interests colliding in non-trivial ways.

* Originally published in *Open Medicine* 2010, 4(1): 31–9, with the permission of the publisher

Appearance also matters. If certain appointments and proximities raise concerns that science is distorted by commercial interests, or favours some types of inquiry over others, the public and practitioners may cease to pay attention to its findings, be disinclined to volunteer to participate in clinical trials, or resent their tax dollars flowing to public organizations that fund such research. Short of outright scientific misconduct, nothing has so potentially chilling an effect on the expansion of science and its appropriate application than the perception that the enterprise has been bought.

Public institutions present a special case because their overarching duty is to serve the public interest–a notoriously difficult concept to pin down with precision. Importantly, there are those who argue that there is no distinct public interest: there are only particular interests, and it is the balance and interplay among them that defines the common good. This view is represented by the neoliberal "Chicago School" of economics and others who are deeply suspicious of government, regulation, broad democratic agendas, and interference in the free market. This is a radical contemporary reformulation of the historical view that the public interest is more than the sum of exchanges among individual interests. That view is the foundation of a wide range of political theories that span the ideological spectrum from classical conservatism and liberalism to social democracy and communitarianism. The nuances of these opposing positions cannot be addressed here; suffice it to say that the difference is highly relevant to the Prigent case.

Dr. Prigent is a long-time drug company executive who has worked for Pfizer since 1995. He is among the senior officers of Pfizer who are registered as lobbyists with the Office of the Commissioner of Lobbying of Canada, and CIHR is listed as one of the targets of Pfizer's lobbying activities (http://www.ocl-cal.gc.ca). Pfizer's primary obligation as a corporation is to make money for its shareholders, and Dr. Prigent's primary professional obligation is to Pfizer. If the choice is between improving the health of the population and making money, both must choose the latter. For a profit-making corporation, any decline in sales is by definition a failure, even if it is attributable to a product being supplanted, to the consumer's advantage, by a competitor's superior product. Any increase in sales is by definition a success, even if the added consumption makes no contribution to health or even has some deleterious effect. Pfizer has an obvious interest in the flow of CIHR funds to science that may lead to drug development, and an obvious interest in diverting CIHR funds away from science that may reveal the comparative ineffectiveness of one of its drugs or challenge the pharmacological therapeutic paradigm. Situationally, Dr. Prigent is bound by the same interests, and the GC appointment places him in a position to argue for the desired steering effect by virtue of GC's power to create and terminate scientific institutes and mount or eliminate programs.

At the Standing Committee hearings, CIHR president Dr. Alain Beaudet explicitly called for the CIHR and private industry to align their agendas. On this understanding, the interests of pharma are the public interest; commercialization and profit in themselves define the successful translation of science into public benefit. The moral arbiter of commercialization is not a set of ethical principles but the health care marketplace. Dr. Beaudet's defence of the appointment has the virtue of clarity: it obliterates any perceived conflict between the mission of his agency and the commercialization imperative.

Yet the public institution he heads is funded by taxpayers who clearly benefit from science that sometimes threatens drug company profits. Hormone replacement therapy for menopausal women and Vioxx were huge commercial successes but by any reasonable account public interest failures.[8,9] These and many other examples make it clear that pharma's interests at times conflict with the public interest as normally understood. That being the inescapable conclusion, the Prigent appointment is defensible only on the neoliberal understanding of conflict of interest–namely that private interests and the public interest essentially coincide, and where the possibility of conflict of interest exists, the remedy is simply to declare rather than avoid it, and rely on individuals to rise above it.

Only the inhabitants of this neoliberal moral universe could fail to see the real and apparent ethical flaws inherent in appointing an active pharma executive to the CIHR GC. Moreover, pharma is not just any commercial entity; it has a long history of documented assaults on scientific integrity and honest marketing.[10] This misconduct has led journal editors to intensify efforts to identify conflict of interest and avoid publishing biased findings. Having witnessed the impact of systematic inattention to both the appearance and reality of conflict of interest, the Obama administration has removed numerous registered lobbyists from public boards.[11] Harvard University has recently instituted strict new policies that limit medical faculty pay for serving on drug company boards and forbid the acceptance of speaking fees from pharma.[12]

Canada is moving in the opposite direction on the premise that the fox, once seated at the henhouse table, will honour its pledge to become a vegetarian. To claim that the Prigent appointment is essential to fulfilling the agency's commercialization mandate is disingenuous. Nothing prevents the CIHR from seeking advice from commercial interests, both pharmaceutical and other. Most universities have technology transfer officers whose mission is the commercialization of academic discoveries. Governments regularly communicate with registered lobbyists unconflicted by dual loyalties but do not appoint them to the Cabinet. Dr. Prigent is an active Pfizer executive and a registered lobbyist. This alone should disqualify him from appointment to the GC, as it now would in the US.

If the ethics and intellectual justification are flawed, the economics are no better. The appointment has been defended on the grounds that pharma exemplifies commercialization in its best form. Those who promote the alignment of the CIHR and pharmaceutical agendas appear to be bedazzled by half of the financial statements–the assets and revenues–but are blind to the liabilities and expenditures. Yes, pharma invests in research and development, creates scientific and marketing jobs, makes profits, and pays taxes. This is only half the story. The liabilities include a great deal of off-label drug use (recently estimated as 20% of all sales,[13] or over $4 billion in Canada), avoidable adverse drug reactions, and consumption of expensive new drugs that are no better than the cheaper ones they have replaced. The US Food and Drug Administration estimates that only a fifth of all new drugs submitted for approval have the potential to add any therapeutic value.[14] The public subsidizes, as tax-deductible expenses, the very marketing practices that promote highly inefficient consumption. By the government's own calculations, the price of generic drugs in New Zealand is less than a quarter of the price in Canada; drugs still under patent are 20% cheaper.[15]

Commercial interests are indeed served by high prices, expanded use irrespective of therapeutic benefit, longer patents, and a happy head office in (usually) another country. It is equally clear that these commercial successes are public interest failures. Of course there are win-win situations–good drugs at reasonable prices used appropriately–but the potential for conflict is obvious, and actual conflicts are many. The assumption that it is possible to align the scientific agenda with the pharmaceutical agenda without one or both overhauling their mission and values is untenable. The CIHR would do well to heed its own analysis: "Interactions between academia and industry have sometimes raised questions of ethics and integrity, as well as concerns that commercialization opportunities need to be properly evaluated and may not always be for the public good."[16]

On general grounds, then, the Prigent appointment constitutes a clear conflict of interest unless the concept itself is to be abandoned as a serious ethical guide to governance structure and behaviour. The selection of a Pfizer official adds yet another layer of provocation. The government chose to appoint to CIHR's GC the representative of a company that recently paid $2.3 billion in criminal fines and penalties for illegally marketing four drugs–merely the latest in a series of malfeasances dating from 2002.[17] I can find no record of Dr. Prigent having opposed or distanced himself from Pfizer's felonies. The Standing Committee majority dismissed the questions posed by NDP health critic Judy Wasylycia-Leis about whether the company's transgressions were relevant to his fitness to serve.

More discouraging than the Prigent appointment in itself is the refusal of either government or the CIHR to acknowledge that the appointment raises even the possibility of conflict of interest. It is one thing to make and defend a decision; it is quite another to refuse to recognize and substantively engage with the very real ethical issues at its core. The Standing Committee chose, for its second hearing on the appointment, to hear from Dr. Jean Rouleau, Dean of Medicine at the Université de Montréal, a CIHR GC member whose own research has been funded by Pfizer and who has negotiated a Pfizer grant to his faculty. Neither he nor CIHR thought that these relationships created either the appearance or reality of conflict of interest. And herein lies the root of the problem: a notion of conflict of interest so stripped of its meaning that those who violate it are as oblivious to their compromised status as the emperor was unaware of his nakedness. In the end, the most disturbing revelation of l'affaire Prigent is the ethical obtuseness that pervades our political and scientific leadership.

References

[1] Munro M. Scientists protest appointment of Pfizer boss to health panel. *Ottawa Citizen* 2009 Dec 7.

[2] Lewis S. Where there's smoke, there's Pfizer: Sparks fly over recent CIHR appointment. *Essays (online)* 2009 Longwoods Publishing.

[3] Sharma AM. Appointment of Dr. Bernard Prigent to the Canadian Institutes of Health Research (CIHR) Governing Council (GC). *Essays (online)* 2009 Longwoods Publishing.

[4] Baylis F. An intractable conflict of interest. *Essays (online)* 2009 Longwoods Publishing.

[5] Lewis S. Well I declare: the emasculation of conflict-of-interest. *Essays (online)* 2009 Longwoods Publishing.

[6] Cassels A. Pfizer eyes Canada: world's biggest drug maker sets its sights on Canadian healthcare. *Common Ground* 2010

[7] Canada. Parliament. House of Commons Standing Committee on Health. *Evidence of Proceedings, meeting no. 47, November 30, 2009.*

[8] Rossouw JE, Anderson GL, Prentice RL, LaCroix AZ, Kooperberg C, Stefanick ML, et al. Risks and benefits of estrogen plus progestin in healthy postmenopausal women: principal results From the Women's Health Initiative randomized controlled trial. *JAMA* 2002;288(3):321-333.

[9] Ross JS, Madigan D, Hill KP, Egilman DS, Wang Y, Krumholz HM. Pooled analysis of rofecoxib placebo-controlled clinical trial data: lessons for postmarket pharmaceutical safety surveillance. *Arch Intern Med* 2009;169(21):1976-1985.

[10] Angell M. *The truth about the drug companies.* New York: Random House Trade Paperbacks; 2005.

[11] No place for (registered) lobbyists [editorial]. *N Y Times* 2009 Dec 3.

[12] Wilson D. Harvard teaching hospitals cap outside pay. *N Y Times* 2010.

[13] Gillick MR. Controlling off-label medication use. *Ann Intern Med* 2009;150(5):344-347.

[14] United States General Accounting Office. *New drug development: Science, business, regulatory, and intellectual property issues cited as hampering drug development efforts* 2006. Report GAO-07-49.

[15] Patented Medicine Price Review Board. *Non-patented prescription drug prices reporting. Canadian and foreign price trends.* Ottawa: PMPRB; 2006.

[16] Canadian Institutes of Health Research. *CIHR's commercialization and innovation strategy, November 2005.* 2005.

[17] O'Reilly C, Capaccio T. Pfizer agrees to record criminal fine in fraud probe. *Bloomberg News.* 2009.

CHAPTER FOUR The Reactionarian: Drug Pricing in Canada

Ontario Generic Drug Wars, Part 1: How It All Began*

Steven Lewis

In the never-ending World Cup of Generic Drug Prices, four teams recently faced off in Group Rx: pharmacists, retail pharmacies, generic drug manufacturers and the Ontario government. In a stunning turn of events, the government – widely expected to finish its customary fourth – went undefeated through the pool, leaving its competitors and the media slack-jawed. No longer content to be the Maple Leafs of drug policy, the government rebuilt its game, combining excellent leadership, sound tactics, a decisive, quick-strike offence and a stout defence. Against this new-found panache, its opponents' classic game – end runs, theatrical dives and wave after wave of attacks – wilted. Bewildered, they found no room around the perimeter, and their fiercest strikes were easily parried. Exhausted and outcoached, their defence in exposed disarray, they left the field bruised, battered and shorn.

* Originally published in *Longwoods Essays*, September 7, 2010

How did it happen? The cracks in the erstwhile champions' games were evident years ago. The pricing was transparently excessive, and everyone knew it. Giant, stock exchange–listed chains barely recognizable as drugstores had a tough time posing as underdogs persecuted by high-handed government. The manufacturers' cause could have done without the litany of pharmaceutical scandals that had piled up over the years: Suppressed research findings. Ghostwritten scientific papers. Grotesque marketing practices and billion-dollar criminal fines. Heavy-handed lawsuits against honest academics. Never mind the distinction between brand names and generics, originators and copycats, "perps" and stalwart citizens. To the public, it was an undifferentiated ethical swamp, and not even a full-court and strangely inept PR campaign could remove the stink.

Add a fiscal downturn and, poof! Instant public policy tenacity – Viagra for the spine, as it were. And, for once, a clear, decisive, take-no-prisoners government communications strategy. No trembling knees, no heading for the hills. Ontario's generic drug prices have been cut in half. Shoppers will survive, and so will Apotex.

But before we anoint heroes and villains, let's examine how things came to be. Ontario's generic drug policy evolved as follows:

- The province regulates the prices pharmacies can charge for generic drugs within the public sector.
- Generic drug manufacturers compete for shelf space and sales in retail pharmacies. Years ago, some enterprising firms began paying rebates to pharmacies to stock and sell more of their products.
- As rebates became more widespread, the government stepped in, not to eliminate the practice but to institutionalize it. It agreed to call the rebates "professional allowances" and capped them at 20% of the wholesale cost. This became standard practice.
- Rebates are not uncommon in the retail world; the difference is that the policy decreed that the pharmacy pocket the entire amount of the rebate. The de facto lower wholesale price was not supposed to reduce prices paid by consumers.
- Prior to the recent policy change, the total paid approached $800 million a year.

No, you have not misread: that's how it was. The government more or less mandated generic drug manufacturers to subsidize pharmacies to the tune of 800 large per annum, with none of the price reductions passed on to consumers. And generic drug manufacturers contentedly went along. The rationale? The kickbacks (excuse me, professional allowances) were essential to the pharmacies' viability – the same logic that justifies bribing Nigerian customs officials and Mexican cops. That is, the (1) dispensing fees for both generic and brand-name prescriptions paid by Ontario Drug Benefit Plan beneficiaries; (2) higher dispensing fees charged on prescriptions covered by private insurance or paid for out of pocket; (3) markup built into the sale price of both generic and brand-name drugs; (4) profits from over-the-counter drug sales; and (5) profits from the sale of magazines, gum, cameras and perfume in the surrounding aisles were collectively insufficient to generate a decent income for the pharmacist and the store. The solution: with the government's blessing, shake down the manufacturers and pocket the difference. Neither the government nor consumers nor third-party insurers had to pay more, and the pharmacies remained afloat. What could be better than a free lunch?

The prospect of a free lunch should raise olfactory alerts. Not many businesses can eat a 20% revenue hit and thrive, but evidently generic "pharma" could, and did. This can only mean that the government had previously botched the regulation of generic prices entirely, gifting risk-free windfall profits to manufacturers (as the brand-name outfits sniffed all along). But this historical failure presented a comely solution: if the pharmacies are suffering, cut them in on the manufacturers' bounty. Problem solved, equilibrium restored; everyone does all right, but no one is enriched beyond reason.

For this to make sense, one must accept the fundamental claim that retail pharmacies could not and did not earn reasonable returns absent the massive rebates. It should be straightforward to subject this claim to an empirical test. But this is pharma, after all, a sector not wholly defined by common sense, transparent data and reliable arithmetic. It is useful to remind ourselves that retail pharmacy is, among other things, a business lobby, and the first rule of every business lobby is to plead poverty. The Chamber of Commerce will have us believe that if we do not cut corporate tax rates, the Canadian economy will soon resemble Albania's. In the early 1990s, the pharmacy lobby issued dire warnings that banning tobacco sales would force many drugstores to close. Fewer pharmacies closed in the year after the ban took place than in the year before, and the net gain in pharmacies (meaning that many new ones opened) remained the same (Taylor n.d.). It is usually unwise to accept any lobbyist's claims without independent verification and analysis.

Who does better than Steven in pointing out the absurdities, the contradictions, the ironies and the ridiculous quirks of our healthcare system?

Danielle Martin

Next in the series: Did retail pharmacy need big subsidies from generic drug makers?

Reference

Taylor, M.C. n.d. Banning Cigarette Sales in Pharmacies Does Not Result in Pharmacy Closures. Ottawa, ON: Physicians for a Smoke-Free Canada. Retrieved September 3, 2010. <http://www.smoke-free.ca/pdf_1/pharmacy.PDF>.

Ontario Generic Drug Wars, Part 2: Did Retail Pharmacy Need Rebates?*

Steven Lewis

Ontario recently overhauled its generic drug policy. In part 1 of this series, I outlined how the previous policy, a key element of which was a massive, mandated subsidy of retail pharmacies by generic drug manufacturers, came to be. This instalment investigates the validity of the claim that these subsidies were essential to the viability of retail pharmacy.

Pharmacies – even the independents – are corporations, and when you are the owner of an incorporated business (as I am), some creative accounting is at your disposal. Say my company's revenues exceed its expenditures by $100,000 in 2010. If I decide that the company I own should pay me $100,000 in salary for 2010, my company's earnings will be zero and will be reported as such. Conversely, if I defer my personal income and take no salary, my company's earnings will be $100,000 and will be reported as such. In the former case, my company looks like a profitless enterprise; in the latter, it appears to be nicely viable. The important point is that if you don't know both my personal income and my company's income, you don't know anything about the viability of my business.

I could find no data that report both pharmacy (corporate) incomes and the incomes of the shareholders (some of whom are owner-operators). The Statistics Canada pharmacy income survey contains only the (self-reported) business bottom line; and if you're with me so far, you know that's only part of the story. So we are left to deduce by other means whether or not Ontario drugstores were ever at risk of going under en masse

* Originally published in *Longwoods Essays*, September 14, 2010

(as opposed to occasional failures due to market saturation, inept business practices, inhospitable location etc.).

Put most simply, businesses get into trouble because their revenues are too low or their costs are too high (or both). Let's focus on a key cost of doing business: staff salaries. If after doing everything it can to increase sales the retail pharmacy sector still finds itself in a precarious state, the focus must shift to cutting costs. This should create downward pressure on hourly wages. Retail pharmacists' wages should be somewhat higher than those of health professionals with similar levels of education and job complexity if profits are robust and somewhat lower if the sector is struggling.

Retail pharmacists in Ontario make around $50 an hour on average (Ontario Pharmacists' Association 2007), and more if they are franchisers or otherwise share in the profits of the store. Compare this with what similarly educated nursing colleagues earn. The top hourly rate for a staff registered nurse in Ontario is about $42 (O'Malley 2009), and the average is several dollars less. (Nursing managers get a pittance extra.) I think nurses have harder jobs than retail pharmacists. Armed with a computer hooked up to the Web, I think I could fake being a pharmacist and avoid doing damage a lot easier than I could fake being a nurse in a hospital (maybe I could fake being a public health nurse more easily). My strategy would be to do nothing but dispense the medications ordered by doctors and Google the answers to questions posed by customers. If Google failed me (or I failed Google), I would redirect the customers back to their doctors for enlightenment. The pharmacy technician would do the actual counting and labelling. In my limited observation, what I would do is not unlike what a lot of these knowledgeable professionals do most of the time. My conclusion is that retail pharmacists are overpaid relative to registered nurses.

Before you burst a vessel, I'm not saying that all retail pharmacists are just pill-counting automatons whose professionalism is subordinate to the mega-chain non-pharmaceutical uber-mission ("We gotta move these refrigerators; we gotta move these colour TVs"). I'm just saying that if you look at it dispassionately, a retail pharmacist's job complexity, risks and levels of responsibility are less challenging than those of a nurse looking after very sick people in a hospital. If your pharmacy is in a dodgy neighbourhood and your clients are cognitively challenged, it's not stress free. But relatively speaking, it's a pretty sweet gig for $100,000 plus per annum.

Which brings us back to the economics of retail pharmacy and the woe-is-us-without-the-rebates argument. A major reason – perhaps the only reason – pharmacists make more money than nurses is because their pay scales are driven by the retail market. If retail pharmacies had been on the brink of financial unsustainability, there's no way they would have bid up pharmacists' wages. Marginally profitable enterprises pay less, not more – ask the people working in daycare centres, private nursing homes and home healthcare agencies.

All along, many more pharmacies were opening than closing, students were clamouring to get into pharmacy programs and drug sales kept rising. I don't doubt that some non-chain stores in small towns or remote areas had a tough go of it. But to concede that the whole sector would have been unviable without these massive rebates is to concede too much. And it is a virtual certainty that the profit windfalls generated by the escalating rebates drove up pharmacists' wages. For once, trickle-down economics seems to have worked.

So, if the case for rebates of this magnitude seems flimsy, why was there no outcry? There is a certain logic to even the most bizarre developments. Generic "pharma" (like brand-name pharma) incurs high fixed costs and low marginal costs. It costs next to nothing to produce an extra pill, so it makes sense that entrepreneurial companies would offer discounts to expand market share. Who can be surprised that the retail pharmacy sector would portray the wallet-fattening rebates as subsistence payments essential to keeping the lights on? (Otherwise they would have been expected to pass on at least some of the discount to their customers.) Having dropped the ball on price regulation in the first place, the government could play Solomon and decree the redistribution of wealth from manufacturers to pharmacies, secure in the knowledge that the former would grin and bear it and the other would just grin. Yes, it could have allowed dispensing fees to rise, but that would show up at the cash register and many people might be upset. So it was a cozy arrangement that caused no political stir.

The inconvenient truth that scuppered the scheme was that its viability depended on unjustifiable retail prices in the first place. It became impossible to ignore the fact that Ontarians (like other Canadians) were paying much more for generic drugs than people in other Organisation for Economic Co-operation and Development (OECD) countries – even the United States, which usually enshrines profiteering in public policy. A house of cards doesn't stand forever, and generic manufacturers do not have an adoring public fan base. One hopes it is not too optimistic to impute good motives to the government: it recognized a flawed system and moved to fix it. Learning late is better than never learning.

Next in the series: Pharmacy – profession or conduit?

References

O'Malley, B.H. 2009. *Nurse Salary in Canada: Registered Nurse Salaries for Nursing Jobs in Canada.* Author. Retrieved September 6, 2010. <http://www.registered-nurse-canada.com/nurse_salary.html>.

Ontario Pharmacists' Association. 2007. OPA 2006 Wage, Benefit and Workplace Environment Survey. Toronto, ON: Author. Retrieved September 6, 2010. <http://www.opatoday.com/index.php?option=com_content&view=article&id=288%3Aopa-2006-wage-benefit-and-workplace-environment-survey&catid=56%3Alink-pages&Itemid=228>.

Ontario Generic Drug Wars, Part 3: The Soul of the Pharmacy Profession*

Steven Lewis

All members of the [Ontario] College [of Pharmacists] have moral obligations in return for the trust given them by society. They are obliged to act in the best interest of and advocate for the patient, observe the law, uphold the dignity and honour of the profession, and practice in accordance with ethical principles and their respective standards of practice.

– Code of Ethics for Pharmacists in Ontario

What a peculiar profession is retail pharmacy. Drugstores whose main business is drugs have gone the way of the corner hardware. Go into London Drugs and the hardest thing to find is the pharmacy, tucked away at the back, forcing you through the aisles of cosmetics, televisions, cameras and magazines on your way to the potions. There is no more honestly named firm in Canada than Shoppers. A Walmart pharmacist in Ontario fessed up to a local doctor that company policy mandates a 35-minute interval between presenting and filling a prescription to allow ample time to empty the customer's pockets. The pharmacy and the pharmacists are increasingly fronts for these retail juggernauts.

* Originally published in *Longwoods Essays*, September 21, 2010

Prior to the recent policy changes, generic drug manufacturers paid Ontario retail pharmacies an average of $100,000 per pharmacist per year in "professional allowances," more honestly described as *rebates* and less charitably termed *kickbacks*. Government policy formalized the rebate rate at 20% and allowed a further 10% markup in the final undiscounted price. So: The invoice price from the manufacturer was $10. The manufacturer paid the pharmacy $2 as a rebate. The consumer paid $11. Hence the pharmacy made $3, or 37.5% ($3 profit on $8 net cost). A 10% markup to cover the costs of inventory and administration is not unreasonable. But a 37.5% profit aligns the pharmacist's interests squarely with increased sales.

How do you spell "conflict of interest"? You would think that a profession dimly aware of the above-cited preamble to its code of ethics would find this unholy pact to conflict with the duty to serve the public good and uphold the honour and dignity of the profession. Not a peep from the official voices of pharmacy (the professional association and the regulatory body). Too many doctors are inept prescribers, and a fifth of admissions of older adults to hospital result from adverse drug reactions. We need pharmacists to offer their counsel, exercise their judgment and communicate with physicians in service of our health and well-being. Overmedication is the spirit of the times; pharmacists must be prepared to question physicians' decisions and stand on guard for prudence and restraint. Yet we were to believe that pharmacists (and/or their employers) whose income significantly depended on volume-based rebates from manufacturers would be unaffected by these arrangements. Discouraging consumption meant no markup profit, no dispensing fee and a 15-minute explanation; getting out of the way generated markup, a dispensing fee and a few minutes of low-intensity chat.

No doubt many fine pharmacists put professionalism above profit, but the system was designed perfectly to encourage timid acquiescence to doctors' orders. Why would we have expected otherwise? Tying their incomes to sales addicted them to volumes and made them part of the pharmaceutical sales force – just as the manufacturers intended.

There is a difference between being in the health business and being in the drug business. A profession dedicated to health would have publicly opposed the institutionalization of the rebates because they compromise objectivity about the products dispensed. Instead the Canadian Pharmacists Association took Ontario Health Minister Deb Matthews to task for urging other provinces to follow Ontario's lead (*Canadian Pharmacists Association Responds to Health Minister's Letter on the Ontario Drug Reform Proposals* 2010).

Pharmacists have been demanding – and to some extent getting – an expanded role in the delivery of healthcare, notably some power to prescribe and renew prescriptions. But they have "*moral obligations in return for the trust given them by society.*" Is their principal obligation to the store owner/rebate payer/shareholder or to the public? It cannot be both. I am in principle in favour of liberating pharmacists (and nurse practitioners, licensed practical nurses and therapists) to use all of their knowledge and skills, advance their careers and expand their good work. But first I have to be confident that they will put my health above their interests should they be in conflict. A profession that willingly tethered its income to my consumption of drugs gives me little confidence that it will uniformly forsake a sale for my well-being. Some pharmacists will; some won't – and I won't know the difference. That's not good enough.

Hence, the profession has some soul-searching to do. It needs to decide what it is – part of the healthcare-is-a-commodity-and-caveat-emptor oligopoly, or professionals who seek to work in an environment and under incentives that reward them to do the right things well, uncompromised by excessive commercial influence. Pharmacy is by no means alone in this dilemma, but its importance is magnified by being part of the fastest-growing health sector with a well-documented history of ethical missteps. Pharmacists enriched themselves by embracing the rebate scheme. I lack the sophistication to understand how this complicity did not conflict with the profession's code of ethics.

Those with a taste for irony will relish the University of Toronto's promoting the PharmD program as the entry-to-practice credential for all pharmacists. That's rich: the solution to the systematic underuse of pharmacists' baccalaureate education is to stuff them with more education. Absurd as it may seem, they'll probably get their way, like the nurses, occupational therapists and physiotherapists got theirs. If the PharmD curriculum concludes with a year of intensive ethical study, perhaps some good will come of this boondoggle.

Finally in the series: Implications for medicare.

Reference

Canadian Pharmacists Association Responds to Health Minister's Letter on the Ontario Drug Reform Proposals. 2010. Toronto, ON: CNW. Retrieved September 7, 2010. <http://www.newswire.ca/en/releases/archive/May2010/03/c7996.html>.

Ontario Generic Drug Wars, Part 4: Lessons for Medicare*

Steven Lewis

In the first three parts of this series, I recounted the recent history of the generic drug policy in Ontario, explored the economics of retail pharmacy and discussed the ethical implications of the previous policy for the pharmacy profession. In this final instalment, I discuss the wider implications of the Ontario story for the system as a whole.

As an artifact of the timing of medicare's introduction and as a consequence of the *Canada Health Act*, Canadians are conditioned to think of hospitals and doctors as the bedrock of publicly financed healthcare and everything else as optional. As a result, drug policy has been highly variable over time and among jurisdictions. There are multiple payers (government, employers that offer drug benefits, individuals out of pocket), and the policy pendulum has swung back and forth between public and private options. Saskatchewan had a universal, tax-funded program for nearly a decade beginning in the 1970s; patients paid only a modest dispensing fee. Today only low-income people and designated groups with special high-cost drug needs have extensive public coverage. Some provincial drug plans, like Ontario's, cover all of their seniors; most do not.

The disparate policy approaches are united by one empirical experience: costs have risen rapidly under all of them. From this, one might infer that it is impossible to contain drug costs without compromising appropriate and effective drug therapy that improves the lot of patients and, in some cases, helps avoid more costly healthcare use

* Originally published in *Longwoods Essays*, September 28, 2010

(e.g., hospital use). Even if one (correctly) disputes this account, one might alternatively infer that in the end, "pharma" is powerful and clever enough to find a way to increase revenues regardless of attempts to curtail its less admirable practices.

These inferences are plausible but not inevitable. Some countries do much better than we do at controlling costs, notably New Zealand. Ontario knew that it could halve generic drug prices because New Zealand had negotiated rock-bottom prices in a much smaller market. Canadian prices are high partly because Canada covers a much smaller percentage of total prescription costs than almost all Organisation for Economic Co-operation and Development (OECD) countries. This fragments purchasing power and erodes governments' resolve to stand firm.

Even more fundamentally, we are ambivalent about the role of drugs in the overall scheme of healthcare. Obviously many drugs are "medically necessary," but they are not defined as such by the *Canada Health Act*. The law thus implies that they are not-quite-fundamentally-core services, hybrid varietals with free market notes. Incessant advertising piped in from the United States fuels further commodification. Pharma spends a quarter of its revenues on marketing (Gagnon and Lexchin 2008), the goal of which is not enlightenment, but sales. (To be precise, we the people spend these enormous sums for the privilege of having drug companies hawk their wares to doctors and pharmacists, and indirectly to us [direct-to-consumer advertising is illegal in Canada]. The costs fall to us because (1) they are tax deductible expenses for pharma, costing the government 30 cents in lost revenue for every dollar spent; and (2) the net marketing costs are passed on to consumers in the form of higher prices.) How would you feel if your local hospital spent 25% of its budget on advertising? How horrified would you be if it worked, and hospital admissions of questionable value skyrocketed? And if you were seeking advice on which car to buy from a trusted independent professional, would you want him to base his judgments on Consumer Reports or the car companies' glossy brochures?

Canadian drug policy is designed primarily not to ruffle feathers, taking its cue from how the Incas dealt with the conquistador Pizarro: pay tribute and hope for peace. We haven't brought drugs fully into the medicare fold, so pharma has multiple sources of revenue and profits from the plurality of options. We do little to narrow the wide variations in practice. We applaud ourselves for maintaining a research-and-development presence in Canada without calculating what it costs in terms of higher-than-necessary drug prices and contemplating whether Canadian research matters much in the agendas of multi-nationals headquartered overseas. We leave billions of dollars on the table by not instituting reference-based pricing on a wide scale. We let others set the price of so-called breakthrough new drugs (ours is the median price among seven comparator countries). No one fully owns the issues, and the buck never seems to stop anywhere. The Common Drug Review and provincial drug formulary committees do their best to promote evidence and rationality, but there remains a vast gulf between ideal and actual drug use. In this context, Ontario's generic policy skirmish should be viewed as symptom relief rather than a breakthrough intervention. Pharma continues to expand its therapeutic terrain as relentlessly as the Sahara desertifies Africa. It is still far more lucrative for pharmacists and pharmacies to acquiesce rather than challenge a questionable prescription. No one is proposing to cap the tax deductibility of marketing expenses or act forcefully to curtail off-label use. No one is convening a summit to recover the $2 billion or so worth of statins uselessly consumed by Canadians without established heart disease to lower their cholesterol levels (Cassels 2010, July 26). Legislating cheaper generic drug prices without comprehensive strategies to improve prescribing merely creates an incentive to crank up utilization. There are no grand plans for improving stewardship of resources, particularly among physicians.

One lesson is clear: wherever a health service is wholly or partly defined as a market rather than a public good, providers will generate demand, costs will rise, practices will vary greatly and people will be harmed. Depending on financing and policy mechanisms, health services defined as public goods are vulnerable to some of the same risks. However, wholly public sector services are far less prone to chaotic and unceasing expansion; the overhead is lower, and both price and cost containment have historically been more effective. Moreover, the drug sector reveals the perils of assuming that the public interest is inevitably served by solutions brokered among diverse public interests.

But, hey, Ontario's made a start. A tawdry regime of sham prices and mandated rebates has been overthrown. Retail pharmacists are less governed by perverse incentives, and their interests are not so closely aligned with those of the manufacturers. There is new funding for value-added professional activity. Patients will get cheaper drugs. Pharmacists in rural and remote areas will get higher dispensing fees. It's not a revolution, but it is an improvement. And if Ontarians are lucky, it will be just the beginning.

Acknowledgment

I gratefully acknowledge the information and insights supplied by three pharmacy professors who wish to remain anonymous. I alone am responsible for the content and opinions expressed in this series.

References

Cassels, A. 2010, July 26. "Cholesterol Drugs Don't Help the Healthy." *The Vancouver Sun*. Retrieved September 9, 2010. <http://www.vancouversun.com/health/Cholesterol+drugs+help+healthy/3323071/story.html>.

Gagnon, M.-A. and J. Lexchin. 2008. "The Cost of Pushing Pills: A New Estimate of Pharmaceutical Promotion Expenditures in the United States." *PLoS Med* 5(1): e1. doi:10.1371/journal.pmed.0050001. Retrieved September 9, 2010. <http://www.plosmedicine.org/article/info:doi/10.1371/journal.pmed.0050001>.

CHAPTER FOUR The Reactionarian: Making the News

Federal Election 2008: Interview (Mock)*

Longwoods roving contributor and democracy revivalist Steven Lewis caught up with the five party leaders in their post-televised debate debrief at an undisclosed location near Toronto, Ontario.

Steven Lewis: As usual, healthcare is front and centre in this election. [*Leaders look at each other quizzically and leaf furiously through their briefing books.*] Medicare is in crisis. The system hangs in the balance. What will you do as prime minister to strengthen this icon of Canadian identity?

Gilles Duceppe: I'm not interested in being prime minister, and healthcare is provincial jurisdiction. Next question.

Jack Layton: More doctors, more nurses, catastrophic drug coverage –

Stéphane Dion: More than more doctors and way, way more nurses than the NDP, and definitely more catastrophic drug coverage –

Elizabeth May: So, you've finally got the Green message.

Layton and Dion: What do you mean?

* Originally published in *Longwoods Essays*, October 14, 2008

May: Your platforms are all recycled. I salute you.

Stephen Harper: Let me be prime ministerial here. The Liberals almost killed medicare by shovelling money at the problems with no success. We've invested wisely and got results. Especially more doctors and nurses.

Dion: But you're just continuing to do what we started in the health accords.

Harper: That's in the past. We've shown the kind of leadership the provinces want.

Duceppe: I agree with that. Write the cheques and get out of the way.

Harper: Exactly. But when we write the cheques with no conditions, the provinces deliver because we clearly respect the constitution. That's the genius of the Conservative approach.

Lewis: How many more doctors do we need? Medical school enrolment has practically doubled in the past five years –

Layton: What the hell?

May: I'm just new here. How could I have known that?

Harper: No way. They're nowhere to be seen. My own doctor is retiring.

Dion: Where's my briefing book?

Lewis: It's a fact, almost double. They'll be graduating soon.

Layton: [*recovering quickly*] Not enough. Should be quadruple.

Dion: Quintuple!

May: Gentlemen, harness yourselves. It's the wrong focus. We need to reduce smoking through education and taxes.

Harper: Let me again show the wisdom of prime ministership. If you raise taxes, people get anxious. Anxious people smoke. It's the only pleasure they have left once you've taken away their jobs in the oil patch. The Green Party may want young people to start smoking. We don't. In fact, we want to put young offenders in jail.

Duceppe: It's not the federal government's business. Smoking is under section 92 of the *Constitution Act*.

Layton: The New Democrats have always respected Quebecers' right to smoke without interference from Ottawa.

Harper: Our record speaks for itself. We're the ones who relieved the provinces of the intolerable burden of reporting to Canadians on how they spent the billions of new federal funding and what they accomplished. We got rid of the nanny state and overbearing federalism that threatens the very fabric of Canada. When Canadians pay their taxes to Ottawa, they want the money to go back to their own provinces with no meddling. Except they have said, very clearly, that they don't want it spent on safe-injection sites.

Dion: Mr. Harper, you didn't get rid of the nanny state, you got rid of the nanny. No child care, no support for families.

Layton: [*aside to May*] Did Dion actually get off a good one?

Dion: And also Mr. Harper, we started writing cheques with no accountability, and you stole our policy and claimed it as your own. I wish I could say I was surprised –

Duceppe: We have nothing to fear but fear itself.

Harper: That's another one of my lines, Gilles. Politicians shouldn't plagiarize –

May: Is it always like this when you guys get together? I feel like drinking the hemlock.

Harper: [*indignant*] If I were your husband, I'd take it!

Lewis: Please, let's get back to healthcare. What will you do to close the technology gap?

Dion: My government will put an MRI in every hospital in Canada with more than eight beds.

Harper: Our plan goes way beyond the Liberal broken promises. We'll put a CT scanner in every 7-11.

Layton: There you go again. Private care for the rich –

Harper: The scans would be paid for publicly.

Layton: Yes, but as a private, for-profit facility, the 7-11 will try to sell Canadians extras they don't need, like Pepsi and shrink-wrapped porn.

Duceppe: Ottawa has no place in the depanneurs of Quebec.

Layton: So our plan is to open state-run convenience stores with CT scanners, ultrasound machines, generic drugs, sigmoidoscopies, all publicly funded.

Dion: [*aside*] Mon Dieu, that's good. Why didn't my dream team think of that? Saboteurs ...

May: Our plan is to build green roofs on every hospital. Solar panels will power the MRIs.

Lewis: Let's turn to catastrophic drug coverage. Romanow called for it. The provinces were all for it, with leadership from Ottawa. Canadians need it. Where is it?

Dion: We're committed to it. It's in our platform.

Lewis: But the Liberal government could have done it years ago. It could have made it a condition of the accord and earmarked money for it.

Layton: Shame! Broken promises! Liberals, Tories, all the same, all the time.

Duceppe: Stéphane, I agree with you. All the Liberal healthcare policies are catastrophic.

Harper: Good one, Gilles.

Duceppe: You can use that in your speeches. Not that you need *permission* ...

May: Time to move on, gentlemen. It's the environment, stupid. Clean it up, ban GMOs, put away the car, get Canadians moving and everyone's healthier. More health, less healthcare.

Layton: [*aghast*] Elizabeth, where's the leadership in that? If everyone's healthier, what will all those new doctors and nurses do? You're out to take away their livelihood. Just like I've always said, scratch a Green and there's dark Tory blue underneath. It's a neo-Con job.

May: Jack, with respect, you need an exorcist. Your head spins faster than Linda Blair's.

Dion: We have the plan for the future. We're going to tax the doctors and nurses and administrators for providing excessive healthcare. They will charge the patients more money. We will give patients a tax cut to pay for the healthcare. So everyone will pay more and everyone will use less. Less for more – that's the Liberal healthcare solution. Just like the carbon tax.

Lewis: Prime Minister, what do you think?

Harper: I'd like to hear more from Stéphane. Keep going.

Layton: [*barely able to contain himself*] Did you say you're going to charge people for medically necessary services?

Dion: My proposal is revenue neutral.

Duceppe: My Quebec includes the *Canada Health Act*. Did I really say that?

Layton: Our position is, we should never have gone in, and we should get out now.

Harper: We will be out by 2011, that's a guarantee.

May: What's this got to do with Afghanistan?

Harper: Elizabeth, we're talking about healthcare. I guess you're too new to understand.

Dion: Let me remind you, the Liberals were always for getting out of healthcare. Mr. Chrétien started it, by cutting transfer payments. Mr. Martin finished the job, adding tens of billions of dollars with nothing expected in return. That's 21st century leadership.

Duceppe: I find myself agreeing with the three of you who won't be prime minister and the one who will. With federalists like you, who needs to separate? Did I really say that?

Lewis: So, let's wrap this up. What's your key healthcare message for Canadians, and how is your healthcare platform different?

May: We're going to strengthen publicly financed healthcare, write cheques and invest in upstream healthcare.

Lewis: So you'd do what every healthcare report has advocated for 20 years.

May: Yes. Like I said, recycling is good. Not as good as cycling, but still good.

Layton: We're going to rescue publicly financed healthcare from the hidden privatization agenda of the Liberals and Tories, write cheques and make Bay Street pay for more doctors and nurses.

Lewis: So, what is that hidden agenda?

Layton: Don't be obtuse. It's hidden, so how would I know? But it's very, very bad for kitchen tables.

Duceppe: We're going to hold the government accountable for writing big cheques with no conditions, so Quebec can accept the cheques, deny the federal government has contributed anything and participate when we feel like it in pan-Canadian initiatives.

Lewis: How is that different from what every other province does?

Duceppe: We are a nation, obviously.

Dion: We're going to restore Ottawa's role in national healthcare –

Duceppe: You mean pan-Canadian. You can't say national.

Dion: I can so say national. National. National. National, national, national.

Harper: We are committed to further increases in transfers with no conditions and allowing the provinces to experiment, innovate and improve.

Lewis: With the economy heading south, where will you get the money?

Harper: Some will come from the tar sands, and the rest from cutting the fat out of cultural spending. You can read all about it in our platform.

ALL: What platform?

Lewis: Thanks to you all. It's a great day for democracy.

The Scary Headlines We Don't See*

Steven Lewis

Recycling isn't always a good thing. News of syringe reuse in Alberta and Saskatchewan health regions provoked the predictable avalanche of concern, outrage, fear and puzzlement. How could it happen? Who's at risk? What's the root cause: penny-pinching? incompetence? negligence?

Naturally, the media are all over it – at least several hundred stories and tens of thousands of Google-generated web results. Thousands of patients fear they may be the unlucky victims of the latest endoscopy and anesthetic misadventures.

Ya gotta wonder. Some things in healthcare are complicated, but some are simple. Wash your hands. Give the heart attack patient an aspirin. Chuck the syringe. How is it that the system does dramatically complex stuff well and screws up simple stuff routinely? Good people quit thinking – it happens to me, it happens to nurses. It's the night watchman's challenge: how do you stay sharp for the ten thousandth iteration of a common and low-risk task? It's not impossible: Six Sigma for aviation; Sick Sigma for healthcare. There's a lot to be pissed about in healthcare – just read Baker and Norton on safety, McGlynn and Katz on the staggering failures of primary care, Sinclair on the Winnipeg

* Originally published in *Healthcare Quarterly* 2009, 12(1): 8-9

baby deaths, pathological pathology in Ontario ... The media spotlight shines on the farces and cover-ups, retells heart-tugging victims' tales and psycho-biographies of perpetrators felled by bad judgment, hubris or both. Scandal! Hearts of Darkness!

Meanwhile, the quality improvement and patient safety mavens ruefully observe yet another absurdity and gamely stick to the script du decade: people are good, systems are faulty; put away the lash and enrol people in collaboratives; re-engineer, don't recriminate. Politicians and administrators face a parallel reality: how does chalking it up to "system error" satisfy the deeply ingrained yearning to make the bastards pay? Quality Improvement, meet the Vengeance Posse. Enjoy your conversation.

So, how should the media report on the syringe reuse debacle? The problem is not so much what the media have said about it – the reporting has been reasonably balanced, noting the very low risk of serious harm and pressing (unsuccessfully) for statements from experts on the odds of being unlucky. The unmet challenge is to interpret the issue in context. How risky is syringe reuse compared with filling your prescription or walking into an emergency room? Should people be more worried about high-profile misdeeds or the risks inherent in substandard everyday care?

Here are some candidates for full monty media coverage – practices that without question harm more people than reused syringes, inconvenience the public and patients, drive up costs or create gaps in the system.

Health Region Knows Handwritten Prescriptions Put Patients at Risk but Allows the Practice Anyway

Despite overwhelming evidence that handwritten prescriptions harm and even kill patients, the local health region has not taken steps to halt this practice in its facilities. Nor has the province required system-wide electronic prescribing and the use of software to alert doctors and pharmacists to contraindicated drug combinations. The thousands of seniors on six or more medications should be extremely worried since they have a 94% chance of suffering an adverse drug reaction.

Doctors Don't Have to Adopt Electronic Health Records If They Don't Feel Like It

Electronic health records are used by fewer physicians in Canada than in any other G7 country, and that seems to be fine with the governments who pay them on our behalf. Many patients have complex conditions treated by several providers, and everyone faces the risk of getting sick away from home and visiting an emergency room in another town. There's almost no chance that their complete health record will be available instantly to the specialist or the emergency team. Customers of banks without ATMs and who enter deposits and withdrawals manually in passbooks and wide ledgers will be familiar with Canadian healthcare practices.

Many Patients Not Allowed to Tell Doctor What's Ailing Them in Single Visit

Patients who inconveniently have several symptoms and health complaints should not bother their doctors with more than one per visit. Many physicians impose the one-complaint-per-visit rule on their patients. Even though some regulatory bodies frown on the practice, it remains widespread. The policy is in response to a fee schedule that discourages doctors from spending time with patients who have complex health issues.

Higher Credentials Result in Less Training for Some Healthcare Workers

Think that newly minted graduate with a master's degree in physiotherapy (PT) has more training than the baccalaureate graduate of old? Think again. PT is just one of several professions that have ramped up their entry-to-practice credential requirements. But it's not a master's degree on top of an undergraduate PT degree; it's on top of any degree. The result? Now it takes six years to turn out a physiotherapist with two years of discipline-specific training, instead of four years to produce one with four years of discipline-specific training.

Of course, the media *should* jump on the syringe reuse story – it is newsworthy, it should not happen, it is a (small) threat to public safety. But it's also important to tally up the harms throughout the system. In Canadian healthcare, more people die every day from avoidable errors than the combined toll from the most high-profile and egregious misdeeds. Canadians should worry more about the general standard of practice than about the prospect of falling victim to brazen or malicious incompetence. And the media could provide a great service by shedding bright and constant light on these routine, persistent and costly failures.

The Conference Board: Rank Amateurs with an Agenda?*

Steven Lewis

The Conference Board of Canada[1] has published in a news release a summary that ranks Canada's health (or is it healthcare? or is it both?) as ninth best out of 16 selected rich countries (the least rich is Italy, where the food, wine and climate are so good that it is hard to imagine why anyone so blissfully located would even notice a little less purchasing power). We get a B. The aforementioned Italy, along with Japan, France, Sweden and Switzerland, gets an A. In a shocking upset, the Americans beat somebody – in this case, get this, *Denmark*. According to a recent UK survey reported on *60 Minutes*, far from being melancholy, the Danes are the happiest people on earth, even though their life expectancy trails ours by three years and Japan's by four and a half. Maybe they're too happy to notice. Maybe they have other priorities, like universally free post-secondary education.

As for the A-list, there are two Axis Powers (Italy and Japan), and two – Switzerland and Sweden – that stayed out of World War II (well, three if you count France). All five countries are rather social democratic, but so is Denmark. By contrast, joining Denmark on the D-list are Ireland, the United Kingdom and the United States. We get a B, but grudg-

* Originally published in *Longwoods Essays*, June 2008

ingly, and the Board notes ominously that we are in danger of tumbling to a dreaded C. Teasingly, the Conference Board released its ranking but not a full-scale report that, one hopes, will, at its promised release in September, reveal the methods, assumptions and data on which it is based. In polite company this would be termed peculiar; in academic circles, irresponsible and even contemptible; in most of the media (Longwoods, of course, excepted), as a gift headline story requiring no further work. Based on essentially no information, can we make sense of the board ratings and rankings?

Tellingly, there are confusions. The lead sentence in the summary is, "Given increasing rates of diabetes and heart disease [this latter is false by the way], Canada has no choice but to adopt a new business model for health care that focuses on both preventing and managing chronic disease." From that, a sentient reader would infer that the board is rating and ranking our healthcare system. But half-way down, the summary states, "It is important to keep in mind that this grade assesses *the overall health status of Canada's population*; it is not intended to rank the health-care system" (italics mine). So what's with the new business model for healthcare if healthcare isn't being evaluated?

If it's health we're examining, let's look at health. Of the 16 chosen countries, Canada ranks second on life expectancy and 11th on infant mortality – the most commonly used composite measures of health. The board is alarmed by our relatively high heart disease and escalating diabetes-related mortality rates. OK, but logically, if we're living longer than everyone but the Japanese and if our tickers and pancreases are letting us down, our other organs must be thriving. We have to die of something (perhaps confusion is a leading cause of death at the board). Why weight some causes over others? There might be a defensible reason, but let us in on it before assigning a number.

Let's compare Italy (A) with Denmark (D). Italy is seventh on life expectancy and 15th on infant mortality. Denmark is 15th and eighth, respectively. So if we're rating health, not healthcare, why are these countries at the opposite ends of the scale? The answer, I suspect, is that the board is conflating elements of both health and healthcare in its method, and come September we might discover precisely how.

The confusion compounds when we look at the Conference Board's prescriptions for success. The board correctly points out that the top-performing countries have progressed by addressing the non-medical determinants of health, among them listing environmental stewardship, health promotion, education, early childhood development, income and social status. By its own assessment then, social democracy seems to be the pathway to population health, but the board pointedly refuses to go there. The solutions are "a new business model for health care," "greater receptivity to innovative technologies and health-care delivery systems," "better information technology" and "new approaches to prevention and management."

I'm a pretty harsh critic of our healthcare system and advocate a major overhaul. Like the board, I'm all for investing in health information systems, managing chronic diseases better and improving accountability. But like anyone familiar with a vast population health literature and a basic understanding of the law of diminishing returns from healthcare, I know that these measures will not reduce health disparities or greatly improve overall health status. The board summary is silent on the one element of healthcare that might make a difference: primary healthcare reform. Instead, it offers up the standard industry tonics of more and fancier gadgets and coded calls for privatization.

Might the Conference Board have an agenda other than improving the health of Canadians? When think tanks promote new business models for health and innovative delivery systems as solutions to problems that, on their own analysis, originate elsewhere, look for the method in the apparent madness. It's usually a call to feed the beast – the diagnostic imaging and drug manufacturers, the private sector management contractors, the advocates of private and parallel healthcare systems. It's perfectly legitimate to tout these reforms, but at least do it forthrightly and explain why Canada should choose this route rather than the broader health-enhancement strategies pursued successfully by others.

I'm new to the rating and ranking game; but in the spirit of the board, I'll give it a go:

Transparency of method	F
Plausibility of ratings and rankings	D
Awareness of factors affecting health	A
Internal coherence	F
Likelihood of prescriptions improving health	F

I'm glad to have the Conference Board in the population health choir, but sad to see its accurate understanding of why some countries are healthier than others dissolve into shilling for industry and solutions destined to raise costs, misallocate resources and miss real opportunities to make a difference.

Note

[1] To read a response to Steven Lewis from the Conference Board, please visit: http://www.longwoods.com/content/19952.

My Evening with the Future*

Steven Lewis

Throw away the crystal ball, and spend an hour with Google Health: the future will be right in front of you. Providers who prefer the pedestal to parity and see themselves as traffic cops on the health information highway are in for the shock of their life.

I intended to compare the online personal health records of both Google and Microsoft, but I couldn't convince Microsoft that I was Phyllis Diller from Scottsdale, Arizona (you have to be a US resident to sign up). Google let me in, and in a few minutes I had my own record. Well, not quite my own. (Health record privacy purists, skip the next paragraph.)

Touch wood, I'm a healthy guy. I don't have any chronic conditions (unless you count seasonal hay fever, a cat allergy and a severe reaction to sopranos), have never had surgery, take no prescription drugs and, having read too much quality and outcomes research, am a bit of a fatalist. There will be no colorectal cancer screening bazooka shoved up my behind unless I get to watch a video of my doctor smiling happily through the procedure. With so little data to enter, I made stuff up – gave myself type 2 diabetes, angina and arthritis and added 10 kilograms – to test the ingenuity of the architecture.

* Originally published in *Longwoods Essays*, April 28, 2009

Hello Frank Gehry. The software leads you through a consumer's garden of neurotic delights – and I mean that in a good sense. You can input your own remarks and notes, set permissions for access, amend or delete entries. You can second-guess the diagnosis or advice you got from your doctor in the seven minutes he spent with you. You can get drug price and therapeutic equivalence comparisons – your own reference-based pricing program is at your fingertips. You can catch contraindicated drug combinations. You can learn your odds of falling prey to various health breakdowns by linking your profile to web-based risk calculators. You are handed the key to a cornucopia of safe information injection sites tailored to your profile.

But, dammit, this is America; and in America nothing good happens unless money changes hands. Some of the featured partner sites offer free advice, but they'll also sell you drugs or other products. Others are more brazenly mercenary: at the Cleveland Clinic site, it's cash for counsel. Want a second medical opinion from MyConsult? That'll be US$565, and it's not insured. The website supplies a sample report so that you can see what you're likely to get: mainly a summary of what you send in and a three-paragraph opinion. I figure a good senior resident could knock one off in half an hour, an hour tops. Bargain hunters can score a nutritional consultation about their gout (honest) for a mere US$95, or two sessions on high blood pressure for US$165.

Perhaps you're more inclined to Blueprint for Wellness, which offers a package of 29 laboratory tests, a wellness questionnaire and a personal wellness report for US$134. TrialX.org will match your condition to a database of 25,000 clinical trials and help you find clinical investigators expert in your condition – all free. It's essentially a dating service for researchers and a potentially vast pool of trial recruits.

To those of us of a certain age for whom a long distance call was a special and costly luxury, this is all a bit disorienting, even creepy. Google has an incentive to choose its partners carefully: it doesn't want to jeopardize its carefully cultivated we're-not-like-the-other-megacorps image. No filter is foolproof, and no interaction is risk free. Nonetheless, the methodologically innocent are far better off with Google as the quality control overseer than heading off solo into a cyberspace full of charlatans.

Still, there are reasons to pause and reflect. Will the model undermine the doctor–patient relationship? Will it fuel an even greater obsession with tests and assessments, luring millions more to the already-vast army of the worried well? What happens if providers act on inaccurate or misleading patient-created information? What jurisprudence will arise from the inevitable litigation when something goes wrong?

Yeah, whatever. Quibble all you want; it's here, it's growing, there will be no pausing and precious little reflecting. It's a predictable workaround, an evening up of the odds against Fortress Healthcare that keeps patients in the dark and puts a firewall between them and their health record. Some enlightened healthcare organizations, such as Group Health Cooperative in Seattle, Washington, put patients at the centre of their e-health strategies. How strangely foreign to the Canadian Way.

Canada's e-health leaders can either ignore it or embrace it. Ignoring it risks dooming the provider-oriented, paternalistic plans to rapid obsolescence. They should take what's good about it – joint production and ownership of health information, the potential to create networks of trustworthy information sites, the linkage to self-management tools tailored to individual profiles, the fantastic communications capacity – and revamp their e-health plans, fast.

You hold us to account, you challenge us, and you help move us forward.

Glenda Yeates

The democratization of knowledge and the desire to be treated like an adult in health-care transactions are irresistible forces. It's a near miracle that Canadians for the most part continue to put up with the arrogance, inconvenience, secrecy and error built into the existing system. We could have seen this coming a decade ago, but we are too often a nation of deer in a world of headlights. Google and Microsoft have set off the alarm. Pushing the sleep button won't cut it much longer.

This Just In: Systems Designed to Fail, Fail*

Steven Lewis

First, there is the disaster that comes to light long after the fact. Then there is the inquiry. Then there is the scathing report that meticulously unearths the causes of the disaster. Then there is the apology (they're allowed now – it's the law!). Then there is restitution. Finally, there is the commitment: never again. And then the same thing happens, somewhere else, again, and again, and again. Canadian medicine – it is quite different in some other jurisdictions – is organized around four fundamental premises. First, doctors are highly trained professionals whose license to practice needs no expiry or renewal date. Second, initial certification examinations are reliable guarantors of lifelong competence and consistent, high-quality practice. Third, it is both unnecessary and unsporting to subject the autonomous judgments of professionals to rigorous and regular scrutiny. Fourth, professional self-regulation is the ideal mechanism for preventing harm.

To quality improvement and harm reduction experts in every other industry, these premises are not merely dubious, but laughable. Yet they persist in medicine, and the inevitable result is that people get hurt. Radiology and pathology are high-stakes diagnostic professions where errors can kill. When massive failures occur, as in the Newfoundland

* Originally published in *Longwoods Essays*, June 9, 2009

and Labrador breast cancer testing debacle of 1997–2005 (!) or the Charles Smith forensic pathology fiasco of 1981–2005 in Ontario (!), the root causes turn out to be depressingly pedestrian. That's what makes them as pathetic as they are tragic.

Even more damning is the repetition. The lid has just come off Quebec's breast cancer diagnostic breakdown. Saskatchewan is cleaning up after a pathologist who may have put thousands of people at risk during five years. It will cost millions of dollars to have every one of his 70,000 images reread out of province, and perhaps tens of millions to settle the malpractice claims. (The notorious Regina lawyer Tony Merchant has already launched a class action suit.) The only difference between these jurisdictions and those so far untouched by the contagion is that the time bombs are on different schedules.

Despite the repeated revelations of system errors that demand system solutions, nothing has fundamentally changed to guarantee safer healthcare and to prevent the birth of gestating misadventures. When push comes to shove, the right to practice shoddy medicine trumps public safety; no one gets to cancel the flight or shut down the assembly line without definitive proof of repeated incompetence. A health region or regulatory body that moves aggressively to suspend a practitioner pending investigation of suspicious results is harassed and condemned for violating due process. The first reflex is not to acknowledge the problem or seek mentorship; it is to lawyer up. The medical association goes to bat to keep the practitioner in the saddle. Physicians and others in the know who would not send their own kids to an incompetent colleague either can't or won't stop yours from ending up in his care.

It's not just a conspiracy between the guilds and the law; it's a systematic failure to manage risk. Built-in redundancy, rigorous peer review, structured continuing education and mandatory re-certification are cornerstones of safety. The higher the stakes, the greater the need for vigilance and tightly organized quality control systems. Geographically isolated professionals are obviously at risk, and many will fail without carefully designed, reliable supports in place. But everyone needs audit, feedback and peer support to perform reliably over time. In medicine, it is well-documented that performance declines with age. The response to this chilling reality has been to let the chips fall where they may – the pathology of denial.

The Saskatchewan case is especially instructive. There were suspicions about the radiologist's competence three years ago. With the regulatory noose tightening around his neck, he volunteered to go for remedial education. No educational program in western Canada stepped up to the plate. After he spent three months at McMaster, the Saskatchewan College received a perfunctory and brief report on his progress and skills that it rejected as inadequate. He returned to practice and, on the evidence to date, his interpretation of every 20th image may have put someone at risk.

The system is designed to fail, and it must be redesigned to succeed. The solution is not to expect physicians to look furtively over their colleagues' shoulders and snitch to the authorities. The remedies must be systemic, obligatory and woven into the fabric of medical education, ethics and organization. Among the obvious requirements are the following:

- Mandatory review of randomly drawn samples of diagnostic interpretations; the frequency and intensity of the scrutiny should be commensurate with the complexity of the practice, known error rates and the consequences of mistakes
- A formal, standardized protocol for addressing competency problems; the first signs of problems should trigger mandatory supervision and intensified case reviews until performance is demonstrably up to snuff
- Beyond certain thresholds of error, automatic suspension followed by the launch of a remediation algorithm
- Specific additional support, review and continuing competency assurance procedures for isolated practitioners
- Transparent reporting to the public of performance results

It is delusional to believe that everything is now out in the open, with nothing more to uncover. It's not just the outliers who cause harm; because medicine is so fraught with unjustifiable variations in practice, it is certain that the errors resulting from "satisfactory" practice far outnumber the misdeeds of the visibly incompetent. The graveyards are filled with anonymous victims whose stories will never surface in a public inquiry. Until professionals take their collective obligations seriously and embrace a culture of safety, prevention will fail, detection will be late and the victims will pile up. If they view peer review, recertification and remediation as violations of sacred entitlements, sleepwalking through mandated processes won't accomplish much.

Sad to say, for radiology and pathology our salvation may come from machines. It is foreseeable that computerized pattern recognition software will be able to diagnose more accurately and consistently than specialists in all but the most unusual of cases. If that day comes, we can be sure that these highly reliable machines will be programmed to self-diagnose and identify anomalies in their own findings and performance at regular intervals, and will be examined, refurbished and re-tested according to strict protocols. In other words, we will treat them and their needs with care and respect, governed by the duty to put patients first. Too bad we don't do the same for fallible diagnosticians and their victims.

A Texas-Sized Spread in Canada or an Exposé on Healthcare Spending in a Poor US County*

Steven Lewis

Atul Gawande is a Harvard-based surgeon and staff writer for *The New Yorker.* He's made big news with an exposé on healthcare spending in a poor county on the US-Mexican border (Gawande 2009). McAllen, Texas, is the poorest county in the United States, with a per capita income of US$12,000. Yet its Medicare – the government program that pays most of the health bills for Americans 65 years and over – costs US$15,000 per senior per year, exceeded nationally only the cost of Medicare in Miami. McAllen has high rates of obesity and other dodgy health indicators. But out in the west Texas town of El Paso, 1,300 kilometres up the Rio Grande, the demographics and health status are similar but Medicare costs are half. Gawande pulls no punches: the higher costs are due to physicians and for-profit clinics exploiting every conceivable opportunity to maximize their incomes. He demolishes the claim that McAllen's cost and utilization patterns can be explained by "defensive medicine" (fear of malpractice) or superior care. Texas has capped malpractice awards at US$250,000, and the doctors in McAllen acknowledge that lawsuits and premiums are way down. Of 25 quality indicators, El Paso beats McAllen on 23.

As Gawande points out, clusters of doctors think and behave differently, producing major variations in practice patterns and costs. Just as greed has turned McAllen medicine into a testing-and-patient-recall factory, Grand Junction, Colorado, and the Mayo

* Originally published in *Longwoods Essays,* June 16, 2009

Clinic in Minnesota have created a culture of quality and restraint that produces first-class results for much less money.

But that's the United States, and we like to believe that the sins of American healthcare stop at the 49th parallel. At the level of provinces or regions, that's probably true: governments allocate healthcare budgets, and the politics of distribution tend to pre-empt two- or threefold variation in total spending between Calgarians and Winnipeggers. The smugness should end there. Our McAllens come in smaller packages. We just need stronger lenses to see them.

Canadian researchers have long documented variations in the use of individual services, such as Caesarean sections and hip replacements. Three decades ago, my home town of Moose Jaw, Saskatchewan, was observed to experience eight times the hysterectomy rate of Regina, 45 minutes down the road. (There were rumours that the local gynecologists were about to start rounding up men.) Practice atlases have reported three- and fourfold variations in surgical rates among Ontario counties. But even these provocative data may obscure even larger variations attributable to individual physicians or practice groups. If a county's propensity to invade your prostate is three times the provincial average, it is possible – even probable – that an individual urologist is 10 times more likely to intervene.

To find our little corners of Texas, we have to analyze overall healthcare use and spending among thousands or tens of thousands of people, not the hundreds of thousands or millions typical of US analysis. US Medicare doesn't allocate funds on population-based formulas or seriously attempt to even out per capita spending. Governments in Canada do more than just process bills; they allocate funding, more or less on an age- and sex-adjusted population basis in most regionalized provinces and by organization elsewhere. Interprovincial variations in total spending are relatively small; and at the level of decent-sized cities, it is highly unlikely that there are Texas-sized gulfs.

Drill down another level or two and the real story emerges. Physicians, especially specialists, tend to cluster in large cities. There are gentrified enclaves of urban Canada that get their primary care from pediatricians, obstetricians and internists. Some general practitioners (GPs) have triple the referral rates to specialists than others. Walk in one clinic with heartburn, and you'll start with Tums; walk in another, and you'll be slated for an endoscopy. Some doctors do annual Papanicolaou (Pap) tests on low-risk women, while others follow the three-year guideline. Some tell sedentary and overweight patients to eat better and exercise; others order periodic stress tests, prescribe a statin and call in a cardiologist.

Many policy makers, managers and practitioners agree that there is a lot of waste in healthcare. The problem is knowing exactly where and why it occurs. If we want to trim the fat from healthcare spending, we have to learn exactly where the avoidable spending takes place. It's not all physician driven, but doctors are the gatekeepers to a huge swath of healthcare spending, and the cascade of costs that originates in the GP office accelerates through laboratories, diagnostic imaging centres, pharmacies, specialists' offices and hospitals.

A well-known concept in health economics is supply-induced demand. Patients tend to trust their doctors, submit to batteries of tests and reappear when summoned to a follow-up appointment. Parts of large urban centres with high concentrations of specialists and abundant technology are potentially mini-McAllens. But so are parts of small-town Canada, where a GP with a local monopoly and few peers in the vicinity can indulge in wildly skewed practices.

> **His contributions to the Canadian healthcare scene are many:**
> ... an early supporter of regional health authorities being the logical unit for delivering integrated care
> ... an early supporter of quality as a core business strategy...
> ... an early supporter of the primacy of primary care as a building block for the whole system
> ... an early supporter of taking a population health focus
>
> *Cathy Fooks*

Gawande went to McAllen because readily available data pointed him there. For all the injustices in its healthcare, at least the United States produces the evidence. President Obama has read Gawande's piece and has begun to use it as an example of why an overhaul of the system is essential. McAllen and El Paso may be this president's Harry and Louise.

Canada needs to map our McAllens and Mayos routinely and develop strategies for reducing the spread of wasteful spending. Disaggregation is key since clinical autonomy is deeply embedded in Canadian healthcare culture, and the one certainty is that groups with similar needs are treated differently. We don't know because we don't look hard enough, often enough. As long as we remain in the dark, not much will get better.

Reference

Gawande, A. 2009, June 1. "The Cost Conundrum." *The New Yorker.* <http://www.new-yorker.com/reporting/2009/06/01/090601fa_fact_gawande?currentPage=all>.

Don't Make Me Gag*

Steven Lewis

Would you commit in writing not to slag your physician on the Internet? A US company called Medical Justice (MJ; http://www.medicaljustice.com/) is hawking a waiver form that gets patients to foreswear anonymous posts to doctor rating websites. I'm your doctor; you're my patient. If you have problems with me or my staff, tell us, tell your friends and family, tell anyone you want through the usual channels. But put it in writing that you won't post it to the Internet. The Internet is a pretty big windmill to tilt against, but MJ claims 1,000 doctors have signed on. The pitch is that the muzzle pact protects doctors from anonymously posted and inaccurate portrayals of their courtesy, promptness, morals and clinical skills. The lawyer in the MJ website video recounts the story of an anonymous post implying that a physician was a child molester. Though the post was a malicious plant from a competitor, not a patient, apparently US law exempts Internet service providers from liability in such cases and they cannot be compelled to remove the alleged defamation.

* Originally published in *Longwoods Essays*, June 2, 2009

This is ugly and outrageous stuff. But the proposed remedy is ethically objectionable in principle and foolish in practice. The flaws are as follows.

First, MJ argues that rating doctors is not the same as rating barbecues. This is formally true: I cannot libel the barbecue, and in any case the barbecue doesn't care. (The manufacturers do, but somehow they have not yet demanded censorship in return for the privilege of purchasing their goods.) MJ goes on to describe the doctor–patient relationship as a precious union of equals whose sanctity and trust are violated by the spectre of anonymous rating. This is patent nonsense: there is a major power imbalance between the parties. The rating sites are popular precisely because the vast majority of patients don't have the nerve to challenge their doctors face to face and fear the consequences if they do so.

Second, the Internet free-for-all has been with us for a decade, and it has created an endless stream of opinions, advice and ratings. Of course, it is full of garbage, lies, rants and ravings. It is also a treasure trove of facts and shrewd observations that skewer privilege and reveal truths absent from the increasingly concentrated mainstream media. The bees have burst from the hive, and there is no getting them back inside. There is no better advertisement for doctor rating sites than the attempt of doctors to suppress them.

Third, like Othello and Lear, MJ mistakes a friend for an enemy. Most people think better of their doctors than their doctors' performance warrants. The overwhelming proportion of assessments on www.rateMDs.com is positive. An avalanche of evaluative literature shows that overall physician performance is in fact mediocre by the standards of evidence-based practice. Misprescribing is rampant, it takes weeks to get an appointment, adverse events abound in hospitals and mental health problems are underdiagnosed and ineffectively treated. Physicians come off far better on the web-based rating sites than in scientific practice profiles. They should be demanding patient ratings, not proscribing them.

Fourth, the public can learn something from the ratings. Themes tend to repeat in both the critical and laudatory commentary. When eight patients tell you that doctor X prescribes penicillin for everything, I doubt they're lying. When 20 of 40 assessments of doctor Y mention misdiagnosis, I'd bet the farm that there's a lot of misdiagnosis going on. When every one of 32 posters says Dr. Z cares, listens and explains, I believe these statements of Dr. Z. Many of the postings are balanced, nuanced and thorough. The critics in particular tend to give reasons for their judgments. Some are scathing and even cruel, but the savage commentary is usually reserved for those who have committed truly barbaric acts.

Fifth, physicians should welcome the feedback, especially if it is anonymous. Patients are disinclined to ruffle their doctors' sensibilities. I like my family doctor, Mick Jutras of Saskatoon, as do 29 of 32 raters on rateMDs.com (http://www.ratemds.com/doctor-ratings/7630/SK/Saskatoon/Jutras). He is intelligent, thoughtful and a good communicator. I did not change my mind because one patient wrote, "He sucks. Totally ignorant. Rude." But I have never had the jam to tell him that same-day access should be the norm (except for the time we were both at a fundraiser with excellent and abundant alcohol), that the laboratory test result communications are erratic or that it is perplexing that Toyota summons my car for screening but his highly automated practice doesn't invite me for the tests that are supposed to be so vital to my well-being. (My optometrist and dentist pester me relentlessly.) Nor has he ever surveyed me. Both he and I have let him down on the quality improvement front. If I thought he and his partners would read the Internet ratings carefully and recognize that the negative feedback is the wellspring of improvement, I'd log on and write.

MJ claims to be in favour of objective physician rating systems, meaning, no doubt, rating systems that they control or endorse. Their real fear is that patients will pay more attention to each other than to the insiders' guild. Don't pay attention to the unwashed who have the gall to write about a condescending ass who interrupts after 20 seconds and can't tell a virus from a bacterium. We'll do the rating and ranking of our own.

But what about malicious content? Yes, it's a problem, and potentially harmful to the innocent. There are remedies, aside from squashing your patients' freedom of expression. The rating sites open their doors to physician comments and rebuttals. Smart ones, such as Saskatoon urologist and medical blogger extraordinaire Kishore Visvanathan, have actually embraced the concept and the technology as a learning tool (http://www.ratemds.com/doctor-ratings/44104/SK/Saskatoon/Visvanathan). Patients can respond to others' posts. Site surfers should be invited to report suspicious content to the administrators or directly to their doctors.

Above all, keep some perspective. False-positive opinions far outnumber false negatives. A patient bent on vengeance has many ways to sully a reputation. And the public are not idiots: if they are at all open-minded about the merits of a doctor, they will read all of the posts and judge on the basis of the body of evidence presented.

If I ran a doctor-rating site, I would add a new category: has your physician ever asked you to sign a MJ-type gag order? If the answer is yes, go elsewhere if you can.

Danny Williams's Ironic Adventure*

Steven Lewis

Newfoundland premier Danny Williams got his heart valve problem fixed in Florida. Reactions were swift, varied and fevered: he's unmasked the house of cards that is single-tier medicare; he's a hypocrite who wouldn't touch the care his government provides to the plebs; he can do what he wants with his money; no he can't, because he's the premier.

First, the facts. Williams had a mitral valve problem that could have been fixed in at least seven Canadian cities. In at least two, surgeons perform the minimally invasive procedure that Williams said was not offered to him. He consulted his physician friends, one of whom practises in New Jersey and suggested a Florida surgeon as the man for the job.

So pick up your pencils and check the response that best describes what he did. Danny Williams

a. made a smart medical choice by carefully weighing his options and having his surgery in the place where he would have the best chance of a good outcome and fast recovery;
b. made a smart geographical choice by having his surgery in Florida in the middle of winter, near his condo where he could convalesce;
c. made a Newfoundland-first political gesture by saying, if it isn't offered in St. John's, I'll not make us look bad by goin' down the road to Toronto;
d. didn't know and didn't care about either the availability or quality of minimally invasive mitral valve surgery in Canada; or

* Originally published in *Longwoods Essays*, March 2010

e. followed the thousands of other Canadians who, over the years, driven by anxiety and relying on reputation, have checked into the Mayo or Cleveland Clinic to nail down a diagnosis, get a second opinion or secure the highest-quality repair work.

I'm thinking d, e and c, in that order. It is consistent with the Williams persona: supreme confidence in his decision-making, quick and decisive position taking, and money enough to get what he wants, when he wants, where he wants. Whatever else he is as a politician, he is no garden-variety obfuscator with his finger perpetually in the wind. It never occurred to him that by virtue of being premier, he needed to consider the broader implications of his decision. *It's my money and it's my heart, and I have an absolute right to go where I want for care – a right I did not cede when I consented to govern.*

No one would care a whit about what Danny Williams did if he weren't premier. But he is, and, like it or not, his flight is freighted with potential political significance. Medicare is the single most important program any provincial government delivers. If a premier's actions betray a legitimate lack of confidence in what medicare can deliver both at home and elsewhere in Canada, it shakes the system to its foundation. The single-payer, tax-financed system stands revealed as a watered-down mediocrity, unreliable when the stakes are high. It confirms that two-tier is essential because a single-tier can't deliver the goods.

On medical grounds, what Williams did was neither necessary nor prudent. This wasn't an evidence-based decision founded on sound knowledge of the availability of services and health outcomes in both countries. It was a guy worth several hundred million dollars doing what guys worth several hundred million dollars often do. If I thought for a moment that he based his decision on sound evidence and a thorough review of all of his options, his choice would give me pause. But it is clear that he did no such thing. He called a pal, got his suggestion and took off. The rich are very different from you and me. They get to spend a lot for a little.

As for any political consequences, he may be correct in assuming that Newfoundlanders are no more inclined to toss out his government than Albertans are inclined to turf theirs. Since his approval ratings routinely trounce those of his counterparts across the country, who's to doubt his instincts? Maybe his constituents love him not in spite of but *because of* how he behaves. He brings a swagger and confidence to his province and relishes a good skirmish. And I suspect he's also banking on the public giving him a thumbs-up for giving the figurative finger to Central Canada: by god, if Danny has to leave the rock, good on him for flying right by those arrogant University Avenue bastards.

It's more interesting to imagine what is not, in fact, true – that Canadian medicare couldn't deliver the valve job and the Williams choice was the right one on all grounds. Would that cut the legs out from under the single-tier medicare system and prove that it's just not good enough anymore? Does any shortcoming undermine the whole enterprise?

The answer is a resounding *no*. Medicare is a public service. If public, tax-financed programs are expected to deliver the highest conceivable standard of service to the entire population with finite resources, no public service will pass muster. It is impossible for every public high school to provide the same quality education that you can get in private schools where tuition is $30,000 a year. The litmus test for a public service is whether it is good enough to satisfy the middle class whose taxes support it and who are more or less obligated to use it. That some rich people opt out of public education proves nothing about the adequacy of public education, just as the lack of capacity to perform certain unusual procedures is no proof of the failure of medicare. The main intent of medicare is redistributive – the healthy and wealthy subsidize the care of the sick and the poor. But the care also has to be good, and throwing all citizens into the same boat creates a community of interest in quality. The collective judgment of the middle class ultimately decides whether the system is adequate. That judgment should be based on both personal experience and systematic evidence. No system will achieve a perfect score on all dimensions; it is the overall performance, and the perception of that performance, that tells the tale. And, of course, it should improve all the time.

The Williams story is interesting not because of its implications for medicare but for its irony. As the facts of this case and a good deal of other research have shown, Canadian medicare is actually very good when life is on the line and organs need a tune-up. We have no shortage of world-class institutions and programs at the glamour end of medicine. If you're really sick in Canada, or if you have a rare and interesting affliction, chances are the system will fawn over you. Who's ahead of the pack in the search for a cure for diabetes? The creators of the Edmonton Protocol. Who identifies the genes responsible for debilitating children's conditions? Take a bow, scientists of SickKids. Who's pioneering robotic surgery? The University of Calgary. Canadian high-end medicine is in the premier league, even if it isn't in the premier's league.

So Danny Williams needn't have gone south for his valve repair – he would have been in excellent hands in Canada. Where he and the rest of us should be concerned is in the more pedestrian precincts of the system: primary healthcare, chronic disease management, the day-to-day care whose quality can make such a difference to so many lives. He decided to forgo the system where it actually performs, and put himself in its hands where it is far more likely to fall short. He's got lots of company there – opinions about healthcare quality tend to be forged in a data-free environment. We need more politicians willing to stir the pot. I'd have cheered if he had gone south in a snit because he couldn't get team-based, evidence-informed, same-day, patient-centred primary healthcare supported by first-class information technology. That's the symbolic stick in the eye that medicare deserves, and the real Achilles heel of the system.

CONCLUSION

Actually, I'd Rather Write about Baseball*

Steven Lewis

I've always hankered to be a baseball writer. It's like health services research, only the data are better, the outcomes are clearer and players pay attention to the findings. A lot of the time nothing important seems to be happening, but drama is just around the corner. The moments of tension are unsurpassed. The field is beautiful, with perfect dimensions. There is no clock, and there are no tie games.

Unlike healthcare, baseball has walked the talk of evidence-based decision-making. Player evaluations are now much more science than art. Salary negotiations typically involve detailed statistical analyses, adjusted to take into account park effects (grass or artificial turf, batter- or pitcher-friendly), era effects (the offence-oriented 30s, the run-starved 60s) and changes in how the game was played (e.g., a premium on power versus speed). You can tell when a great season is probably a fluke (e.g., pitchers who begin with great win–loss records but few strikeouts are not great bets for long and successful careers). And talk about a culture of disclosure: the line score has runs, hits and errors. Because it is cerebral does not mean that it is predictable.

In baseball, the best teams win 60% of the time and the worst 40% (occasionally there are exceptions). No other sport has such uncertainty of outcome. On any given day, there is hope. Compared to other sports, baseball has less testosterone and more wit and personality, not least because even the best players fail much of the time. Can you imagine a football trash-talker matching the quip of Steve Hovely, a ballplayer of no distinction: "Baseball is a lot like religion. Great game, bad owners"? If your workday involves watching Vladimir Guerrero throw, you've got one helluva job.

* Originally published in *Longwoods Essays*, January 11, 2011

AFTERWORD

Virtuosity in Health Policy

Terrence Sullivan

Those of us in the world of health policy comprise a splendid and slightly ragtag collection of folks who ply their trade from different ports of origin. Some enter from politics, others from health services leadership directly and still others from the research end of the continuum. What is more, we disparate critters often have more in common with each other than with our professional or disciplinary colleagues who span the waterfront from law, social science, epidemiology, management, politics and journalism. But what distinguish the journeymen from the virtuosos are three particular attributes.

The first is a deep understanding of how the legislative, regulatory and administrative processes work in healthcare. Such a person must comprehend how the institutional arrangements and incentives are intended to act in the delivery system and how they operate in reality. Second, one who understands these matters well must have the capacity to take complex issues in the organization, financing and delivery of health services and render them simple, sensible and even imaginable to other actors in the field through clear analysis using a variety of analytical tools. This turns out to be no small task since many in our delivery system believe that the current organization fell from the sky fully formed, that it is more or less all workable with more money or more efficiency and that all major transformations should therefore be resisted, by threat of political retribution, professional jihad or continuous shroud waving with the public. The virtuoso can take a health policy issue, simplify and articulate it with clarity and work to move the issue, its causes and its potential remedies into the unforgiving light of public and political discourse. This brings me to the last attribute, which is the personal drive, motivation and public interest that health policy activists bring to the debate. Being knowledgeable is one thing. Having the capacity to analyze and articulate is another. But possessing the motivation to craft and thrust a line of opinion or analysis into the public debate in a timely fashion is to advance the public discourse and illuminate better decision-making. Steven Lewis illustrates these attributes with distinction.

This country is short of individuals such as Steven who seize the opportunity and create debate. Working effectively and opportunistically with a variety of research and policy organizations and governments in this country and abroad, Steven operates like a one-man policy apparatus pushing forward new ideas.

Dear friend and colleague, Esteban, the Dos Equis of Canadian health policy, we congratulate you on getting old. But, as you know, 60 is the new 40. So enjoy the fruits of your virtuous life of running and living well. And continue to contribute prolific material to the Canadian health policy world and be the important, iconic gadfly that you have become.

Co-authors of Steven Lewis

Stephen Leeder, MD, PhD
Director, Menzies Centre for Health Policy, and Professor, School of Public Health, University of Sydney
[co-author of: *Why Health Reform?*, page 19]

Colleen Maxwell, PhD
Department of Community Health Sciences, University of Calgary
[co-author of: *Decoding Mazankowski: A Symphony in Three Movements*, page 33]

Denise Kouri
Executive Director, Canadian Centre for Analysis of Regionalization and Health
[co-author of: *Regionalization: Making Sense of the Canadian Experience*, page 41
Categorical Nonsense, $p < .05$, page 156]

Nandita Chaudhuri
Primary Health Services Branch, Saskatchewan Health
[co-author of: *Extreme Makeover: Can We Achieve Rapid Improvement in Canada's Healthcare System?* page 75]

Bonnie Brossart
Health Quality Council, Saskatchewan
[co-author of: *Extreme Makeover: Can We Achieve Rapid Improvement in Canada's Healthcare System?* page 75]

Gill White, MD
College of Medicine, University of Saskatchewan
[co-author of: *Extreme Makeover: Can We Achieve Rapid Improvement in Canada's Healthcare System?* page 75]

Jeanette Edwards
Director of Community Development for the Winnipeg Regional Health Authority and served as Program Chair of the National Primary Health, Care Conference
[co-author of: *Primary Healthcare: The All-Too-Quiet Revolution in Waiting*, page 92]

Colleen Flood
Associate Professor, Faculty of Law, University of Toronto; Canada Research Chair in Health Law and Policy
[co-author of: *Courting Trouble: The Supreme Court's Embrace of Private Health Insurance*, page 162]

Testimonials contributed by:

Jack Altman earned a doctorate in Biopsychology from the University of Chicago and worked nearly 30 years as a teacher, researcher, clinician and administrator. He is a past-president of the Public Health Association of British Columbia and was one of the original members of the steering committee of the B.C. Healthy Communities Network. His professional positions included provincial director of the Heroin Treatment Program for the B.C. Alcohol and Drug Commission, director of a public health unit in the City of Vancouver Health Department and Vice-President of Community Health Services for the various incarnations of the Vancouver Regional Health Board. **(page 164)**

Morris Barer was the inaugural Scientific Director of the Institute of Health Services and Policy Research (one of the 13 Canadian Institutes of Health Research). He was the founding (and is currently) Director of the Centre for Health Services and Policy Research at UBC. He is also Professor in the School of Population and Public Health. He is a fellow of the Canadian Academy of Health Sciences and a member of the Board of Trustees for the Canadian Health Services Research Foundation. Dr. Barer has served on the Federal/Provincial/Territorial Advisory Committee on Health Services, as senior editor for Health Economics with the journal Social Science and Medicine and as a consultant to a number of Ministries of Health across the country and internationally. **(page 144)**

Lillian Bayne is an independent consultant working in the field of health policy, planning and research. Lillian has been a Regional Director General with Health Canada and an Assistant Deputy Minister with the Ministry of Health in BC where her portfolios have included intergovernmental health relations, professional regulation, Aboriginal health, mental health and forensic psychiatric services and population and public health. Lillian has chaired numerous provincial and inter-jurisdictional committees, panels and boards, including the erstwhile *F/P/T Advisory Committee on Health Services* where she first met Steven, who served as a highly valued external expert committee member. **(page 36)**

Bonnie Brossart has been working for over 20 years in Saskatchewan's healthcare system. Trained as a health economist, she spent her first decade as a health services researcher and has been with the Health Quality Council (HQC) since its launch in January 2003. Prior to becoming CEO in 2007, she served as Deputy CEO for over three years and co-led the Saskatchewan Chronic Disease Management Collaborative, one of the province's largest quality improvement initiatives ever undertaken. Before joining HQC, she was a health services researcher with the Health Services Utilization and Research Commission (HSURC) of Saskatchewan, a large tertiary hospital in Calgary, and the Saskatchewan Ministry of Health. **(p. 72)**

Robert Evans is a lifelong leader in academia and an internationally esteemed health economist. His groundbreaking comparative studies of healthcare systems and funding strategies have shaped policy in Canada and provided insight to governments and health agencies worldwide. A decorated academic, Professor Evans is the recipient of Canada's highest honour for lifetime achievement, as an Officer of the Order of Canada. He also served as a member of the British Columbia Royal Commission on Health Care and Costs in 1990, and of the National Forum on Health, chaired by the prime minister of Canada, from 1994-1997. His canonical works, "Strained Mercy: The Economics of Canadian Health Care" and "Why Are Some People Healthy and Others Not? The Determinants of Health of Populations" are considered classics in the field. **(p. 144)**

Ken Fyke has 45 years of experience in Canadian health services. In 2001, he was Commissioner and author of "Caring for Medicare-Sustaining a Quality System," the Report of the Commission on Medicare in the Province of Saskatchewan. He served as a member of the British Columbia Royal Commission on Health Care and Costs, Closer to Home, 1990-91, as the founding Chair of the Board of Directors, Canadian Blood Services (CBS), 1998, and as a Deputy Minister of Health in the provinces of Saskatchewan and British Columbia, working with governments led by several political parties. Ken led the Victoria Health Project, which received national recognition and an international award for its innovations in community-based care. **(p. 112)**

Cathy Fooks is the President and CEO of The Change Foundation. Based in Toronto, the Foundation is dedicated to independent analysis and informed debate on current and emerging health issues. Prior to her position at the Foundation, Cathy was the founding Executive Director of the Health Council of Canada where she was responsible for implementing the Council's mandate of reporting to Canadians about healthcare renewal. She has held executive positions with the Canadian Policy Research Networks, the College of Physicians and Surgeons of Ontario and the Institute for Clinical Evaluative Sciences. **(p. 232)**

Dennis Kendel served as President of the Saskatchewan Medical Association in 1979, just seven years after entering practice as a family physician in Saskatoon. In the interval since then, Dennis has served as the President of Medical Staff at St. Paul's Hospital in Saskatoon, President of the Medical Council of Canada, and President of the Federation of Medical Regulatory Authorities of Canada. Dennis has also served on many health agency Boards, including the Board of the Health Services Utilization Research Commission, an agency which engaged Steven Lewis as its inaugural CEO. Dennis has served on the Board of Directors of the Health Quality Council of Saskatchewan for the past 10 years and continues to serve on that Board as well as on the Board of the Health Council of Canada. **(p. 188)**

Denise Kouri is a policy analyst, researcher and evaluation consultant based in Saskatoon, working on topics in health and social development. She also holds a part-time appointment as Evaluation and Research Coordinator with the University of Saskatchewan's THRP, a health promotion project in Mozambique. She has an interdisciplinary background, with a Bachelor of Science degree in Mathematics and a Master of Arts in Sociology and Social Studies. Denise is the former director of the National Collaborating Centre for Healthy Public Policy in Montreal. Before that she was director of the Canadian Centre for Analysis of Regionalization and Health, a national organization based in Saskatoon. **(p. 58)**

Kira Leeb is Director, Health System Performance at the Canadian Institute for Health Information (CIHI). Kira has held several positions within CIHI since she started in 2000. While at CIHI, Kira has overseen the production of serial reports, such as Health Care in Canada and Health Indicators as well as numerous special reports. From 2006-2008, Kira was seconded to the Health Council of Canada where she supported the Council's mandate to report on health care renewal. Kira holds a MA in Psychology. **(p. 9)**

Dr. Danielle Martin is a family physician. She is a Clinical Staff at Women's College Hospital and a lecturer in the Department of Family and Community Medicine at the University of Toronto. Danielle's policy expertise and passion for equity have made her an emerging leader in the debate over the future of Canada's healthcare system. A recipient of the Canadian Medical Association Award for Young Leaders, Danielle sat two terms on the Health Council of Canada. In 2006, the Ontario College of Family Physicians recognized her as one of three New Family Doctors of the Year. In May 2006, Danielle helped launch Canadian Doctors for Medicare, the voice for Canadian physicians who believe in *a high quality, equitable, sustainable health system built on the best available evidence as the highest expression of Canadians caring for one another.* **(p. 100, 200)**

Kimberlyn McGrail is an assistant professor at the University of British Columbia, an associate director of the UBC Centre for Health Services and Policy Research, a senior researcher with Statistics Canada and an associate with the Centre for Clinical Epidemiology and Evaluation. Kim's current research interests are in variations in healthcare services use and outcomes, aging and the use of health care services and understanding healthcare as a determinant of health. She has collaborated with provincial and federal policy- and decision-makers, including the BC Ministry of Health Services, the Health Council of Canada and the Canadian Institute for Health Information. Kim was the 2009-10 Commonwealth Fund Harkness Associate in Health Care Policy and Practice. **(p. 144)**

Dr. Tom Noseworthy is the former Vice President, Medical Services, and CEO of the Royal Alexandra Hospitals, and Chair of the Department of Public Health Sciences, Faculty of Medicine and Dentistry, University of Alberta. He is also former Head of Community Health Sciences, University of Calgary. In 2007, Dr. Noseworthy was named by the Governor General as a Member of the Order of Canada for contributions to health policy and medicare. In January 2012, Dr. Noseworthy assumed the position of Associate Chief Medical Officer for Alberta Health Services, responsible for Strategic Clinical Networks and Clinical Care Pathways. **(p. 178)**

Roy Romanow was born, raised and educated in Saskatoon. He was first elected to the Saskatchewan Legislature in 1967. Between 1971 and 1982, Roy Romanow served as Deputy Premier of Saskatchewan. On November 7, 1987, Roy was acclaimed Leader of the Saskatchewan New Democratic Party. On November 1, 1991, he was sworn in as Premier of Saskatchewan, a post he held until the spring of 2001, at which time he retired from active political life. On April 4 2001, Roy was appointed by Prime Minister Jean Chrétien to head the Royal Commission on the Future of Health Care in Canada. In 2003, Roy was made an Officer of the Order of Canada. **(p. 11)**

Terrence (Terry) Sullivan is the Chair of the Canadian Agency for Drugs and Technologies in Health (CADTH) Board of Directors. He is the former president and CEO of Cancer Care Ontario, a position he occupied for seven years. From 1993-2001, Terry was president of the Institute for Work & Health, a private not-for-profit institute affiliated with the University of Toronto, which he developed into North America's leading research centre on work-related injury. Terry has held senior roles in the Ministry of Health and Long-Term Care, Ministry of Intergovernmental Affairs and the Cabinet Office. He served two successive first ministers of Ontario as executive director of the Premier's Council on Health Strategy. **(p. 245)**

Glenda Yeates was appointed Deputy Minister of Health Canada in April 2010, after serving as Associate Deputy Minister of Health Canada since May 2009. Prior to this appointment, Glenda served as President and CEO of the Canadian Institute for Health Information (2004-2009), Deputy Minister of Health in Saskatchewan (1999-2004), and as Saskatchewan Deputy Minister of Social Services (1997-1999). She held various Assistant and Associate Deputy Minister positions in Saskatchewan Health, and a number of senior posts in the Saskatchewan Department of Finance. Glenda has served in the past as a board member for Carleton University, the Ontario Change Foundation, and the Canadian Health Services Research Foundation. **(p. 28, 64, 226)**

Index

Notes

Page numbers in italic refer to a table. The letter "n" following a page number indicates that the information can be found in a note on that page; e.g., 60n1 indicates note 1 on page 60.